SLAVERY:
The African American
PSYCHIC TRAUMA

By Sultan Abdul Latif and Naimah Latif

Published by
Latif Communications Group, Inc.
in conjunction with
Tankeo, Inc.
6 N. Michigan Avenue, Suite 909
Chicago, IL 60602
(312) 373-6397

Cover photo by Ted Gray

SLAVERY:
The African American
PSYCHIC TRAUMA

By Sultan Abdul Latif and Naimah Latif

Published by
Latif Communications Group, Inc.
in conjunction with
Tankeo, Inc.
6 North Michigan Avenue, Suite 909
Chicago, IL 60602
(312) 373-6397

ISBN 0-9640118-0-8
Printed in the United States of America

Dedication

This is a
    Tribute to our
    Ancestors, our
    Native land, and the
    Kingdoms and
    Empires from which we
    Originated

For Grandfather Luther "Tankeo" Anderson and Grandfather Sip Charles, two great black patriarchs who dared to be men. And for cousin Charles "Chuckie" Meredith, whose untimely passing made us remember the value of close family ties.

This book is dedicated to our parents, without whose support and encouragement this work would not have been possible; to our African ancestors, whose bravery and strength enabled them to survive the Middle Passage and create new life in America; to our children, who represent all of our hopes for the future; and to those descendants yet unborn, who will carry on a proud family legacy, by the grace of Almighty God.

Our sincere gratitude to all of the
Tankeo, Inc.
stockholders, whose financial support made the publication of this book possible. And thanks to the following patrons for their financial support: Muhaimen Karim, Gus Redmond.

Acknowledgements

Special thanks to Cheryl Charles of the Boston Globe for an outstanding editing job. Thanks also to the following who provided editorial assistance: Lois Anderson, Yvonne Brooks, Jimell C. King, Deborah Luckey, Barbara Pement, Khalilah Rafat, Nafi Rafat, Valorita Amatullah Rauf, Falahuddin Shams, Dr. Muhammad Sohna, Michael Ward, Rashid Yahya, Hajji Dhul Yaqub, and Nycemah Yaqub.

Thanks to Dr. Florestee Vance for assistance in preparation of the Psychic Trauma Test, and thanks also to the following organizations and institutions who provided participants for the sample test group:

African American Griot Society, Chicago

Maple Park Methodist Church, Chicago

Members of the Omega Psi Phi Fraternity, Chicago graduate chapter

Operation PUSH, Chicago Headquarters

Chicago Vocational High School

Our sincere gratitude to Dr. Muzafar Ahmad Zafar, African American historian and lecturer, whose extensive travel and research throughout Africa provided important documentation for this book. Thanks also to others who provided valuable research assistance: Willie Dixon, Ted Gray, Abdul Karim, Deborah Luckey, Falahuddin Shams, Kevin Ward, and Nycemah Yaqub. Thanks to Mildred Trimuel of Builders Letter Service for business support services. Thanks to photographer Ted Gray for outstanding photographic reproduction. Special thanks to Fareeda Hardy of Paperwork, Inc. and Granville T. Ware of Extech Company for their important technical help. And thanks to Attorney Robert W. Porter for expert legal assistance.

Contents

Table Of Illustrations

Table of Illustrations

Foreword

The monstrous legacy of slavery profoundly interrupted the normal course of economic and psychological development in Africa. Millions of people were captured and sold abroad into slavery. Those who remained behind did not receive a better treatment. They fell into the jaws of imperialism and were treated as slaves in their own country. These cruel tragedies never affected the profound feeling of brotherhood that indigenous Africans have always had for their African American brothers, because they share a common ancestry and a strong sense of history as builders of great civilizations of antiquity.

Perhaps, the most disturbing question often raised by contemporary European scholars of African history is in regard to the creation of Egyptian Civilization. If Africans were the architects of Egyptian Civilization, they argue, how can their present condition as compared to that of the Europeans be explained? An in-depth examination of the history of the rise of the Arabs in the seventh century as an outstanding contributing force in advancing the frontiers of human knowledge, particularly in the areas of science, mathematics, astronomy, architecture, and commerce, will render such a question virtually impotent, considering the deplorable condition of the Arabs as we enter the 21st century. Having abandoned the universal teachings of justice concerning brotherhood, they began to undermine gradually the structures and spirit in which the formidable institutions of their people were grounded. Consequently, their dignity as a people was destroyed and their future thrown into the dustbin of history. Similarly, Africans, having reigned for centuries, started to experience some difficulties generated by internal contradictions. The enemy seized the momentum and from there, successive invasions ensued which ultimately led to the downfall of Egypt. In his book, *The African Origins of Civilization, Myth or Reality*, Cheikh Anta Diop argues:

"When Herodotus visited it, Egypt had already lost its independence a century earlier. Conquered by the Persians in 525 (B.C.), from then on it was continually dominated by the foreigner: after the Persians came the Macedonians under Alexander (333 B.C.), the Romans under Julius Caesar (50 B.C.), the Arabs in the seventh century, the Turks in the sixteenth century, the French with Napoleon, then the English at the end of the nineteenth century."

"Ruined by all these successive invasions, Egypt, the cradle of civilization for 10,000 years while the rest of the world was steeped in barbarism, would no longer play a political role. Nevertheless, it would continue to initiate the younger Mediterranean peoples (Greeks and Romans, among others) into the enlightenment of civilization. Throughout Antiquity it would remain the classic land where the Mediterranean peoples went on pilgrimages to drink at the fount of scientific, religious, moral and social knowledge, the most ancient such knowledge that mankind had acquired." (p. 10)

However, after the disintegration of Egypt, powerful states such as Mali, Ghana, and Songhay emerged in the Western part of Africa. In the fifteenth century, when the Portuguese, Dutch, English, French and Danes established trading posts on the West Coast of Africa, the institutional organizations of the African states were often equally efficient and often superior to those of the European states. Constitutional monarchies were already in place, with a Common Assembly in which the various social strata had adequate representation. During this period, Africans could satisfy their economic needs without having to embark upon building a society dedicated to change and invention. This situation opened the way for Renaissance Europe to see Africa as vulnerable, and an easy prey for conquest. Thus, a new relationship, master-slave, sprang into being. Africa became the reservoir from which the labor force that built the economic foundation of America was forcibly extracted.

Of all the havoc that the institution of slavery had created, the psychological damage seems to be far more devastating because it generated in the African American one of the deadliest character flaws -- a crisis of identity! Fanon explains: "*I am talking of millions of men who have been skillfully injected with fear, inferiority complexes, trepidation, servility, despair, abasement.*" Identity crisis is an embodiment of confusion, fear, and inferiority complex combined with an extreme sense of hopelessness.

The question is, can African Americans as a people overcome their present condition? The authors of the book *Slavery: The African American Psychic Trauma,* have made an excellent analysis of the African condition prior to the institution of slavery in contrast to the present condition of African Americans. Historic evidence seems to indicate that human progress is primarily contingent upon the kinds of organizational structures designed to foster specific goals. It can be rationally argued that there has never been a civilization that achieved meaningful development without sound organizational structures as a basis for development and an appropriate ideology as a guiding principle. The enterprise of science, technology, government, commerce and the military-industrial complex are offsprings of particular organizational and ideological structures. The following areas should therefore constitute the basic foundation of any strategy that will be geared toward the resolution of conditions of African Americans: (1) to establish sound organizational and ideological structures, (2) to promote a consistent and systematic process of educating the people, (3) to create, by means of an appropriate ideology, a new African American, and (4) establish an economic system that will reflect the primary aspirations of African Americans. All these require an educational system conducive to the achievement of the aforementioned goals.

Education may be briefly defined as the consistent and deliberate liberation of human intelligence. When human intelligence is liberated, the people concerned are able to look at the world from a particular perspective. This implies the ability to gather facts, to arrange them logically, to examine them, and to analyze and draw from them significant conclusions. Clearly, the application of this scientific process to the desperate condition of African American people will then be attainable. Consequently, African Americans will be able as a people to reconstruct a political direction and forge a new economic order. What does this new economic order mean? It is important to state from the beginning that the new economic order being proposed is not a free enterprise system as we understand it. The new economic order should be erected upon: (1) partnership (cooperation), (2) government as a direct reflection of fundamental national interests, and ultimate power (political and economic) in the hands of the people, and finally, (3) politicians should be accountable to the electorate.

In conclusion, it should be recognized that the success of any strategy is to be judged by the achievement of the goals and objectives for which it was designed to accomplish. The logical implication of this statement is that no plan of action has ever succeeded without strong emphasis upon the special role that scientific knowledge should play in our daily endeavors to direct governmental, cultural, historic, political, and economic activities. This view is an embodiment of Nkrumah's statement, "Seek ye first the political kingdom and every other thing will be granted." It may be also said that African-Americans must seek the economic kingdom first and every other thing will be added on to it.

Muhammad Mustapha A. Sohna, Ph.D

Dr. Muhammad Sohna was born in The Gambia, West Africa. He served on the Detroit / Africa Economic Development Task Force as an advisor to the Mayor of Detroit, Michigan on international trade between Africa and the city of Detroit and wrote a philosophical guideline for trading with Africa. He has traveled extensively in the course of historical research and served as Researcher for the Center For Black Studies at Wayne State University, Detroit. He assisted in teaching a public policy course entitled, "The Black Community and Public Policy." He is an independent motivational speaker and organizer. He is fluent in several languages, and served in The Gambia as an educator. He was also a Regional Secretary of the Gambian Teachers' Union.

INTRODUCTION:
What Is Psychic Trauma?

STOLEN
FROM
AFRICA:
250 MILLION
PEOPLE!

0A

Journey On A Slave Ship

    This layout of the Brookes, a 320-ton vessel, was built to accommodate 451 people, yet carried as many as 609 slaves on one voyage. Journeys through the Middle Passage on ships such as this were for many Africans the beginning of a never ending nightmare. (Drawing from a pamphlet by Thomas Clarkson, London, 1839, Carnegie Institution of Washington. Picture courtesy of DuSable Museum of African American History file, Chicago, Illinois.)

INTRODUCTION:
What Is Psychic Trauma?

PSYCHIC: Pertaining to the mind or soul; mental as distinguished from physical or physiological.
TRAUMA: A severe emotional shock, having a deep often lasting effect on the personality.
(From Webster's New Collegiate Dictionary).

These two words have been used by psychologists to describe what happens to victims of extreme psychological abuse. We believe it perfectly defines the distressed mental condition that African Americans find themselves in today.

What happens when a close-knit, harmonious community is shattered by strange looking foreign invaders, who kidnap a number of its citizens?

What happens to those citizens who are smuggled away, locked in chains, and shipped off to a foreign land, where they are murdered, tortured, raped, beaten, and forced to labor in the fields under the lash of a whip and the constant threat of death?

What happens to them when they are forced to have sex with each other for the purpose of producing babies, who are then snatched away and sold, like puppies, to strangers?

What happens to their children, who learn to live in mortal fear of their captors, and who grow up being taught that they come from a people who are ugly, stupid, and commanded by God to live as servants?

What happens to these children, when they are raped by their captors, and forced to give birth to their captors' babies, then told that the offspring from these rapes are superior because they look more like the captors?

And what happens to the children conceived through rape, who are taught that the only way they will be treated with any kind of respect is if they can look, speak, and act like their captors?

What is the mental condition that develops as a result of such an experience?

We believe it is *Psychic Trauma*.

SYMPTOMS LIKE PRISONERS OF WAR

Psychologists today understand the emotional trauma experienced by survivors of rape and violent assault. In his book, *The Wretched Of The Earth*, Algerian psychiatrist Franz Fanon examines the mental disorders of his patients who survived the violent Algerian revolution in North Africa. He notes that victims of torture experienced everything from extreme paranoia to psychosomatic illnesses. Recent psychological studies show that victims of child abuse often must go through intense psychotherapy in order to behave like normal adults, particularly when they have lived through brutal beatings and sexual assault.

Prisoners of war, who are kidnapped and held hostage and tortured under the threat of death are also known to experience Post Traumatic Stress Syndrome. This causes everything from violent flashbacks to extreme depression, especially when they are forced to witness the murder of their comrades by their captors.

Generation after generation of African Americans have been told that, in spite of the violence, the European invasion of Africa and the enslavement of their foreparents were really, in the end, for their own good. They've been taught that Europeans brought "salvation" to their "uncivilized" ancestors. They've been made to believe that, as a result of genetic mixing with Europeans, African Americans are a better looking race of people.

The psychological trauma from slavery has never been addressed, and the resulting emotional scars have been passed down, generation to generation. Psychic Trauma is a malady suffered by every African American, regardless of sex, occupation or religion. Very few manage to rid themselves of its effects, because society continues to reinforce the trauma.

STRIVING FOR WHITE APPROVAL

Those who have achieved positions of economic status in society and intermingle regularly with whites may protest, "I know I don't have a problem. This must pertain to those 'lower class' blacks."

Often it is the so-called "successful" African Americans who are traumatized most. Many African Americans have achieved high status in various professions. However, as noted psychologist Dr. Alvin Poussaint states in his book, *Why Blacks Kill Blacks:*

Despite these major gains, there are many blacks who are still ashamed of their skin color. This is particularly true of those who associate with important whites. They seem to almost have two personalities, one for whites, one for blacks. Around whites, they might sell out psychologically, by trying to hide their "Negro characteristics." They will talk with an Oxford accent around them, then switch to "soul brother" talk when they're around their own. Some of them didn't use the terms 'black' and 'Afro-American' until key whites had used them in public. A few continue to be so hung up on white approval that it is unlikely they will ever change." (Page 20)

Many books have been written by psychologists and sociologists examining the destructive influences of "ghetto life."

This is not another one of those books.

This is not another study of "the problem" concluding with, "All we have to do is make white folks treat us right and we'll be OK."

Our premise is that African societies, before the European invasion, enjoyed harmonious families, advanced education, well organized governments, productive economies, and a strong spiritual base, which led to high moral values. It was only after the devastating slave experience and the enforcement of a destructive European culture and system of values that Africans became traumatized.

This is not another book to give blacks ammunition to attack whites or any other racial group for their problems.

This book was written to address how African Americans were drastically transformed by slavery, and to provide steps on how to undo the damage. At the end of certain chapters are special activities designed to help remove the damaging attitudes and behaviors caused by psychic trauma. These activities can help African Americans produce a new generation of trauma-free adults, who are prepared to create a new society.

No approval from any other group is necessary -- these are things that each person can do to change his or her own condition!

The first step to ridding oneself of the damage from slavery is to first recognize signs of it within yourself. At the end of this chapter is the "Psychic Trauma Test." There are no right or wrong answers.

The important thing is to be absolutely honest. Take the test -- not for others, but for yourself, in private, and see how deeply YOU have been affected.

DO YOU HAVE PSYCHIC TRAUMA?

ACTIVITY:
Take The Psychic Trauma Test

Survey Questions   SA A U DA SD

(Circle the number which best describes
how you feel about each statement.   4 3 2 1 0
Strongly Agree (SA)=4;
Agree (A)=3;
Unsure (U)=2;
Disagree (DA)=1; and
Strongly Disagree (SD)=0

1. While watching an African American
being interviewed on a television program,
when I notice that the person is using
"incorrect" grammar with a very heavy "black
dialect," I get embarrassed.   4 3 2 1 0

2. When speaking to whites, I consciously
try to alter my grammar and pronunciation
so that I sound more like them, "proper."   4 3 2 1 0

3. When stopped by white police officers in
traffic, I feel fearful.   4 3 2 1 0

4. When I hear an African-American leader
speaking forcefully or aggressively, I feel
uncomfortable.   4 3 2 1 0

5. When a white man wearing a business suit speaks to me in an authoritative tone, I have difficulty looking him in the eye.   4 3 2 1 0

6. When competing with whites, whether in business, on the job, or academically, I believe they will probably perform better than I.   4 3 2 1 0

7. When I go to events where I am the only black person in attendance, I feel self conscious.   4 3 2 1 0

8. I believe I would be further along in my career if I were white.   4 3 2 1 0

9. I hesitate to take on certain professional responsibilities because I don't believe I have the ability to master them.   4 3 2 1 0

10. If I were to suddenly lose my present means of employment, I think I would have great difficulty surviving.   4 3 2 1 0

11. When a member of the opposite sex whom I want to attract sees my hair before it is pressed or permed, I feel embarrassed and unattractive.   4 3 2 1 0

12. I think I would be more attractive if my skin were a few shades lighter.   4 3 2 1 0

13. The people I find most attractive tend to have lighter skin and curly or straightened hair.   4 3 2 1 0

14. When a white member of the opposite sex finds me attractive, I consider it a greater compliment than when a black member of the opposite sex finds me attractive.   4 3 2 1 0

15. I feel resentment when I see an attractive black member of the opposite sex romantically

involved with a white person of my sex.   4 3 2 1 0

16. I feel that I am more attractive than my
darker skinned associates.   4 3 2 1 0

17. When I see Africans in films expressing
their own cultural rituals and activities,
I see them as repulsive.   4 3 2 1 0

18. I think blacks who were brought to America
from Africa became more "civilized" than those
who remained in Africa.   4 3 2 1 0

19. When I consider traveling abroad to
become more "cultured," my first choice is
a place in Europe, such as Paris or London,
rather than a place in Africa.   4 3 2 1 0

20. I found myself defensively making excuses
for my answers as I filled out this
questionnaire.   4 3 2 1 0

*Now, add up your score, and enter the
total here:*   _____

Psychic Trauma Test Analysis

Score of 0
You appear to have eliminated problems related to
fear of whites and low self esteem due to the African
American slave experience. You have learned to be
proud of your racial identity and have a healthy
sense of self worth.

Score of 1-20
You have taken some steps toward developing a
positive self image. However, your attitudes are still
affected by racial prejudice in society.

Score of 21-40
Many of your perceptions are influenced by preoccupation with what whites may think and do. This could be having a negative effect on your self esteem.

Score of 41-60
You are struggling with feelings of inferiority, and your self esteem has been greatly damaged. This could affect your ability to reach personal and professional goals.

Score of 61-80
You have suffered extreme trauma. You have accepted your presumed inferiority as a matter of fact, and may unconsciously act out the role by purposely performing below standard or seeking out demeaning relationships. You will have to work hard to change deeply ingrained self hatred.

Review your test answers and note the questions on which you scored the highest. Questions 1-5 examine automatic acceptance of whites as authority figures, leading to fear of white disapproval. Questions 6-10 examine feelings of personal inferiority to whites and unwillingness to step out of one's "proper place" to strive for higher goals. Questions 11-16 examine rejection of African features and preference of European features when determining physical beauty standards. Questions 17-19 examine rejection of the African identity, while desiring to identify more with Europe and European culture. Question 20 examines the tendency for denial. It is often difficult to admit problems. However, honesty will help you overcome the effects of psychic trauma.

Think of personal experiences which may have influenced your current attitudes. Share this test with a friend and discuss your scores.

Throughout this book, we will refer to the questions raised in this test, and show what happened to create such attitudes and beliefs in the African American mind.

Now, in order to understand the brainwashing process which led to this condition, let us go back to the beginning, and examine the people who were taken away to a foreign land and remade into slaves.

0B
King Tut
Many say that African Americans descend from ancient Egyptians such as King Tutankhamun (1361 B.C. - 1352 B.C).

CHAPTER ONE
The Stolen African Past

1A
Doorway To The Past
This gateway into an old temple is an example of how ancient Egyptian kings left the history of their glory on the walls of the skyscrapers of their time. (Reprinted from Illustrated Africa, North Tropical and South, by William D. Boyce, Rand McNally & Company, Chicago, IL, 1925.)

CHAPTER 1
The Stolen African Past

AFRICA ... at one time known as Upper and Lower Egypt ... a beautiful green landscape with plush forests and colorful animals ... what may have once been the elusive Garden of Eden. It was a place of many nations, where people intermarried and traded cultures and traditions.

There have been a multitude of lies spread under the guise of "education." World history, as taught by Europeans, is full of false tales of Africa being a "dark continent" of "savages" waiting for Europeans to come and "civilize" them.

But, to discover the real history of human civilization, one has to go all the way back to mankind's beginning.

THE REAL ADAM AND EVE

"So God created man in his own image, in the image of God he created them. God blessed them and said to them "Be fruitful and increase in number; fill the earth and subdue it. Rule over the fish of the sea and the birds of the air and over every living creature that moves on the ground."

The Bible, Genesis, Chapter 1, Verses 27 & 28. (Taken from the Holy Bible, New International Version.)

American anthropology textbooks promote a theory that modern man evolved from an ape or an ape-like creature. Illustrations in those books cleverly show ape-like people with brown protruding faces and stooped shoulders, said to have been found in Africa. They are believed to be the evolutionary link between man and ape.

We also see pictures of hairy cavemen with pale skin, straighter noses and an upright posture, said to have been found in Europe. These Caucasian looking, upright people, we are told, are the first fully evolved human beings.

A student may wonder, "If these white cave men are the first true people, where did black folks come from?"

The unwritten message is that black people were in Africa, swinging through the trees like apes, perhaps not quite yet evolved into modern man. The implication is that blacks are somewhere between apes and white people on the ladder of evolution.

For years, archaeologists who believed in the theories of evolution as taught by English naturalist Charles Darwin sought to prove that modern man first evolved in Europe. However, archaeological findings and scientific studies have forced European historians to admit that Africa, not Europe, is the birthplace of all mankind. The oldest human skeleton, a small female, was discovered in East Africa. It is calculated to be perhaps more than 100,000 years old. Scientists have named her "Lucy."

According to an article published in the January 1988 edition of *Newsweek Magazine*, recently scientists conducted a study of human DNA (Deoxyribonucleic acid) the material responsible for genetic composition. Starting out with the theory that all human beings descend from one male and one female, they set out to systematically trace DNA codes to find the original "Eve."

The scientists presented their hypothetical "Eve" as most likely a "dark haired, black skinned woman." They traced through an international assortment of genes and followed a trail of DNA that led them theoretically to a single woman from whom they believe all people descended.

Scientists date their Eve, based on DNA research, at about 200,000 years old. They have reached the obvious conclusion that all humanity belonged to a single black group, prior to the flood of Noah's time. Their evidence indicates that "Eve" lived in "sub Saharan Africa." Meanwhile, other geneticists are trying to trace humanity back to a scientifically derived Adam. They intend to trace a hypothetical trail of DNA to find the man who is commonly regarded as the "great father" of all people.

It is interesting to note that after studying DNA material, scientists have concluded that it is composed of something like clay or mud. Religious scriptures, both the Bible and the Quran, (the Islamic holy book, sometimes spelled "Koran" by Westerners) had already declared the same thing centuries ago.

"And surely We created man of dry ringing clay, of black mud wrought into shape."
The Quran, Chapter 15, Verse 27.
(Taken from The Holy Quran, Arabic Text and English Translation.)

The first human beings, dark skinned and living near the earth's equator, produced the chemical melanin, which is responsible for dark skin pigmentation and protects the skin from the sun's ultraviolet rays. Since Africa was the place of mankind's origin, dark skin was the natural state of the original man. Dark skin, dark hair, wide noses and wide lips remain dominant genetic traits among the races of man today.

THE DEVELOPMENT OF RACE

A study of physical geography shows that the continents at one time were all one land mass, called Pangaea. During this time, known as the Triassic period, prehistoric animals could travel across this great supercontinent from one end to the other.

Then, about 180 million years ago, the continents began to move apart, and the position of each body of land in relation to the sun and surrounding bodies of water affected its climate. Human beings, just like animals, developed physical characteristics to adapt to the environment.

People who migrated to the northern, colder regions where the sun was farther from the earth and the ultraviolet rays were not as intense lost the need to produce melanin. The result, after a period of centuries, was a loss of pigmentation, resulting in what we call "white" skin.

Some European historians still insist that Europe laid the foundations for early man's development. But as historian John Henrik Clark states in his introduction to John G. Jackson's book *Introduction To African Civilization:*

Civilization did not start in European countries and the rest of the world did not wait in darkness for Europeans to bring the light ... There is not a single book in existence with a title incorporating the words, "World History" that is an honest commentary on the history of the world and its people. Most of the history books written in the last five hundred years have been written to glorify Europeans at the expense of other people. The history of Asia has been as shamefully distorted as the history of Africa. (p. 3)

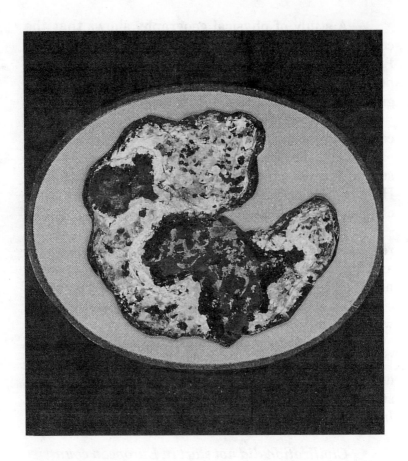

1B

Pangaea Map

Scientists calculate that more than 180 million years ago, during what is known as the Triassic Period, the earth was one big land mass, allowing prehistoric animals to travel from one continent to the other. The later shifting of the continents during the Jurassic Period, created climactic changes which affected the physiological development of animals on each continent. This map, drawn by Sultan A. Latif from a composite of geographical sketches, illustrates that the continent of Africa, once it broke away to become a separate body, is actually four times the size of the United States.

Just as man's birthplace was in Africa, so was man's first development. The evolution of man into organized societies actually began around 10,000 B.C. Archaeological findings indicate that perhaps more than ten centuries ago, mankind learned how to control the use of fire and to manufacture stone implements for hunting. Clothing was made from animal skins and food was obtained from hunting, fishing, and farming. Homes were built with bricks, made from straw and dried grass mixed with mud. Written communication, now called Hieroglyphics, introduced to the world the first form of writing.

In an article published in the November 26, 1982 edition of the *Chicago Sun-Times*, scientists ponder new information revealed by radar which indicates the probable existence of civilizations even before the rise of ancient Egypt. The article, written from Washington, D.C. by Al Rossifer Jr., states:

The powerful Earth-watching radar carried aboard the space shuttle a year ago revealed ancient, buried riverbeds known previously only to Stone Age people in what now is the driest part of Egypt, it was reported Thursday.

A team of eight scientists said the dramatic subsurface terrain -- buried several feet under a sheet of featureless sand -- shows that the climate in the eastern Sahara was vastly different tens of thousands of years ago.

The findings of the shuttle radar in the Arabian Desert of southern Egypt may explain some of the tales going back to ancient Egyptian times of lost oases or the great "Bahr-bela-ma," or large river without water, the scientists said.

They said tools provide abundant evidence of episodic human occupation in the area dating back

200,000 years or more. The Stone Age artifacts indicate the ancient rivers were sites for early human occupation. The desert was largely abandoned about 5,000 years ago when very arid conditions set in.

This discovery presents a more complete picture of the history of mankind. The Adam and Eve of the Bible represent not the beginning of all human life, but the beginning of a new five thousand year dispensation, three thousand years of which have already passed. There have perhaps been many dispensations of mankind, and remnants of older civilizations possibly existed during the time of Adam and Eve. (This explains some Biblical mysteries, such as, where did Cain and Abel's wives come from?)

THE AFRICAN ROOTS OF EGYPTIAN DYNASTIES

According to the map on the opposite page, the land mass where civilization began was first called Chem (Northern Ethiopia) and Nubia (Southern Ethiopia). This Ethiopian empire extended across the vast continent of Africa, and was considered two lands. Cities rose up along the Nile river. This ancient land, also known as Abyssinia, laid the foundation for the Egyptian empire.

The Egyptians made their appearance on the stage of history about 10,000 years ago. Despite attempts by European writers (with the help of Hollywood) to claim Egypt as part of Europe's heritage, archaeologists and historians have proven through drawings, statues, ancient writings and human fossils, that ancient Egypt was, without a doubt, African. Its people had the same physical characteristics of Africans today.

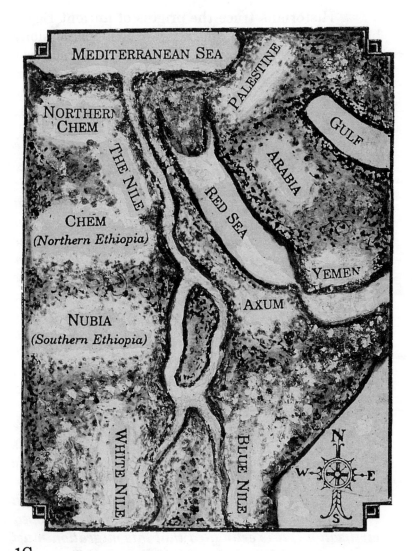

1C
Chem & Nubia Map
According to this map, drawn by Sultan A. Latif based on a composite of historical documents, the Ethiopian Empire encompassed what later became Upper Egypt and Lower Egypt. This map shows how Africa was divided prior to the first Egyptian Dynasty, and how the land around the Red Sea (important in many Biblical events) connects Arabia, Palestine and other areas of the "Middle East" to the old empire.

Historians trace the origins of ancient Egypt back to the northern migration of Ethiopians along the Nile River. During this period, Africa was divided into a series of small feudal kingdoms. Jackson goes back 5,000 years, beginning with the legendary king who founded Egypt and who the people later rose to the status of a god:

The Edfu Text is an important source document on the early history of the Nile Valley. This famous inscription, found in the Temple of Horus at Edfu, gives an account of the origin of Egyptian civilization. According to this record, civilization was brought from the south by a band of invaders under the leadership of King Horus. This ruler, Horus, was later deified and became ultimately the Egyptian Christ. The followers of Horus were called "the Blacksmiths," because they possessed iron implements. This early culture has been traced back to Somaliland; although it may have originated in the Great Lakes region of Central Africa. In Somaliland there are ruins of buildings constructed with dressed stone, showing a close resemblance to the architecture of early Egypt. Professor Arthur G. Brodeur, in his The Pageant of Civilization, *has conjectured that the ancestors of the South Egyptians came originally from this region; that they entered the Nile Valley through Nubia, and brought with them a well-developed civilization. It is estimated that this migration must have occurred long before 5,000 B.C. (p. 93)*

The basis of Egyptian chronology, Jackson states, is a book entitled *History of Egypt,* by Manetho, a learned Egyptian priest of the Temple of Sebennytus. He was commissioned by Ptolemy Philadelphus, King of Egypt in the third century B.C.

to write a history of Egypt from the earliest times up to his own day. Although a great part of this history was lost in the destruction of the Alexandrian Library, some of the information, such as the lists of kings of Egypt, survived.

Jackson quotes Egyptologist W.M. Petrie's calculation that the first Egyptian dynasty arose in 5500 B.C. Egyptian civilization dominated the world scene for 5,000 years before falling to foreign invasion from Persia. Then the great continent of Africa was dominated by a series of flourishing west African kingdoms right up to 1500 A.D.

Up until the 27th dynasty (beginning 525 B.C.) Egypt was ruled by the dark-skinned ancestors of today's descendants of Africa. After that time, the country was taken over by Persians, and since that time, Egypt has rarely been free from foreign domination. But the achievements of the people prior to that time were astounding.

How vast was the time of African rule before the rise of Europe! Let us look at the number of years covering the ancient Egyptian dynasties. The following dates are compiled by Petrie.

DYNASTY   YEARS IN POWER (Before Christ)

DYNASTY	YEARS IN POWER (Before Christ)	
I	5500 B.C. -	5300 B.C.
IV	4780 -	4500
VI	4275 -	4075
XII	3580 -	3370
XVIII	1587 -	1328
XIX	1328 -	1202
XX	1202 -	1102
XXI	952 -	749

XXII	725	-	664
XXVI	664	-	525
XXVII	525	-	405
XXX	378	-	342

According to historian Cheikh Anta Diop, author of *The African Origin of Civilization: Myth Or Reality,* some modern Egyptologists have grouped the 30 Egyptian Dynasties into four periods:

1) The Old Kingdom   Dynasties I-VI
2) The Middle Kingdom Dynasties XI-XIV
3) The Empire   Dynasties XVIII-XX
4) The Saite Age   Dynasties XXVI-XXX

MENES UNITES UPPER AND LOWER EGYPT

The Golden Age of Egypt began when the father of African king Menes or Aha Mena defeated the Asian invaders of the northern kingdom, and his son King Menes became the first pharaoh of the united kingdoms of Upper and Lower Egypt. His rule began Dynasty I, during which five powerful kings ruled. The political unification of Egypt played a significant role in the social and political development of Egypt. According to the booklet, *A Salute To Historic African Kings and Queens,* published by Empak Enterprises, Inc.:

In addition to uniting Egypt, Menes is also credited with founding the ancient city of Memphis which was located between the two kingdoms. Because of its central location, Memphis was one of Egypt's leading cities, and it served as the capital for a considerable period of time. The city was named after Menes, and its ruins lie not far from present day Cairo ...

Governmental and social institutions were also developed during Menes' reign, which endured with comparatively little change for almost two millennia. Furthermore, hieroglyphic writing developed immensely during this period, as well as technical skills and other arts.

Prior to the rule of King Menes, many petty kings ruled over small territories in Upper and Lower Egypt. All these kingdoms were united in time by marriage and conquest, as Jackson explains. So-called "modern" world history teaches that Africans had no means of formal education. However, the fact is that Egypt had surpassed the world in scholarship and learning.

In Egypt, priests were the royal chroniclers and keepers of records. They were the learned class. Egyptian priests were physicians and embalmers, lawyers and law givers, sculptors and musicians. Under the teachings of these versatile men, the Egyptians became a prosperous and moral people.

Look at the difference between the scandal ridden religious leaders of today, and some of the brilliant priests of ancient Egypt.

IMHOTEP: THE REAL FATHER OF MEDICINE

Imhotep was prime minister to King Zoser of the third dynasty (5345 B.C. - 5307 B.C.). In addition, he was an astronomer and magician and also held the post of Chief Physician. He built mankind's first hospital, called the Temple of Imhotep. Sufferers from all over the world came to it for healing, prayer, and peace. Imhotep, a multi-genius, was known as "one who comes in peace." He is the true Father of Medicine, (not the Greek Hippocrates, who came along 2,000 years later). But Imhotep's teachings were absorbed by the Greeks, who studied in Egypt.   One of Imhotep's most famous sayings is still being quoted today: "Eat, drink and be merry, for tomorrow we die."

Medicine in ancient Egypt concentrated on the art of healing, as opposed to today's practice of treating the symptoms of a sickness. Apparently, Egyptian thought was more advanced than today's "modern" medicine, and physicians such as Imhotep practiced holistic healing techniques. This idea of holistic healing (healing of the body, mind, and spirit), is just now beginning to be accepted in today's medical circles.

Why have we allowed African-American children to be discouraged from entering the field of medicine, when they descend from the world's first and greatest physicians?

KHUFU: BUILDER OF
THE GREAT PYRAMID

The Egyptian's knowledge of mathematics and astronomy was amazing. One of Egypt's greatest wonders was the building of the Great Pyramid. This happened during the reign of the Pharaoh Khufu. Khufu was one of history's most outstanding personalities.

The height of the Great Pyramid is one billionth of the distance from Earth to the sun. This is a unit of measure that wasn't even calculated accurately in modern times until 1874. The pyramid was possibly used as a vault for the preservation of scientific instruments and of standard weights and measurements rather than a tomb.

Inside the Great Pyramid, according to Jackson:

> *There is a granite slab, which evidently served as a standard of measure. The length of the slab is one millionth of the distance of either pole from the center of the Earth. This invariable distance, only recently determined by modern science, is the basis of the metric system. The distance from each of the poles to the center of Earth is 3,949.79 miles. From this measurement, we are enabled to calculate the circumference of Earth through the poles, which is 24,817.32 miles ... This fact was known to the Egyptian astronomers six thousand years ago. (p. 99)*

The Great Pyramid itself took 20 years to build. The project employed one hundred thousand men, working three months at a time. There are misconceptions that workers were slaves, however, in reality they were very organized teams of construction crews.

Consider today's tallest skyscrapers and elaborately designed buildings. Modern architecture still requires the use of steel beams for support and electrical wires for inside heating and cooling. However, pyramids were designed to make effective use of solar energy, storing hot air in the warm season and releasing it during the cooler season. This maintained a comfortable inside temperature at all times (and no electric bills!) The mathematical correctness of each brick fitting together made nails and screws unnecessary. Scientists are still exploring some of the amazing qualities of the pyramids.

1D
Black Man In A Chariot
This painting was found on a wall of an ancient Egyptian tomb built over 5,000 years before the birth of Christ and said to be the tomb of "Prince Mena." This could possibly refer to Menes of the First Dynasty, 5500 B.C. It reveals the presence of dark skinned Egyptian citizens during his reign. (Reprinted from Illustrated Africa, North, Tropical, and South, by William D. Boyce. Copyright 1925, Rand McNally & Co.)

THE END OF EGYPT'S FIRST GOLDEN AGE

Egypt's first Golden Age ended in 4163 B.C., at the death of King Neterkere, the last ruler of the Sixth Dynasty, Jackson notes. From 4163 to 3554 B.C., the period covering the Seventh through Tenth Dynasties, the Nile Valley was in a state of chaos.

Diop, in his book, *The African Origin of Civilization: Myth or Reality,* examines the political and social evolution of Egypt during its various cycles of development. He states that Egypt's strong Monarchy gradually evolved into the old feudal system. A class system developed which created a wide gap between the rich and poor and the Sixth Dynasty finally ended with mass uprisings and rebellions. Diop observes the forces which led to Egypt's decline:

Obviously, division of labor on the basis of craftsmanship already existed. The cities doubtless were active centers of trade with the eastern Mediterranean. Their idle poverty stricken masses would take an active part in the revolt. The mores of the nobility created a special class of men: servants contracted for varying tenure. The text describing these events shows that the country had plunged into anarchy; insecurity reigned, especially in the Delta with the raids by "Asiatics." The latter monopolized the jobs intended for Egyptians in the various workshops and urban building yards.

The wretched of Memphis, capital and sanctuary of royalty, pillaged the city, robbing the rich and driving them into the streets. The movement soon spread to other cities. (p. 205)

According to Diop, the major cause of the

rebellion was the taking over of the economy by foreigners. (This is a conflict which often surfaces in urban riots of today.)

He states that the spread of violence and theft throughout Egyptian society caused the collapse of the Old Kingdom.

A major portion of African history has already occurred at this point and, although classism, greed, and oppression have played a major role in Egypt's fall, European whites have been nowhere around.

If one learns nothing else from studying Egypt's past, one should at least realize that blacks in power were guilty of many of the same abuses as whites in power. A black face at the helm of government is not the only criterion African Americans should strive for in seeking self determination. To prevent internal conflicts, the leaders of a country must develop a system which provides fairly and equitably for all the people, without major class distinctions and unfair privileges for a few.

Political unrest and revolt of the masses prompted many of the royal class to flee south toward the original homeland, Diop asserts.

The dynastic period of Egypt, the Middle Kingdom, extended from the time of the Sixth through Fourteenth Dynasties. It was a turbulent period where confusion reigned, and often several rulers claimed the throne at the same time.

According to Jackson, when King Amenemhet IV of the twelfth dynasty died childless, leaving no heir to the throne, this presented a great problem. In Egypt, as in many African nations, the kingship was inherited through the daughter of the monarch. (In some cases the daughter would marry the son, and this brother/sister, husband/wife relationship was the means whereby families kept royal power within the family.)

In this case, King Amenemhet's widow, (who was also his sister), Queen Sebeknefrure, was to marry a member of the nobility from the capital city of Thebes, and transfer the power of the throne to him. However, when she married a commoner from Lower Egypt, the Theban nobility protested, and a rival ruler challenged Queen Sebeknefrure's new husband's right of succession. The nation erupted into a civil war, which lasted nearly one hundred years.

As one ruler sat on the throne at Thebes, a rival ruler sat on the throne at Memphis, and the armies of both regimes attacked each other up and down the Nile Valley. The divided, war torn Egypt presented a grand opportunity for invasion by a horde of nomads from Asia, known as the Hyksos or "shepherd-kings," or "rulers from other lands." Weakened by war, Lower Egypt fell to the Hyksos, who then moved up the river and captured Thebes. These "shepherd kings" dominated Egypt for about 150 years, spanning the time of the Fifteenth, Sixteenth, and Seventeenth Dynasties.

Here the term "Asian" must be clarified. During this period, as maps of the time show, the area now called "Asia" was actually considered part of Africa. Europeans later redrew boundaries, and used terms such as "Middle East," "Asia Minor" or "Arabia" to separate the people who live on the peninsula between the Black sea and the Mediterranean Sea from the people of Africa. According to the *Thorndike Barnhart Advanced Dictionary,* Arabia is defined as the large peninsula in Southwest Asia, which now includes Saudi Arabia, Yemen, Southern Yemen, Kuwait, Oman, Qatar, and the Union of Arab Emirates. However, in ancient times, all of these lands were considered part of the old empire of North Africa.

THE RACIAL ROOTS OF PRESENT DAY NORTH AFRICA

Much of today's political conflict in Northeast Africa and the area across the Red Sea, commonly referred to as the "Middle East" can be traced back to events narrated in the Bible. Many groups are claiming some sort of Divine rights to control various territories, based on their claims to be descendants of the original inhabitants of the land.

But many who control Northeast Africa today have no connection with the people referred to in Biblical scriptures. They are actually descendants of various foreign people, some of whom migrated to Egypt, some who were captured in battle and brought to Egypt as slaves, and some who invaded Egypt and overthrew existing regimes.

In the book *Great Black Leaders,* edited by Ivan Van Sertima, author Legrand H. Clegg II looks at the reunification of Egypt after a period of invasion and war, in a chapter entitled "Black Rulers Of The Golden Age." He observes that confusion from the various wars and conquests may lead historians to disagree as to the racial origin of Egyptian rulers between the thirteenth through seventeenth dynasties. He points out:

Scholars are generally agreed however, that about 1600 B.C., around the time of the late Seventeenth Dynasty, there arose a family in Upper Egypt that would be strong enough to expel the Hyksos and ultimately consolidate Egypt. Two

*commoners, Senakhtenre Tao and his wife Tetisheri,
became rulers of Upper Egypt at this time. No one is
certain how they achieved this power...he may have
usurped the throne. In any case it is clear that he and
his wife founded the most powerful line of rulers
Egypt was ever to know. Their descendants reigned
for three hundred years. (p. 148)*

Seqenenre Tao and Ahhotep I, the son and
daughter of Senakhtenre Tao and Tetisheri, began a
great war of liberation against the Hyksos people. It
was the youngest son of Seqenenre Tao and Ahhotep
I, named Ahmose I, who continued this war of
liberation and finally drove the Hyksos out of Egypt.
His reign begins the Eighteenth Dynasty.

Clegg II asserts that evidence indicates
Senakhtenre Tao and Tetisheri were of Nubian
origin, and concludes that each member of this royal
family was black. Portraits and statues of eighteenth
dynasty rulers tend to confirm this belief. Clegg adds
that the people of Upper Egypt and Nubia (the
country south of Egypt) grew close together during
the period of Hyksos domination.   Apparently
recognizing the Semitic invaders as a common
enemy, the North and the South forged a strong
political alliance.

So, again, the "Nubians," the black people,
after driving out the "Hyksos," were in control of
Egypt.   A significant question is, who were the
Hyksos -- the "shepherd kings" from the east?

Many historians, seeing the word "Semitic"
attached to these people, may go seeking white faces
similar to those who currently call themselves Jews
and who control Israel today. But the identities of
those who were the Hebrews of ancient times, and
who were chased out of Egypt into the Sinai desert

by the armies of Ahmose I, can be traced to another
group of black people, some of whom ended up in
America along with members of many other African
nations.

A student of African ethnology can recognize
the many descendants of these "shepherd kings"
walking the streets of America today. States William
D. Boyce in his book *Illustrated Africa, North,
Tropical, South:*

*Among the people of Senegal are the Fulani...
They are found in many parts of West Africa. The
Fulani are light brown, or reddish brown, and some
historians believe they are descended from the
Shepherd Kings of Egypt. (p. 254)*

Some historians have argued over whether
Fulanis are mixed with white or whether they are
truly "Negro." But, with so many variations of skin
tone, hair texture, and shapes of the lips and noses,
how can anyone really define a "Negro" race? Racial
classification seems to be more of an invention by
Europeans to identify a race of "non-people" whom
they could enslave. Africans belonged to many
different ethnic groups. It is estimated that perhaps
forty percent of the Africans brought to America
were Fulanis.

Fulanis have remained pastoral people
throughout the ages, herding their livestock from one
pasture to another, Boyce notes. During the
seventeenth and eighteenth centuries, when the
European slave trade was at its zenith, African
farmers and herders, out in the rural areas far away
from densely populated cities, were often easy prey
for slave catchers.

QUEEN HATSHEPSUT LEADS EGYPT TO A NEW GOLDEN AGE

The third phase of Egyptian history, the period covering the Eighteenth through the Twentieth Dynasty, is known as "The Empire," Jackson states.

The Eighteenth Dynasty saw the rise of another Golden Age in Egypt. Many notable leaders, both male and female, made enough shrewd moves during this period to keep Egypt in its position as a dominant world power.

In *World's Great Black Leaders,* Danita R. Redd offers an analysis on Queen Hatshepsut:

Hatshepsut, a great Black leader of Africa's Golden Age, has been called "the first great woman in history." In addition, she is the only woman known to have actually ruled Kemet (Egypt) as the "Living Horus" (pharaoh)... She was loved, admired and respected by most of the masses and elites of ancient Kemet. Hatshepsut was also a profoundly religious person, and commissioned stupendous and awe-inspiring construction projects in honor of the gods. (p. 166)

Hatshepsut, whose family history stretched back to the Seventeenth Dynasty, was a positive force during this period, and Egypt's prominence grew.

QUEEN TIYE: GREAT ROYAL MATRIARCH

Another influential figure of this era was Queen Tiye, the Great Royal spouse of Amenhotep III, who ruled Egypt as queen along with her husband, and as queen mother on the ascension of her son to the throne.

In *World's Great Black Leaders,* author Virginia Spottswood Simon sheds light on this power behind the throne, in the chapter entitled, "Tiye: Nubian Queen of Egypt:"

In Tiye, dark brown skin graced wide-arched brows, high cheekbones and a nose with delicately flared nostrils. Full lips curved above a slightly jutting jaw...

Constantly and in many ways, Pharaoh Amenhotep III expressed love for his black queen. The gifts he lavished on her made Tiye wealthy in her own right...

More than a lover though, Tiye was a capable, educated woman. Her library of papyrus scrolls contained religious, historical and scientific texts, poetry and stories. She must have mastered much of their contents. For her opinions commanded respect and she exerted informed political influence throughout her half-century as queen consort and queen mother of the most powerful nation of her day. (pp. 206, 207).

International trade reached great heights during the reign of Amenhotep III (1538-1501 B.C.) From Syria, timber was imported and large, sturdy ships were built. Obviously, during this period a lot of overseas travel went on. Traces of pyramids have been discovered in South and North America, showing that people from this era traveled there.

After the death of her husband, Tiye's son, Amenhotep IV became ruler. Simon observes that Tiye remained a stabilizing force in the government while her son's religious innovations caused him to neglect Egypt's foreign affairs and defense. It was Tiye with whom Kings of Asian states negotiated for military protection from Egypt.

AMENHOTEP IV: "WORSHIP ONE GOD"

During his reign, Amenhotep IV had abolished the hundreds of gods of Egypt, and worshipped only one god, Aton, whose symbol was the flaming disc of the sun.   Amenhotep IV then renamed himself "Akhnaton" (also spelled "Ikhnaton") meaning devoted to Aton. He ignored the warnings that priests of the disallowed cults were rising up in rebellion.

Hostile armies invaded the nation, toppling him from power. He died, possibly poisoned by his enemies, and the Aton cult was abolished.

Although the monotheistic Aton religion was crushed in Egypt, it did not perish altogether. History reports that a young Egyptian priest, Moshe (Moses) had become a disciple of Akhnaton. When monotheism was suppressed in Egypt, he led a group of followers out of the country and into Palestine.

According to the historian Manetho, Moses taught that it was a terrible error to present the Deity in the form of animals, as the Egyptians did, or in the shape of a man, as was the practice of the Greeks and of other African nations.   For that reason, Moses recommended that the Deity be worshipped without emblems.

It was after this period of prosperity that Egypt took a turn toward excessive tyranny. Diop explains that although Akhnaton's religious reforms failed, his absolutist policy survived and was consolidated under the Nineteenth Dynasty with the deification of Ramses II. He states:

With the deification of Ramses II, feudal privilege and royal absolutism reappeared ... The

*temples again profited from immense holdings,
endowed with immunity which empowered them to
dispense justice to their tenants... At the same time
they received tens of thousands of Aryan slaves
branded with a hot iron. These were the only cases of
slave labor force in Egypt for large scale production...*

*So it was as a prisoner of war, transformed
into a slave, chained and branded that the white man
first entered Egyptian civilization. (pp. 211, 213)*

The descendants of these white prisoners were
to be freed under a later administration.   Their
presence in Egypt led to Egypt's later fall to foreign
domination, beginning with Twenty sixth Dynasty
ruler Psammetichus, according to Diop.   During the
reign of Ramses II, white foreigners were recruited
into the auxiliary armed services.   The Egyptian
army began to lose its nationality, and rapidly
became a force of free mercenaries or semi-slaves
commanded by national officers, with only a few high
commanding officers remaining Egyptian.

AHMOSE II: EGYPT'S LAST AFRICAN PHARAOH

The last African pharaoh to reign in Egypt was
Ahmose II (569-525 B.C.) of Libyan ancestry.   The
land known as Libya today was at one time occupied
by the Watusis, a race of tall, dark skinned,
gracefully dignified African people.

King Ahmose II, whom the Greeks called
Amasis, was a great statesman, but he could not save
his country from foreign domination.   After his
death, early in 525 B.C., the kingship fell to Psantik
III, and after a few months the land of Egypt was
overwhelmed by the armies of King Canbyses of
Persia.   This ushered in the 27th Dynasty.

1D

Ramses The Builder

*These are statues in Luxor, Egypt, are of the Pharaoh Ramses II.
He was known to have erected more temples and monuments
than any other Pharaoh, perhaps to assure himself a place in
history. Note the broad nose and full lips on the figure on the
far right. (Reprinted from Illustrated Africa, North, Tropical,
and South, by William D. Boyce. Copyright 1925 by Rand
McNally & Company.)*

Many of The present light complexioned inhabitants of Egypt descend from these foreign invaders. However, there are still many Egyptian citizens who look like the original natives. From the reign of Menes of the First Dynasty to Amasis was a span of five thousand years. No wonder dark skinned people make up a great portion of the population of Egypt.

However, Europeans want so badly to claim this great civilization, that most of the ancient Egyptian monuments have been purposely mutilated. One may look at Egyptian statues today and wonder why everything has remained intact on these figures, except the noses on their faces. The fact is that Napoleon, during his invasion of Africa, saw the features on the Egyptian Sphinx and other statues. To hide their true identities, he took his cannons and blew off the distinguishing negroid noses.

1F
The Egyptian Sphinx
The Sphinx, said to have been built during the Fourth Egyptian Dynasty, is conspicuously missing its nose. However, the lips and head shape still reflect its Negroid origin.

ACTIVITY:
Expand Your Vision Of The Past

Most history books used in American schools present the past from a Eurocentric perspective. The study of "Black history" is generally confined to the period after the European slave trade. This gives most students a distorted impression of the past and minimizes the great influence of African people on world history.

To broaden your sense of African history, review the chart below. The shaded in areas represent periods of African domination of history and culture. In upcoming chapters, these periods in history will be discussed in more detail. Study the chart. Do you detect any noticeable patterns? If so, based on this chart, what developments would you predict for the future?

History At A Glance
6000 B.C. (Before Christ) - 2900 C.E. (Christian Era)

| ██ African | | | European | //// Transition |

6000	5900	5800	5700	5600	5500	5400	5300	5200	5100
5000	4900	4800	4700	4600	4500	4400	4300	4200	4100
3000	2900	2800	2700	2600	2500	2400	2300	2200	2100
2000	1900	1800	1700	1600	1500	1400	1300	1200	1100
1000	900	800	700	600	500	400	300	200	100
0000	100	200	300	400	500	600	700	800	900
1000	1100	1200	1300	1400	1500	1600	1700	1800	1900
2000	2100	2200	2300	2400	2500	2600	2700	2800	2900
?	?	?	?	?	?	?	?	?	?

B.C. --->

<--- C.E.

CHAPTER TWO
Europe's First Rise To Power

2A

St. Maurice of Rome
The name Maurice is derived from Latin and means "Like A Moor." Maurice, a general of Rome, died a martyr's death for Christianity and is now a principle saint of central and southern Germany, parts of France, Switzerland, Spain and Italy. (Reprinted from World's Great Men of Color, Volume II, by J.A. Rogers. Copyright 1972 by Macmillan Publishing Company.)

CHAPTER TWO
Europe's First Rise To Power

Now, after five thousand years of African high culture and civilization, we experience the first rise of Europe.

If you study the Bible from a purely historical point of view, you'll see that it is actually at about the time of the end of the Seventeenth Egyptian Dynasty that the Old Testament begins its chronology of human events.

In the first chapter, Genesis, humanity is traced from Adam and Eve to Noah and his descendants. According to many theologians, the span of time from the creation of Adam and Eve to the present is only about six thousand years.

Just consider all the existing artifacts -- great stone monuments, well preserved mummies, ancient hieroglyphics, etc. -- which scientists date back more than eight thousand years. Obviously there is a discrepancy in the accounting of time somewhere. European theologians continue to try to develop theories to explain why their Biblical teachings don't seem to agree with the chronology of events as discovered through scientific research.

There is nothing in European history or culture that gives a clue as to the beginnings of mankind. None of the theories which attempt to place Europeans at the center of human civilization ever coincide with archaeological findings. Out of all of the cultures arising from the various continents, it is the Africans who can actually trace their history back to Biblical traditions. Author Henry H. Mitchell notes that Ethiopians claimed to have "walked with God" longer than any other race. In his book *Black Belief,* he quotes Diodorus Siculus as saying:

*"The Ethiopians conceive themselves to be of
greater antiquity than any other nation; and it is
probable that, born under the sun's path, its warmth
may have ripened them earlier than other men. They
suppose themselves also to be the inventors of divine
worship, ·of festivals, of solemn assemblies, of
sacrifices, and every religious practice. They affirm
that the Egyptians are one of their colonies." (p. 25)*

Recall the first chart of Egyptian dynasties
from the years dating from 5500 B.C. Compare this
to the chart below, from the book *Black Presence In
The Bible* by Rev. Walter Arthur McCray, which
dates the people and events in the Bible.

PEOPLE	YEARS IN POWER (B.C.)		
Mesopotamia	2100	-	1200+
Egyptians	2100	-	1200
Judges	1200	-	1000
United Monarchy of Israel	1000	-	850
Armaeans (called Syrians)	850	-	800
Independence of Israel			
and Judah	800	-	745
Assyrians	732	-	609
Egyptians	609	-	605
Chaldeans	605	-	538
Persians	538	-	332
Greeks	332	-	165
MacCabeans	65	-	63
Romans	63 B.C. -		AD+

Again it appears that the dark people of Africa
dominated ancient history, until the Persian period
of domination from 538 to 332. The Greeks did not
come to power until 332 and later the Romans gained

control from 63 B.C. until the Dark Ages.

Historical evidence also confirms the fact, as many African Americans have claimed, that African people are indeed part of the original "Hebrews" of the Bible.

Many ancient African religious teachings are parallel to the teachings in the Bible. These traditions were passed down through oral historians, and as family groups migrated, they carried these teachings with them.

The Fon and the Yoruba people of Africa have an ancient religious tradition that God made man from clay. The Yoruba have a name for God which means "the Owner of the best clay."

Mitchell relates how the Ashante people of Africa believe that when creation was finished, God provided for laws and customs to regulate human life. Still another Ashante tradition tells how Tano, like Jacob, deceived his blind father and obtained his older brother's inheritance. The older brother Bia, was then forced to make do with the arid stretches of the Ivory Coast, while Tano received the rich inheritance of Ghana. This has geopolitical implications comparable to the assignment of Esau to the desert wastes of Seir and Edom as described in the Bible in Genesis.

The Dogon people, who live just above the Ashante, trace their beginnings back to a being considered a kind of demigod, named Nommo. He descended to earth in an ark, with eight ancestors and a supply of animals and plants. This story is remarkably similar to Noah and his ark.

All of these traditions date back centuries before Europeans ever set foot in Africa. And while many African traditional religions mirror Biblical teachings, none of the creation stories, flood stories, or tales of the prophets can be found anywhere in ancient Europe. Europeans as a whole do not appear on the world scene until much later in the history of mankind. As stated by McCray in *Black Presence In The Bible*:

"The existence of whiteness and the development of "white" people occurred later in the history of humanity. In other words, the evidence -- Biblical evidence, archaeological evidence, and DNA-wise evidence -- points in the direction that Blackness is humanity's norm and whiteness is the exception, rather than the rule, the derivation, not the origination."

In *Introduction To African Civilization*, John G. Jackson states that the first civilization of Europe was established on the island of Crete. The ancestors of the Cretans were natives of Africa, a branch of western Ethiopians. Around 1700 B.C., this civilization reached its highest point of development. The people were not white, he noted, but a dusky color. He added:

Throughout Crete were attractive and comfortable homes, well constructed ports and fine, paved roads... The people had considerable leisure time, so they engaged in music, dancing, theatricals, athletic contests, and other forms of entertainment, and had a considerable amount of leisure time. There was no powerful priesthood. They worshipped their gods in caves or on hilltops, but built no great temples.

Around 1400 B.C., this splendid culture was laid to ruins by an invasion of semi-barbarous Greeks from the north. Upon the ruins of the Cretan culture,

*the Greeks in later times built their own civilization.
These Greeks were the first civilized white people.
(p. 77)*

As stated by historian Joseph McCabe, in the
book, *Life Among the Many Peoples of the Earth:*

*"Four thousand years ago, when civilization
was already one or two thousand years old, white men
were just a bunch of semi-savages on the outskirts of
the civilized world. If there had been anthropologists
in Crete, Egypt, and Babylonia, they would have
pronounced the white race obviously inferior, and
might have discoursed learnedly on the superior germ
plasma or glands of colored folks." (p. 26)*

The ancient Egyptians were considered by
Greek and Roman scholars as Ethiopians. (The name
Ethiopia actually derives from the Greek word
"Ethiops" meaning "burned faces." Prior to the
coming of the Greeks, this land was known as
Abyssinia.) Egypt rose up from ancient Ethiopian
civilization, which had developed along the Nile river
for centuries. So, when the Greeks first encountered
Ethiopians, what they found among the dark people
was far from "primitive." These people enjoyed
indoor bathrooms and plumbing systems, where
drains were constructed with faucet jointed pipes
superior to anything known in ancient Rome. In
fact, they were not surpassed in modern times until
the middle nineteenth century.

Unfortunately, today's society is unable to
benefit from the great knowledge acquired by these
people. Much of the culture of Africa has been lost
because of the destruction of ancient records. The
Egyptian city of Thebes possessed a magnificent

library. This library, with all its precious records, was destroyed by an invading Assyrian army in 661 B.C., during the time of the twenty fifth dynasty, when Ethiopian kings were in power. From 525 B.C. to 332 B.C., Egypt was under Persian control. Then in 332 B.C., the Nile land succumbed to Greek military man Alexander "The Great." During his invasions, great libraries in several African cities were burned and looted, and their literary treasures were lost forever. It is apparent that every aspect of European philosophy on everything from geography to theology has been used in the massive cover-up of human history. This is so as not to acknowledge that during the greatest portion of world history, Europeans were not even present.

FACTS HIDDEN BY EUROPEAN CHRISTIANITY

European Christian theology has been especially geared to omit certain facts, in order to keep hidden the true origin and development of mankind. European religious teachings of ancient history present a very limited view of the ongoing political and social developments prior to the recorded life and ministry of a man known as Jesus. If one were to calculate modern human existence as beginning six thousand years ago, according to European theologians who use the Bible as a reference book, a careful study of history proves this to be physically impossible -- especially since the construction of the Great Pyramid by Khufu occurred nearly eight thousand years ago.

Scholars such as Henry H. Mitchell and Rev. Walter Arthur McCray who have deciphered the names and locations referred to in the Bible have

pinpointed the genetic history of the ancient people
of the book. The facts show, without a doubt, that
the people of Noah, and Ham, and David, and
Solomon, and Elijah, and Moses, and Jesus were the
people of Africa.

Just as African oral historians or "griots" of
today recite history according to family lineages, so
did those of centuries ago. They recounted the
histories of the people according to "so-and so, who
begat so-and-so, who begat so-and-so." Alex Haley, in
his book *Roots* recalled how the griot who recited the
history of his Kinte family clan in Gambia, west
Africa, spoke in the style of the Old Testament of the
Bible.

In addition to being recorded on written
scrolls, the events of the Bible were passed down by
oral historians, who memorized centuries of family
genealogies as a means of tracing time. They
recalled the migration of family clans from one place
to another. One can study a map of Africa and
match the names of places with the area to which
they referred to discover the people's identities.

Genetic lines can be traced back to Noah, who,
after the flood according to Biblical accounts, was the
father of Shem, Ham and Japeth, whose descendants
made up the people of the Old Testament. Let us
examine Ham, the son who is considered the father
of Black people. According to McCray, in *The Black
Presence In The Bible:*

*"Names in the Bible are usually impregnated
with much meaning. The meaning of some of these
names make reference to a person's or nation's
racial/ethnic origin. This is particularly so in the case
of the personal name of an individual. An example of
an identifying Black personal name is "Kedar" ("Very*

*Black") or "Phinehas" ("The Negro" or "The Nubian").
An example of a people or national name is "Cush"
("Black") and an example of a place name is
"Tahpanhes" (Jeremiah 43:7 "Palace of the Negro") or
"Ham", indicating hot, heat, black." (p. 54)*

According to the references in the Psalms,
Ham is synonymous with Egypt, McCray continues.
Psalms 78:51 speaks of God smiting the first born in
Egypt, which it parallels with the "tents of Ham."
Psalms 105:23 and 27 speak again of Egypt being the
"Land of Ham" which served as the place of Joseph's
sojourn and Moses' miracles. Psalm 106:22 speaks
also of the "Land of Ham" where the reference is to
the Israelites, who forgot the wondrous works which
God, their Savior, had done for them in Egypt.

It is clear from the Hebrew poetry of Psalms,
states McCray, that Ham is Egypt in Africa. It is at
this point that the Bible stands in stark contrast to
those scholars who do not want to associate Egypt,
Africa, with Black people.

Kush, (sometimes spelled Cush), a descendant
of Ham, is also identified as Black, and Moses' Black
wife is twice called "Kushite woman" (Numbers 12:1).
"Ham" the person is the ancestor of "Ham" his people
(both in Canaan and in the aboriginal heart of
Egypt), who are the ancestors of Mizraim (Lower and
Upper Egypt). These verses concur with the
archaeological studies pointing to Egypt's Nile Valley
as the birthplace of human civilization.

THE DESCENDANTS OF HAM

Following is a genealogical chart of Ham, as
outlined in *The Black Presence In The Bible*. Note
that Ham's descendants affected and influenced the

Hebrew-Israelite-Judahite people more than any other nation in the Old Testament. These descendants would include the Egyptians, Canaanites, Babylonians, and others.

Noah
/
Shem   Ham   Japeth
/
Kush----Mizraim (Egypt)----Put----Canaan
/   /
Seba--Havilah Sabtah--Raamah--Sabteca
/
Sheba--Dedan

It is possible that the people of Seba, the Sabeans, are to be identified with more than one place in the ancient world. It has been identified both with Meroe in Upper Egypt and Sheba in South Arabia.

McCray also suggests that Raamah is located in Southwestern Arabia. The name Sheba, he states, apparently refers to two or three different progenitors of one or more Arabian tribes and/or places. As a Hamitic descendant, Sheba is referenced to Seba and are the Sabaeans in Yemen, southwest Arabia. They were rich people and their home was a land of extensive commerce. They exported gold, frankincense, and other valuables.

The Queen of Sheba has been a most notable figure within and outside Biblical history. The visit of this powerful and beautiful Black woman to King Solomon is recorded in 1 Kings 10:1-13. It is said that she was Queen of Egypt and Ethiopia.

Apparently much of the Old Testament

occurred during the period between the eighteenth and thirtieth Egyptian dynasties.

Moses' revolutionary defiance of the Egyptian Pharaoh ushered in a new era for the Hebrew people. However the struggle between the slave and the free in ancient Egypt was not based on color, in terms of white against black as in modern times. Back then, both the oppressor and the oppressed were Africans; Egypt was a mosaic of various types of people of color.

Diop ponders over the ethnic identities of Biblical peoples, and their historical significance:

> *To determine the worth of Biblical evidence, we must examine the genesis of Jewish people. What then, was the Jewish people? How was it born?...*
>
> *Those who would become the Jews entered Egypt numbering 70 rough, fearful shepherds, chased from Palestine by famine and attracted by that earthly paradise, the Nile Valley.*
>
> *Although the Egyptians had a peculiar horror of nomadic life and shepherds, these newcomers were first warmly welcomed, thanks to Joseph.*
>
> *According to the Bible, they settled in the land of Goshen and became shepherds of the Pharaoh's flocks. (p.5)*

Tracing the origins of the Semitic people, one can go all the way back to Noah's three sons, Shem, Ham, and Japeth. The Bible, (Genesis 10 through 12), lists the genealogical descendants of Shem. It traces Abram, (who later became Abraham), the great patriarch of the Jewish, Christian, and Muslim religions, back to Shem. And Abraham was the father of Isaac, who was the father of Jacob -- who later was named Israel. The children of Israel are believed to be the original Hebrew people. Israel's son Joseph was first brought to Egypt as a slave, sold by his half brothers. According to the Bible, he later rose to become an important government official under the Egyptian Pharaoh, before the great migration out of Egypt by the Hebrews. But if Ham was the great father of all Black people, and Shem was Ham's brother, what could Shem have been? As a matter of fact, what must Noah have been? In North Africa four thousand years ago, the Hebrew people were still dark skinned. They represented just another ethnic group.

So, who were the enslaved Hebrew tribes in the Biblical story of Moses and the Exodus? This is a point in history worth exploring. At the time of Moses, Ramses II was in power. In *The African Origin of Civilization, Myth Or Reality*, Diop describes the political climate of the time:

> *After the death of Joseph and the Pharaoh "Protector," and facing the proliferation of the Jews, the Egyptians grew hostile ... If we are to believe the Bible, they were employed on construction work, serving as laborers in building the city of Ramses. The Egyptians took steps to limit the number of births and eliminate male babies, lest the ethnic minority develop into a national danger which, in time of war, might increase enemy ranks.*
>
> *So began the initial persecutions by which the Jewish people was to remain marked throughout its history. (pp. 5, 6)*

In a land where tremendous wealth invites greed and opulence, the struggle of the ruling class to maintain its control over the poor masses often leads to extremes of cruelty. One could compare violent

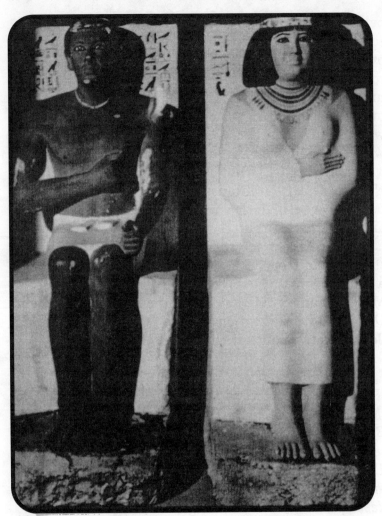

2B

Joseph and His Wife

A painted sculpture from a tomb at Medum, is calculated to have been carved around 2500 B.C. It illustrates how the Pharaoh of Egypt, to show his royal favor, gave Joseph an Egyptian name and married him to the daughter of the priest of the great national temple of On (Genesis 41:45). This carving shows that Joseph was a dark skinned negroid-looking man. According to the Bible, (Genesis 39:6,7), Joseph was considered well built and handsome.   (From the library collection of Ms. B. D. Luckey, Special Education Consultant.)

steps to cut down and control America's black male population, (beatings, lynchings, jail, etc.), with Egypt's policy to kill Hebrew male babies. Both are examples of unspeakable cruelty.

Perhaps one could conclude that the takeover of the Egyptian empire by Persians in the Twenty Seventh Dynasty was a dose of Divine punishment for Egypt's oppression of its weaker subjects.

Meanwhile, Moses and his followers headed east across the Red Sea and out of Egypt. In his book, *God, The Black Man, and Truth,* author Ben Ammi takes a look at the Hebrew migration and its significance to Africa:

Many of the descendants of Abraham followed Moses from Egypt, but some remained in Egypt while others migrated south and westward, according to Joseph Williams. Another scholar, Edmond D. Morel, identifies the Fulani of West Africa as "lineal descendants of those Hyksos and Hebrew migrants." Those migrating Hebrews explain why traces of Hebrew culture can be found throughout west, central and east Africa. Many scholars believe the ancestors of the Fulani, Ashanti, Ewe, Yoruba, Bantu and other peoples were in fact early Hebrew Israelites.

Many Israelites were also driven out of their land by the Romans in 70 C.E. and thereby migrated gradually to the surrounding nations of Africa. We know that many west Africans, especially the Ashantis, are direct descendants of the ancient Hebrews because of the strong Hebrewisms that have been identified in Ashanti tribal customs, including similar sounding words, similarities in marriage and child-birth customs, observance of the Sabbath (Saturday) as well as the name Ashanti from the words "ti," which in the west African tongue means

"race of" and Ashan, a town in the domain of Judah
(see Joshua 15:42). (pp. 9,10)

⁓Judah, according to the Bible, became one of
the "lost tribes" of Israel. Many Ashantis, as well as
Fulanis, Ewes, Yoruba, and Bantu, were taken out of
Africa and brought to America as slaves. In the
1960's Ben Ammi led a group of African Americans
back to Africa to inhabit present day Israel. The
group, known as the African Hebrew Israelite
Nation, has settled in Israel and parts of Africa, and
its members consider themselves descendants of the
ancient African Hebrews.

ROME BRINGS DESTRUCTION TO AFRICA

The rise of Europe ushered in an era of race
and color consciousness that still taints human
relations across the world. The rise and fall of Rome
affected Africa then and influences the world events
of today. With Roman soldiers came massive
destruction.

Carthage, a city-state, was established on the
North African coast in the year 814 B.C. Carthage
was one of the great cities of the ancient world, but
tragically after three wars waged by Romans, it was
finally destroyed. In 146 B.C., the city of Carthage
was captured by Romans and completely destroyed by
fire. According to historian John G. Jackson in his
book *Introduction to African Civilizations,* the library
of Carthage, said to have contained 500,000 volumes
dealing with history and science, was totally
destroyed.

Perhaps the reason Rome attacked Carthage
with such ruthlessness was because it feared the
might of legendary military genius Hannibal, leader

of Carthage and Commander of its armed forces. In the book *Great Black Leaders,* edited by Ivan Van Sertima, author Wayne B. Chandler writes in the chapter entitled "Hannibal: Nemesis of Rome:"

> *For fifteen long years Hannibal had been the scourge of Rome. He had inspired consternation among the noble senators and stark terror among the Roman populace. In battle after battle he had dealt the Roman army decisive defeats, until he had succeeded in shaking the very foundations of the mighty Empire...*
>
> *Hannibal's tactical feats have awed the military strategists of many different lands and centuries; his identity has fascinated as many historians. He single handedly put his nation on the world's historical map, for without his existence, Carthage would be unknown save to a few erudite historians. (p. 282)*

After the destruction of Carthage, the Romans established a group of five provinces in North Africa, called Africa Romana. The ancient Libyan inhabitants of this region, originally a branch of western Ethiopians, became intermixed with Phoenician, Greek and Roman immigrants, which further explains today's lighter complexioned north African people.

During this period of Roman oppression, ancient Hebrew traditions state that the people of Israel were anticipating the coming of a great liberator, a "Messiah" who would free them from the control of the Roman government.

Although the Israelites were expecting a powerful political leader or a military strategist, Jesus represented neither. Yet, his teachings of peace through spiritual reformation were seen as dangerously revolutionary to the government. He pointed out the hypocrisy of the religious leaders of the day, boldly exposing how they misused the laws and regulations brought by Moses to exploit and oppress the people.

Those first Egyptians to accept the teachings of Jesus were called Coptics. Their conversion was really a reestablishment of the monotheistic teachings of Imhotep and other Egyptian ancestors who discouraged idol worship and preached doctrines of peace.

In the book *Peoples and Cultures of Africa,* edited by Elliott P. Skinner, author A.J. Davis explains the evolution of Egyptian religion in a chapter entitled "Coptic Christianity:"

Christianity, which eventually became the religion of the original Egyptian race -- the Copts -- first entered the country through the missionary campaign of St. Mark ... The teaching of the "Man from Nazareth" displaced the ancient pagan religion, although it took several centuries to do this completely...

The years between the influence of Mark in Egypt and the persecutions of about A.D. 300 saw a great transformation in Egyptian thought and feeling. The efforts of those who followed the teaching of Jesus of Nazareth soon went far beyond the expectations or even the hopes of those who were close to him, and with this success over the Old Egyptian God, Amon-Re (Light of the World) there followed Egyptian disenchantment with their "sacred animals" and disillusionment with the old worship of rocks ...

The idea held in pre-Christian Egypt that God is one and that the numberless names, idols, and

*images all pointed to aspects of the same principle
found its way into the new religion ... The Egyptian
idea of eternal conflict and the difference between
good and evil supported the teaching in the new
religion of hell and heaven. (pp. 678, 680)*

Other African nations also adopted Jesus'
teachings of a spiritual rebirth through repentance
and a reformation of behavior. Ethiopia, with its
long history of spiritual leaders and prophets, was
another nation which was influenced by the ministry
of Jesus.

History records that after years of persecuting
the followers of Jesus, the Roman empire embraced
a religious belief which it claimed as Christianity,
and the Christian church became an arm of the
Roman government.

Coptic Christianity, as practiced in Egypt,
promoted the belief that Christ was created by the
Father and was therefore subordinate to Him.
However, this conflicted with orthodox Roman
Church belief which taught that Christ was co-
eternal and co-equal with the Father. The Roman
occupation of Egypt created an ideological conflict
regarding the nature of Jesus, which caused the
Christian Church of Egypt to split in two. In the
year 451 C.E., at the Council of Chalcedon, Church
authorities rejected the Coptic Christian teachings
and voted that Christ was to be considered as the
Son of God, part of the Trinity, with two distinct
natures, one human and one Divine. The Coptics of
Egypt were then considered heretics, and were
isolated from the rest of the Church.

Racism was not an integral part of the
Christian religion at first. In fact, the earliest
religious figures were portrayed as black, a testimony

of the race of Mary and the Hebrew people. Many of the early saints, much admired in Rome during the formation of the Roman Christian church, were also black.

Some African American historians, born and bred under the yoke of American racism, interpret the conversion to Christianity by Africans as just a European scheme to destroy "traditional African religions." However, Christianity itself was first an African religion, then was adopted and distorted by Europeans. The racism was developed as a part of the religion much later, mainly to excuse the European slave trade. But, initially, the teachings of Jesus represented a continuation of the spiritual reformation which occurred throughout the history of mankind.

ROME'S DECLINE AND FALL

The rise to power of the early Christian church catapulted civilization into a major decline. As part of the Roman empire, the leaders of the primitive Christian church were, for the most part, according to John J. Jackson, ignorant, bigoted religious fanatics who embarked on a course promoting faith and destroying knowledge.

But the Roman society was not built to last. They were greatly deficient in the areas of pure science and abstract thought, although they made some strides in the industrial arts. But, the defects of Roman civilization overshadowed its virtues and, in due time, led to its disintegration. The main shortcomings of Rome were slavery, militarism, and a bad fiscal system.

The Roman ruling class tried to forestall the impending fall of the nation by abolishing the old

pagan cults and making Christianity the state
religion, but this was of no avail. Old Roman rituals
and beliefs crept into Christian teachings and became
incorporated with Christianity itself.

The infusion of Roman culture into Christian
doctrine can be accredited in a large part to the
Apostle Paul. Paul, according to the Bible, claimed
to have had a profound spiritual experience while on
the road to Damascus. He then sought to join Jesus'
Apostles, whom he had previously persecuted, and
began to preach in the Synagogues in an effort to
convert the Jews.

He and the other Apostles weren't having
much luck with conversions, however. The followers
of Jesus were being beaten up, stoned and killed for
trying to spread Jesus' teachings of peace.

So Paul, after receiving only halfhearted
acceptance among the original Apostles of Jesus, and
after three years of unsuccessful preaching among
the Jews, decided to change his strategy. After
enduring intense persecution, the Apostles had
scattered abroad to other cities, but were still
preaching to the Jews only. However, as J. D. Shams
notes in his book, *Where Did Jesus Die?:*

*By this time Paul had despaired of the
conversion of the Jews. So he determined to preach
openly to the Gentiles. Nevertheless this was against
the teaching of Jesus; he had strictly prohibited his
disciples, saying:*

*"Go not unto the way of the Gentiles and city of
the Samaritans enter ye not. But go rather to the lost
sheep of the House of Israel."...*

*Despite being opposed by the disciples, he
continued preaching to the Gentiles and was
successful in his mission. The disciples, who were*

bitterly persecuted, eventually agreed with him that he should continue his work among the Gentiles and they would preach to the Israelites.

He further realized that to ensure success amongst the Gentiles, the teaching propounded by Jesus and practiced faithfully by him and his disciples must be modified. He saw that the ceremonies and rites of the Mosaic Law could never be accepted by those who were not Jews. With characteristic boldness, therefore, he declared the abolishment of the Law with all ceremonials and ordinances and gave a new direction to Christianity which became a complex of his own active imagination, Roman thought and Greek philosophy. (pp. 52-53)

Shams observes that Paul's deviations from Jesus' teachings in order to accommodate the Romans was hotly debated by the rest of the Apostles. While Jesus taught that spiritual reformation came through sincere repentance, prayer, good deeds, and observance of the commandments given by Moses, Paul taught that the only thing required to get to Heaven was belief that Jesus acted as a sacrificial lamb, dying for the sins of mankind. This was an easy faith for the Gentiles to follow, since they already believed this about their own gods. Shams states:

At the festivals of Adonis, which were held in western Asia and in Greek lands, the death of the god was annually mourned with a bitter wailing, chiefly by women; images of him dressed to resemble corpses were carried out for burial and then thrown into the sea or into springs. In some places his revival was celebrated on the following day. At Alexandria they

*sorrowed not without hope, for they sang that the one
lost would come back again. In the great Phoenician
Sanctuary of Astarte at Byblus the death of Adonis
was annually mourned -- but next day he was believed
to come to life again, and ascend to heaven in the
presence of his worshippers ...*

*The central idea behind the worship of Adonis
was the death and resurrection of this god; he was
killed by a boar, but the boar was an incarnation of
himself, and thus the god was both executioner and
victim, an idea propounded in the Epistle to the
Hebrews wherein Christ is described as high Priest,
who to put away sin, sacrificed Himself. (pp. 61, 63)*

In addition, there was the worship of Attis, the
Good Shepherd, son of Cybele, the Great Mother,
sometimes known as the virgin Nana, who conceived
him without the union of a mortal man, like the
story of the Virgin Mary. According to Roman belief,
in the prime of his manhood he mutilated himself
and bled to death at the foot of his sacred pine tree.
During the Spring festival of Cybele, held from
March 22 to 25, a pine tree was felled on March 22
and to its trunk an effigy of the god was fastened.
This effigy was later buried in a tomb, where it
remained until March 24th, the Day of Blood. In this
part of the ceremony, the High Priest, impersonating
Attis, drew blood from a human sacrifice. In the
olden days, Shams notes, the priest was actually
hanged or slain, to perform the act of sacrificing
himself.

When comparing these pagan religions to St.
Paul's presentation of Jesus and the crucifixion, it
appears that his version of Christianity is simply a
copy of many previously held Gentile beliefs. The
Romans' acceptance of Christianity as presented by

Paul demanded no change in their behavior and therefore did not lead to the moral reformation of Roman society.

One of Rome's major pagan festivals, the feast of Saturnalia, was held on December 25, around the winter solstice. This celebration was marked with wild, drunken parties. Once the government adopted Christianity, they turned this festival into a celebration of the birth of Jesus, a tradition which is carried on in the Western world to this day (complete with the wild, drunken parties).

As time passed, this religion, created by Paul and accepted by the Romans, became the conquering religion of the Roman Empire. Shams observes that the pagan beliefs and practices continued, merging of the worship of Attis into that of Jesus. Finally, in the year 325 C.E., about three centuries after the crucifixion, at the Council of Nicaea, Jesus was officially recognized by the Church as God. At this point, all Roman art depicting Jesus, Mary, and other Biblical characters, portrayed them as looking like Romans.

Roman attitudes toward domination through military rule and the practice of slavery continued. Rome's fall has often been blamed on barbarian invasions, but they are not totally to blame for its collapse. Among the barbarians who invaded the Roman Empire were a Teutonic tribe called the Vandals. In 411 C.E. they attained official status as subjects of the Roman Empire,and were given grants of land. Geneseric, King of the Vandals, was given rule over certain provinces in Africa Romana. He treated the Africans harshly, seizing the wealthiest African nobles and making them slaves to his sons and top followers. He took the best African land and parceled it out among the Vandals, leaving the

2C

Entrance To the Temple Of Luxor
*One of the entrances to the Lotus Column Court of the Temple
of Luxor in Egypt had pillars of enormous height. The size of
the building can be best understood by comparing the height of
the man standing at the bottom, right side. (Reprinted from
Illustrated Africa, North, Tropical, South, page 216, by William
D. Boyce, Copyright 1925 by Rand McNally)*

African people with land of inferior quality. He then charged them high taxes. (Does this sound familiar?)

It has been said of the Vandals, "They found Africa flourishing and they left it desolate, with its great buildings thrown down, its people reduced to slavery and the Church of Africa -- so important in those early days of Christianity -- practically non-existent."

Now we know what "vandalizing" really means.

By the end of the fifth century, Europe had begun the long night of the Dark Ages, which lasted 500 years (500 C.E. - 1000 C.E.)

So, now here we have another 500 years where Europeans were virtually absent from the stage of world history. And during that time, Africa flourished. What caused Africa to rise to prominence again? And what happened, after 1000 years of world supremacy, that caused Africa to fall again to European conquest? The real story behind the African slave trade is exposed in the next chapter, "A Hidden Spiritual Heritage."

CHAPTER THREE
A Hidden Spiritual Heritage

3A

The Royal Court Of Abyssinia

At the top, an Abyssinian Empress is attended by two of the members of her court. At the bottom, on the left is the Prime Minister. At the right is the Court Page. These pictures leave no doubt as to the race of the Abyssinian people. (Reprinted from Illustrated Africa, North, Tropical, South, page 421, by William D. Boyce, Copyright 1925 by Rand McNally)

CHAPTER THREE
A Hidden Spiritual Heritage

Mention African religion and usually the image of beating drums and barefooted, mask-wearing black bodies dancing wildly around a fire come to mind. Some vague notion of "voodoo" or something is connected with this picture, and many African Americans breathe an inward sigh of relief that they have been "saved" from all that "pagan" worship.

This, of course, is another big lie used to get African Americans to excuse the European slave trade with the thought, "Well, at least we found God."

Just think -- now, how is it that the people whose great stone monuments stand as wonders of the world today are suddenly running around the jungle with spears and loincloths? Even some African American writers fail to see how inconsistent this is: On the one hand, they claim Egyptian civilization as African, then on the other hand they state that the Africans who were captured and enslaved by Europeans could not read or write, wore little clothing, and worshipped idols.

Apparently something is not being told here. So, let us add the missing pieces and give a more complete picture of the rise and fall of Africa.

AFRICA'S SPIRITUAL REBIRTH

It seems that much of Africa's recent history is tied to a revolutionary movement beginning in the latter part of the sixth century. In 571 C.E. (Christian Era) the birth of Muhammad Mustapha in Arabia heralded a new system of religion that profoundly affected the course of human events. This new religion, called Islam, spread like wildfire.

The teachings of the religion appealed to all classes of people. Islam recognized Moses and Jesus as prophets of God, but strictly forbade worship of symbols, idols or human beings. The doctrines of equality and brotherhood were cherished by the oppressed. And its encouragement of followers to seek knowledge was in stark contrast to the repression of thought under the Roman Christian church. In fact, Islam's stress on seeking knowledge led to the rise of many world renowned scholars, whose works are admired to this day.

As the earlier genealogical chart shows, the people of the North African region, which later became Arabia, share a common Hamitic ancestor with the people of Egypt. The African origins of Arabia are explained by John D. Baldwin, in his book, *Pre-Historic Nations:*

At the present time Arabia is inhabited by two distinct races; namely descendants of the old Adite, Kushite, or Ethiopian race, known under various appellations, and dwelling chiefly at the south, east, and in the central parts of the country, but formerly supreme throughout the whole peninsula; and the Semitic Arabians -- Mahomet's race -- found chiefly in the Hejzas and at the north. In some districts of the country these races are more or less mixed, and since the rise of Mahometism the language of the Semites, known to us as Arabic, has almost wholly superseded the old Ethiopian or Kushite tongue; but the two races are very unlike in many respects, and the distinction has always been recognized by writers on Arabian ethnology. To the Kushite race belongs the purest Arabian blood, and also that great and very ancient civilization whose ruins abound in almost every district of the country. (pp. 73, 74)

The appearance of the earlier Arabian people show evidence of an African ancestry. In his book *The Arabs*, author Dr. Bertram Thomas asserts:

The original inhabitants of Arabia ... were not the familiar Arabs of our own time, but a very much darker people. A protonegroid belt of mankind stretched across the ancient world from Africa to Malaya. This belt, by environmental and other evolutionary process, became in parts transformed, giving rise to the Hamitic peoples of Africa, to the Dravidian peoples of India, and to an intermediate dark people inhabiting the Arabian peninsula. in the course of time two big migrations of fair skinned peoples came from the north, one of them, the Mongoloids, to break through and transform the dark belt of man beyond India; the other, the Caucasoids, to drive a wedge between India and Africa. (p. 339)

Although the physical features of many Arabs today are slightly more European, the history of the Arabian people is intertwined with that of the Africans. Cheikh Anta Diop, in his book *African Origin of Civilization*, traces the ancestry of Muhammad all the way back to an Egyptian woman and traces many of the practices in Islam to ancient Egypt:

The 30 day fasting period already existed, as in Egypt ... There were also sacred springs and stones, as in Moslem times. Zenzen, a sacred spring. Kaaba, a sacred stone. The pilgrimage to Mecca already existed. The Kaaba was reputed to have been constructed by Ishmael, son of Abraham and Hagar the Egyptian (a Negro woman), historical ancestor of Muhammad according to all Arab historians. (p. 127)

Arabia, although today it is viewed as separate from Africa, was at one time part of the old Egyptian empire. Similarities in culture, traditions and even appearance of the Arabs and the Egyptians are perhaps evidence of this. Often Islam is portrayed by western writers as an "Arab" religion, forced upon some Africans at the point of a sword. But many Islamic practices and beliefs are common to ancient African religions. The heritage of the founder of Islam is rooted in Africa.

Muhammad Mustapha was born in Mecca, Arabia. His father, Abdullah, was an Arab, who died before Muhammad's birth. Not much is recorded about Muhammad's mother, Amina, but some accounts indicate she may have been an Ethiopian. The Arabs claim descent from Abraham, great grandson of Shem, Noah's oldest son. The Bible, in the book of Genesis, gives a genealogical account of Abraham's descendants. Abraham and Hagar had a son, Ishmael. Ishmael and his wife had a son, Kedar. (Genesis 25:13). As noted in Chapter One, Kedar in Hebrew means "very black." Kedar is the son from whom the Arab tribe of Muhammad Mustapha claims to descend. Abraham, like his ancestor Noah, must have been dark skinned.

Abraham's descendants from his wife Sarah are considered to be the ancestors of the Jews. Abraham and Sarah had a son, Isaac. Isaac and Rebekah had a son, Jacob. And Jacob and Rachel had a son, Joseph. Joseph became a high official in the Egyptian kingdom during the period of the Sixteenth or Seventeenth Dynasty. The carved statue of Joseph (see Chapter Two, page 68) is a good indication of how Abraham and his descendants may have looked. It also gives a clue as to how Muhammad and his people may have looked.

3B

Arab Types

According to historical traditions, Arabs share a common Hamitic ancestor with Egyptians and Ethiopians. Arabia was at one time part of the old Egyptian Empire. These photos, taken in Morocco, illustrate the African genetic influence on Arabian people. The photo at the top is identified as an Arab. The photo at the bottom is considered a "Negro" Arab, possibly the result of a mixture of Arab and African. (Reprinted from Illustrated Africa, North, Tropical, South, page 49, by William D. Boyce, Copyright 1925 by Rand McNally)

MUSLIMS SEEK REFUGE IN ETHIOPIA

Just like the early Christians who declared their allegiance to Jesus and sought to follow his teachings, the earlier Muslims were also harassed, beaten, and tortured. When the persecution became unbearable, Muhammad assembled his followers and sent them to Abyssinia. He told them that they would be safe there, because the king was a just king who respected the belief in one God.

So, the earlier Muslims migrated to Abyssinia, a place of high culture and learning, where peace and human rights were held sacred. This was the turning point in the spread of Islam, which planted the seed for the Golden Age of Africa.

Even those who did not believe Muhammad to be any divinely led ruler recognized his reputation as one who was honest and truthful. He became known as The Truthful One. When he related the words which he said were told to him by God, they were recorded in what is now known as the Quran, the Islamic book of scripture. All the verses Muhammad spoke were said to be what he heard directly from God, through the angel Gabriel.

Various people from different tribes began to accept his teachings, and the followers of Islam steadily grew. One of the well known first followers of Muhammad was an Ethiopian named Bilal. He was a companion of Muhammad, and fought in some of the earlier wars in defense of Islam. He became a powerful general and led the Muslim army to many great victories. Later, Muhammad appointed him as an Ambassador. His deep, rich voice earned him the distinction of being the first "Muezzin," the person who announces the call to prayer during each of the five daily prayer times for Muslims.

The first efforts to spread this new movement to entire nations came through diplomatic letters Muhammad sent to the rulers of the day, inviting them to accept Islam as their faith. These letters document the changes in the political climate since Egypt's golden age. In his book *The Life Of Muhammad,* author Hazrat Mirza Bashir-Ud-Din Mahmud Ahmad translates this letter sent by Muhammad to the Negus (a title reserved for the royal head of state), King of Abyssinia:

LETTER TO THE NEGUS, KING OF ABYSSINIA

In the name of Allah, the Gracious, the Merciful, Muhammad, the Messenger of God, writes to the Negus, King of Abyssinia. O King, peace of God be upon you. I praise before you the one and only God. None else is worthy of worship. He is the King of Kings, the source of all excellence, free from all defects, He provides peace to all his servants and protects all his creatures. I bear witness that Jesus, son of Mary was a Messenger of God, who came in fulfillment of promises made to Mary by God. Mary had consecrated her life to God. I invite you to join with me in attaching ourselves to the One and Only God and in obeying Him. I invite you also to follow me and believe in the God who hath sent me. I am His Messenger, I invite you and your armies to join the Faith of the Almighty God. I discharge my duty hereby. I have delivered to you the Message of God, and made clear to you the meaning of this Message. I have done so in all sincerity and I trust you will value the sincerity which prompted this message. He who obeys the guidance of God becomes heir to the blessings of God." (p. 120)

3C

Muhammad Mustapha's letter to the Negus, King of Ethiopia
This is a photocopy of the actual letter sent by Muhammad
Mustapha, who is known as the Holy Prophet of Islam, to the
Negus, King of Ethiopia. The letter was kept sealed in an ivory
box by the government of Ethiopia for 1,000 years. (Reprinted
from Letters From The Holy Prophet, page 49, by Sultan Ahmed
Qureshi, Copyright 1986 by Noor Publishing House.)

During this time, much of the area which had been part of the old Egyptian Empire was under foreign domination or was controlled by the Roman government. Many of the leaders responded with hostility when contacted by Muhammad and scoffed at his invitation to accept the teachings of Islam. However, when the Negus received Muhammad's letter, he showed very great regard and respect for it. The land of Abyssinia was a place where many prophets had brought spiritual teachings. Moses had said that God told him:

"I will raise up for them a prophet like you from among their brothers; I will put my words in his mouth, and he will tell them everything I command him. If anyone does not listen to my words that the prophet speaks in my name, I myself will call them into account."
The Bible, Deuteronomy 18:18,19

"Their brothers" is interpreted by some scholars as a reference to the Arabs, who are descendants of Ishmael, the brother of Isaac, ancestor of the Jews. Jesus had told his followers:

"But when he, the Spirit of truth, comes, he will guide you into all truth. He will not speak on his own; he will speak only what he hears, and he will tell you what is yet to come."
The Bible, John 16:13

The Negus, being a Christian, could have recalled these prophesies, and may possibly have recognized Muhammad as the person to whom they referred. He held the letter from Muhammad up to his eyes, then ordered that the letter be placed in an ivory box, saying, "While this letter is safe, my kingdom is safe."

What he said actually proved true. For the next thousand years, in spite of wars in surrounding territories, the kingdom of Abyssinia remained untouched.

Muhammad sent two more letters to the King of Ethiopia in which he preached the message of Islam. The Ethiopian ruler was quite moved by these letters. According to the book, *Letters of The Holy Prophet* by Sultan Ahmed Qureshi, the Negus wrote this letter in response to Muhammad:

TO MUHAMMAD, PROPHET OF ALLAH. MAY PEACE BE ON HIM.

From As'hama, the Negus.
May peace be on you O Prophet of Allah! May blessings and favors of Allah be on you. Allah, except Whom there is none worthy of worship, Who has shown me the way of Islam and has guided me.

O Prophet of Allah! I had the honour of seeing your esteemed letter. Whatever you have written about Isa Jesus (A. S.) I swear by the Allah, Lord of earth and Heaven, that Isa (A.S.) is nothing more than that. I have well understood all these things which you have conveyed to me. Your cousin and his companions are my close companions.

I bear evidence that you are a true Prophet of Allah. I have taken bai'at (oath of allegiance to Allah and His Prophet) at the hand of your cousin, for the sake of Allah and have become a slave of Islam. O Allah's Prophet! I send my son Arha to you. If you will so order, I will present myself to you. May peace and blessings of Allah be on you. (pp. 52, 53)

The conversion of the king of Ethiopia to Islam paved the way for strong diplomatic relations between Ethiopia and Arabia for centuries to come.

In spite of the destruction brought by Roman armies, Africa was experiencing growth and development during these years while Islam was in its infancy. As Europe was passing through its Dark Ages, Africa was experiencing the beginning of a new age.

THE GOLDEN AGE OF AFRICA

The Golden Age of West Africa covers a span of time from the beginning of the eighth Century to the end of the 18th Century. Africa enjoyed more than 10 centuries of thriving civilization under four great trading empires. In *Introduction To African Civilization,* Jackson states them as:

WEST AFRICAN EMPIRE	YEARS OF RULE	
Ghana (The first great empire of the Medieval Sudan)	700 C.E.-	1200
Mali (Absorbed the empire of Ghana and expanded Westward)	1200 -	1500
Songhay (Slowly took over Mali empire)	1350 -	1600
Kanem Bornu (Last great African empire before European take over)	1600 -	1700

The Ghanaian Empire of the Medieval era originated in the western Sudan, in a region northeast of the Senegal River and northwest of the Niger river. At the height of its power, it ruled over lands stretching westward to the Atlantic Ocean; Eastward to the south bend of the Niger River; Southward to the port near the headwaters of the Niger; and Northward into the sandy wastes of the Sahara Desert. In its heyday, Ghana covered the area that would include the modern nations of Guinea, Senegal, Mali, and Mauritania.

The founders of Ghana were a people known as the Soninkes. They consisted of groups of tribes related by a common ancestry, and each tribe contained a number of family groups or clans. The main family groups were the Sisse, Drame, Sylla and Kante.

The clans employed an organized system of division of labor which was instrumental in regulating the various functions of government. For example, as relates historian John G. Jackson in *Introduction to African Civilizations:*

> *The Sisse was the clan of the ruling class; from it was chosen the principal political officials and the governors of provinces. The Kante clan provided the artisans, who engaged in metal working, such as blacksmiths, goldsmiths, silversmiths, etc. Other clans specialized in such activities as agriculture, fishing, animal husbandry and the manufacture of clothing. (p. 200)*

The Kante clan of artisans and iron workers surfaces again many times throughout history, and has a tremendous impact on present day African Americans.

Besides iron, Ghana possessed a seemingly inexhaustible supply of gold. The ruler of the empire was considered Commander-in-Chief of the army, the head of the state religion, and chief dispenser of justice.

The Ghana empire had its beginnings in the year 300 A.D., when the Berber invaders from North Africa ruled the region. Then the leader of the Sisse clan of the Soninkes organized a revolution and ousted the Berbers. The Soninke people laid the foundation for the Ghana empire, growing in power over generations by employing the simple principle of cooperation between families. Like many kingdoms of the past, Ghana built an empire by annexing other kingdoms. The year 700 A.D. saw the development of a full-fledged kingdom, the first great empire of the Medieval Sudan.

The story of Ghana provides a blueprint for present day African Americans. Empires are built gradually, by family groups coming together, combining skills and talents to create a strong society. By organizing their skills and manpower, these societies are able to control their economy. This is the foundation for independence.

In contrast to the thriving Ghanaian empire, Arabia at this time was in a most barbaric state. According to Hazrat Mirza Bashir-Ud-Din Mahmud Ahmad in his book *The Life Of Muhammad*, Arabs were given to excessive drinking of alcohol, and gambling was the national sport. While they were much interested in the art of language, their knowledge of history, geography, and mathematics was practically nothing. There was in the whole of Arabia not a single school. It was said that in Mecca, only a few individuals could read and write.

Women in Arab society had no status and no

rights. Because sons were preferred, many people put their baby girls to death. This was a violent society, where tribal wars resulted in wide-scale bloodshed. Slavery was widespread. Weak tribes were conquered and made into slaves. Women slaves were used to satisfy sexual desires. In terms of civilization and social advance, the Arabs were a very backward people. Their chief occupation was trade, and for this they sent their caravans to far off places such as Abyssinia, Syria, Palestine, and even India.

In spite of their backwardness, the religion of Islam produced a miraculous change in the people of Arabia. This philosophy, which forbids drinking and gambling, also preached equality of men and women and the right of the poor to share in the wealth of the rich. It soon spread to North Africa, and in time the country of Morocco became part of a growing Islamic empire.

AFRICAN MOORS BRING LIGHT TO EUROPE

The Moroccans (or Moors, as they were called), became a powerful force in the civilizing of Europe. It began with the conquest of Spain under Moorish general Tarik. An army of twelve thousand Africans was recruited and placed under his command. When ten thousand Senegalese soldiers clad in shining white uniforms, all riding graceful white horses, came galloping into Spain in perfect unison, the sight was too awesome for the Spanish soldiers to withstand. They laid down their arms in surrender, refusing to fight such a powerful force. Tarik's army captured all of Spain -- quite a conquest for Africa.

The Moors laid the foundation of a new civilization in Spain. There they introduced the silk industry. In the field of agriculture, they were highly skilled and introduced rice, sugar cane, dates, ginger, cotton, lemons and strawberries into the country. Ibn Khaldun, a Moorish expert on agriculture, wrote a valuable treatise on farming and worked out a theory of prices and the nature of capital.

How Spain flourished under African rule! In the eighth century, education was universal in Spain under the Moors, who followed the prophet Muhammad's command to "seek knowledge." However in the rest of Europe, still under Roman Christian rule, 99 percent of the people were illiterate. In Spain, there were 200,000 homes, 800 public baths, many colleges and universities and many royal palaces surrounded by beautiful gardens.

In the tenth century, Cordova, Spain, was very much like a modern city, because of the influence of these Africans. The streets were well paved and there were raised sidewalks for pedestrians. At night one could walk for ten miles by the light of lamps flanked by an uninterrupted extent of buildings. And this was hundreds of years before there was a paved street in Paris or a street lamp in London!

As the Moors brought modern civilization to Europe during the dark ages, the Ghanaian empire enjoyed great prosperity in the tenth and eleventh centuries. Its efficient armies discouraged invaders and maintained internal peace while the rich lands produced ample crops of cotton, millet and sorghum. Its capital city, Kumbi, became a great trading emporium.

By the middle of the eleventh century, the empire of Ghana had reached its peak. But the neighbors of Ghana envied its wealth and began to raid its fringes, causing a sudden decline.

EUROPE BECOMES RELIGIOUS
BATTLEGROUND

As the barbarous pagan tribes in north and east Europe engaged in bloody warfare throughout the seventh through twelfth centuries, the church of Rome and the rising Islamic forces were battling to gain supremacy in the land. The outcome of their struggles was an unexpected massive religious conversion which confuses many historians to this day.

According to the book *The Thirteenth Tribe*, by Arthur Koestler, European Jews first appeared in about 740 C.E. (Christian Era). The people of eastern Europe known as Khazars lived between the Caucasus and the Volga (the area which is now Poland, Hungary and Czechoslovakia). They are described as white complexioned with blue eyes and flowing reddish hair. They occupied a strategic position at the gateway between the Black Sea and the Caspian during a time of rising invasions from the barbarian tribes of the north -- the Bulgars, Magyars, Pechenegs, the Vikings and the Russians -- and the advancing Arab armies from the east.

The Christians diligently sought to convert the Khazars to Christianity and the Muslims sought to convert them to Islam, both for politically strategic reasons. Koestler explains:

At the beginning of the eighth century, the world was polarized between the two super-powers representing Christianity and Islam. Their ideological doctrines were welded to power-politics pursued by the classical methods of propaganda, subversion and military conquest. The Khazar Empire represented a Third Force, which had proved

*equal to either of them, both as an adversary and an
ally. But it could only maintain its independence by
accepting neither Christianity nor Islam -- for either
choice would have automatically subordinated it to
the authority of the Roman Emperor or the Caliph of
Baghdad. (p. 59)*

According to Koestler, The Khazars had been
exposed somewhat to the Jewish faith by Hebrew
refugees who had fled to eastern Europe to escape
religious persecution under the Emperor Romanus.
The Khazar King sought to remain a politically
neutral force between the Christians and the
Muslims. According to Arab and Hebrew records,
after consulting with a Jewish scholar the King
realized that Judaism was a religion which was
respected by both Christians and Muslims. As Jews,
he reasoned, the Khazars would not be considered
pagans and barbarians, as were the other eastern
European tribes, but would be regarded as people of
the holy scriptures.

Around 740 C.E., the Khazar King, his court
and the military ruling class embraced the Jewish
faith and Judaism became the state religion of the
Khazars.   Nearly two centuries later, a Jewish
heritage had become well entrenched in the Khazar
culture.   Koestler relates that in 929, Hasdai Ibn
Shaprut, the chief minister of the Caliph of Cordoba
discovered that a Jewish kingdom existed in eastern
Europe.   Hasdai wrote to the Khazar king of the
time, King Joseph, to inquire as to which of the Lost
Tribes of Israel they belonged. Joseph sent a letter
in reply. Koestler notes:

*Though a fierce Jewish nationalist, proud of
wielding the 'Sceptre of Judah', he cannot, and does*

*not, claim for them Semitic descent; he traces their
ancestry not to Shem, but to Noah's third son,
Japheth; or more precisely to Japheth's grandson,
Togarma, the ancestor of all Turkish tribes. 'We have
found in the family registers of our fathers,' Joseph
asserts boldly, 'that Togarma had ten sons, and the
names of their offspring are as follows: Uigur, Dursu,
Avars, Huns, Basilii, Tarniakh, Khazars, Zagora,
Bulgars, Sabir. We are the sons of Khazar, the
seventh...' (p. 72)*

So now a clarification can be made. The
Hebrews were a race of people who had settled in a
certain part of Northeast Africa. Judaism is a
religion founded by Moses, a Hebrew, which espoused
monotheism and refuted the many pagan practices in
Egypt at the time. Many Europeans are Jews, but
the Hebrews of the Bible are Africans. The white
Jews who were victims of Hitler's policy of Jewish
extermination from Europe and who are claiming
rights to present day Israel are in fact descendants
from those earlier European converts. They are not
the Hebrews of the Bible. Koestler reflects on this
discovery:

*This has led several historians to conjecture
that a substantial part, and perhaps the majority of
eastern Jews -- and hence of world Jewry -- might be
of Khazar and not of Semitic origin ...*
*If so, this would mean that their ancestors
came not from the Jordan but from the Volga, not
from Canaan but from the Caucasus, once believed to
be the cradle of the Aryan race; and that genetically
they are more closely related to the Hun, Uigur and
Magyar tribes than to the seed of Abraham, Isaac and
Jacob. Should this turn out to be the case, then the*

*term 'anti-Semitism' would become void of meaning...
The story of the Khazar Empire, as it slowly emerges
from the past, begins to look like the most cruel hoax
which history has ever perpetrated. (pp. 16, 17)*

The descendants of the Khazar Jewish
converts spread throughout Europe and later gained
economic power and influence in many European
countries.

MANDINKAS ESTABLISH MALI EMPIRE

The State of Mali, once part of the empire of
Ghana, rose to prominence upon the weakening of
the empire from outside attacks. The new state of
Mali was established by the Mandinka people. It's
capital city, Kangaba, was located on the Niger River,
about 250 miles south of Kumbi. The Mandinkas
(Sometimes spelled Mandinke or Mandingo) play a
special role in later African-American history.

King Sundiata, the first great ruler of Mali,
came to power in 1230. Sundiata traces his ancestry
all way back to Bilal, one of the first followers of
Islam. Sundiata also embraced Islam and Mali
became the first Muslim state in the Sudan. He
gained control of the salt and gold trade and stressed
agricultural expansion. He turned many of his
soldiers into farmers, training them in the raising of
poultry and cattle. With an adequate food supply,
the empire was strengthened. (Perhaps today's rulers
should study his program.)

Sundiata, after his death, was succeeded by his
son Wali, who adopted the title "Mansa" (meaning
Emperor or Sultan). This title was later transferred
to his successors.

Perhaps one of history's most famous rulers

was Mansa Musa, who ascended the throne in 1307. During his twenty five-year reign, he gained fame throughout Africa, the Middle East, and Europe. He was known as a devout Muslim, but was not fanatical. He adopted a policy of tolerance toward his non-Muslim subjects, although it troubled him that many of them still worshipped many gods.

According to some accounts, Mansa Musa rose to power after his uncle, who was ruler of Mali before him, took a fleet of 200 ships on an expedition headed west across the Atlantic ocean and never returned. Only one ship came back from this journey. It could be presumed that the others arrived on the continent of America and made it their home. Later on, we will discuss evidence of this.

The greatest event in the reign of Mansa Musa was his famous pilgrimage to Mecca in 1324. It was a spectacular event. All Muslims are required, if they can, to visit the Holy land of Mecca. After months of preparation, Mansa Musa set out with an entourage of 60,000 toward Mecca. To finance his journey, 80 camels were loaded with 300 pounds of gold dust each. He also took with him a staff of cooks to prepare elaborate meals for the entire assembly at each rest stop. During his journey, he spread so much gold around that the economies of the surrounding countries were greatly affected. His journey aroused great curiosity (and later led to visits from foreigners seeking ways to get some of the wealth). When Mansa Musa and his entourage reached Cairo in July 1324, the Sultan of Egypt held a grand celebration. After visiting the holy cities of Mecca and Medina in Arabia, Mansa Musa returned to Cairo and lavishly distributed the gold and other gifts. This elaborate pilgrimage was talked about for years, and Mansa Musa gained widespread prestige.

When Mansa Musa died in 1332, he was succeeded by his son Mahan, who unfortunately was neither as wise nor as able as his father. During his reign, Mali went into a decline. The great Mali city of Timbuktu, known worldwide for its outstanding centers of learning, was captured by enemy forces and burned.

In about 1475 the Songhay Empire arose. In a series of battles, Mali struggled to maintain its supremacy. In 1481, Portuguese sailors landed on the Atlantic coast of Mali and the Mali government attempted to hire the Portuguese as mercenaries to fight the rising nation of Songhay. This proposed alliance never took place, but the Portuguese did, however, gain an opportunity to observe the tremendous wealth of African cities. It also set into motion the later disaster suffered by the entire continent of Africa. The slave trade grew and was able to flourish as a result of rival African nations attempting to gain supremacy by enlisting the aid of European invaders.

THE SCHOLARS OF SONGHAY

Mali finally disintegrated and was replaced by Songhay. In the year 1464, Sunni Ali The Great rose to the Songhay throne and an age of great achievement began. The city of Timbuktu was restored as a center of commerce and culture, home of the renowned University of Sankore, which attracted scholars and students from distant lands.

The city of Jenne became a part of the empire through Sunni Ali's marriage to the widow of the town's ruler. At the University of Jenne, there was a great medical school which produced physicians and surgeons of great skill. Among the difficult surgical operations performed successfully by doctors in Jenne was the removal from cataracts from the eye.

By his death in 1492, Sunni Ali The Great had become one of the most famous rulers of his day. Askia Muhammad came to power upon the death of Sunni Ali. Intellectual progress reached a peak. The Songhay empire grew to cover an area larger than the continent of Europe. The revival of education was a major factor in this remarkable expansion. Chancellor Williams describes the influence of African education in his book, *The Destruction of African Civilization:*

> *Three of the principal centers of learning were at Jenne, Gao and Timbuktu. At the head of the educational system at Timbuktu was the world famous University of Sankore, drawing students from all West Africa and scholars from different foreign countries. It was especially noted for its high standard of scholarship and, therefore, exacting admission requirements (about which there were some complaints).*
>
> *The University structure consisted of a (1) Faculty of Law, (2) Medicine and surgery, (3) Letters, (4) Grammar, (5) Geography, and (6) Art. (Here "Art" had to do with such practical training as manufacturing, building and other allied crafts. After the basic training the expertise required was through the traditional apprenticeship system in the various craft guilds. (p. 205)*

These were highly prestigious schools, and one had to achieve a certain academic standing to get in. Consider some of America's prestigious schools today, such as Harvard or Yale or Princeton. The University of Sankore, which attracted top students from all

over the world, surpassed even these schools in its
reputation for scholastic excellence.

In the schools, colleges, and universities of the
Songhay Empire, courses were given in astronomy,
mathematics, ethnography, medicine, hygiene,
philosophy, logic, prosody, diction, elocution, rhetoric,
and music. Professor Ahmed Baba, a faculty member
at the University of Sankore in Timbuktu, was a
major scholar. He was author of more than forty
books on such diverse fields as astronomy, biography,
and theology.

The study of Islam and the Quran, along with
law and literature, was at the core of the University's
curriculum. Since the Quran was written in Arabic,
Arabic became the language of the Muslim religion,
much as Latin had become the language of the
Christian religion in Europe. In addition, Arabic was
also the language of trade and commerce. By using
a common language in the world of business and
education, the people of Songhay were able to work
around tribal language differences and expand the
empire for a long time.

THE DECLINE AND FALL OF SONGHAY

Askia Muhammad died in 1558 at the age of
97, and was succeeded by his sons. Unfortunately,
because of their misrule, the empire began to fall
apart. The weakening of the Songhay empire came
at a critical time in history. Just as Europeans began
explorations abroad in search of wealth, Songhay was
in the midst of power struggles with neighboring
states who were fighting for dominance.

The death of Askia Muhammad marked the
beginning of the end of the Songhay Empire, and set
off a chain of events which eventually caused the fall

of Africa and aided in the massive enslavement of African people. Askia's sons fought each other for succession to the throne. They were wasteful and indolent, and mismanaged government affairs so badly that citizens within the empire begin to revolt.

Sibling rivalry and immorality caused the decline of the empire, according to some chroniclers of the time, states Thomas A. Hale, author of *Scribe, Griot and Novelist.* In his book, he quotes one narrator's view that the decadence of the Songhay government was manifest during the reign of Askia Ishaq II, (1588-1591), grandson of Askia Muhammad.

According to Hale, during Ishaq II's reign, one citizen, who had been exiled to the salt mines in Teghazza, reportedly fled to Marrakesh. From there he wrote to the Sultan of Morocco to ask him to invade the Songhay empire and take it over, due to the ineptness of Songhay's leadership.

Hale explains that the Moroccans began pressuring Askia Ishaq II to give up control of the Teghazza salt mines, a continuing source of revenue for Songhay.   This was the time of the Spanish Inquisition and there were fierce battles between the Islamic Moors and the Christian Spaniards.   The Sultan of Morocco indicated that if ownership of the salt mines were handed over to the Moroccans, the revenues would then be used to help finance wars against the Christians.

Ishaq II refused, and the two nations went to war. The two armies met on April 12, 1591, and Ishaq II's soldiers were forced to retreat. As Ishaq II led his army across the river to the right bank at Bara, near Asongo, he was overthrown by his brother Balama Mohammad Gao.

Ishaq fled west toward the country of the Gourma, where he was well received at first. But his hosts assassinated him one night soon after his arrival.   In analyzing the Moorish invasion of Songhay, Hale observes:

One immediate result of the invasion was a general rise in political and moral disorder in the empire. Groups on the fringes revolted. For example, the Bambara sacked Djenne. Es-Sa'di underscores the change wrought by the disintegration of Songhay rule by noting:

"Faith was transformed into infidelity; there was not a single activity forbidden by God which was not practiced openly. People drank wine; they engaged in sodomy, and as for adultery, it had become so frequent that its practice had almost become legal. Without it, there was no elegance, no glory. It was so bad that the children of the sultans committed adultery with their sisters.

"They say that this happened for the first time at the end of the reign of the sultan, the just, the prince of the believers, Askia El-Hadj Mohammed, and that it was his son Yousef-Koi who invented this kind of debauchery...

"It is because of these abominations that God took vengeance by sending to the Songhay the victorious Moroccan army. So the roots of this people were separated from the trunk and the punishment which it endured was of those which are exemplary..."

This interpretation of the causes of the empire's downfall catches the reader's attention not only for the morality that it reveals, but also because these are the first references to deviant sexual practices--in this case incest--in the chronicles. (pp. 119, 120)

The fall of the Songhay empire in 1591 was one of the cataclysmic events of West African history,

Hale asserts. It was the first to fall to the greater firepower of an invading country that obtained some of its soldiers and weaponry from Europe. It's demise marked the beginning of the end of a regional system of government which had survived for many centuries without significant outside interference.

Western historians say that prior to the slave trade, Africans were engaged in "tribal wars," (an expression which conjures up the old image of grass skirt-wearing natives in the jungle hurling spears.)

Such an explanation hardly gives an accurate picture of the real state of affairs within the empire. This was an immensely wealthy nation, and with the death of a powerful ruler, control of the kingdom was up for grabs. Unfortunately, the breakup of the united kingdom of Songhay allowed Europeans to come in and do much of the grabbing.

The Hausa, Yoruba, Fulani, Mandingo, Kru, Ashanti, Ewe, Bantu; the Moor, the Senegalese, the Gambian...all were taken prisoner and held captive on slave ships bound for America and other parts of the Western world. The irony is that today's African American, cut off from the continent for hundreds of years, has no memory of any ethnic or national affiliation. African Americans have intermixed and intermingled between themselves and other races so much that there can be no tribal distinctions. The very identities under which African nations raised the banner of war have been completely removed. Perhaps this is another case of Divine retribution.

However, African Americans still identify themselves as descendants of Africa, but are unburdened by the prejudices of nationalism and tribalism which divides Africa today. They now have an opportunity to reunite with their African born brethren and help to develop a new united Africa.

ACTIVITY:
Be Your Favorite Figure From History

Just as today's national leaders must make critical decisions concerning economics, health care, national security, and social reform, the great leaders from the past were often faced with the same issues. Envision yourself as one of the leaders listed below, in a meeting with your top government advisors. What kind of discussion might you be having regarding the following questions?

Menes - How should the new government of a united Egypt be structured in order to include local leaders and prevent future civil wars?

Khufu - How will the building of the great pyramid affect the economy? How long is the project estimated to take to complete? How many jobs will it create?

Hatshepsut - How can religion be promoted through the building of monuments?

Tiye - What should Asian states be required to give in return for military protection from Egypt?

Hannibal - What kind of military training should soldiers receive to prepare them for the cold journey across the Alps on elephants?

Sundiata - How will taking money from the military and putting it toward agricultural training affect national defense?

Mansa Musa - What provisions should be made for the running of government in the King's absence during the trip to Mecca? What countries should be visited along the way to establish diplomatic ties?

Askia Muhammad - What should be the educational requirements for professors at the world renown Universities of Jenne, Gao and Timbuktu? Which languages should they speak?

CHAPTER FOUR
The Columbus Conspiracy

4A

A Sample Of Moorish Architecture
The famous Muhammad Ali mosque in Cairo, Egypt, built during the Golden Age of Africa, is characteristic of the type of the mosques built in Moorish Spain. (Reprinted from Illustrated Africa, North, Tropical, South, page 185, by William D. Boyce, Copyright 1925 by Rand McNally)

CHAPTER FOUR
The Columbus Conspiracy

Most American history books state that the European Renaissance, beginning around the fourteenth century, was the catalyst for revolutionary thought. Scientific discoveries paved the way for new inventions, we are taught. Before that time, Western historians agree, Europeans were experiencing the "dark ages" of barbaric ignorance.

Because Western education is so Eurocentric, most American students have no idea of the important events going on throughout the rest of the world during the middle ages. Credit for bringing Europe out of its darkness belongs largely to the Moors, the Africans.

"DISCOVERY" OF AMERICA?

The death of kings often marked the beginning of a new era for a nation. Just as Sunni Ali's death in 1492 marked a new period of expansion under Askia Muhammad, the year 1492 also heralded another event in history. Christopher Columbus, who had studied in Moorish Spain, had been exposed to the teachings of the Quran, the scripture of the Muslims. Muslim scholars were able to deduce from observations and certain Quranic verses that the earth was round. In the 55th chapter entitled "Al Rahman," in the 18th verse God is referred to as "The Lord of the two Easts and the Lord of the two Wests."

The earth, being round, creates a condition in which every spot on earth in relation to other spots is an East and a West. The east of the Eastern Hemisphere is the West of the Western Hemisphere,

and the West of the Western Hemisphere is the East
of the Eastern Hemisphere, and thus there are two
Easts and two Wests. This phenomenon could not
exist if the earth was flat, as Europeans believed at
that time. They feared that if one sailed too far in
any direction, one would fall off the edge.

During this period, Europe was in a frenzy to
catch up with other nations in international trade.
India was a hot spot for new merchandise, and
Columbus reasoned that, if the earth was round, he
could sail west and perhaps find a short cut to the
east, and discover a new trade route to India. So, he
set out with this aim in mind, and the results
changed the course of human history.

Columbus became lost at sea was guided to the
shores of what is known today as America. He was
confused as to where he had landed. Mistaking this
parcel of land to be a piece of India, he called the
inhabitants "Indians," an erroneous label that the
people of the continent carry to this day. But,
although Columbus did not reach India, his journey
somewhat proved to Europeans the theory that the
west could be reached by traveling east. However,
African explorers already knew the Earth's shape. In
Introduction to African Civilization, John G. Jackson
reports:

> *The Arab historian Abufeda (1273-1332)
> describes the world as spherical in shape and tells of
> ships that had circumnavigated the globe. An African
> scholar, Al Omari, in a work published in Cairo
> about 1342, tells of mariners of the Mali Empire
> crossing the Atlantic Ocean to the New World during
> the reign of Mansa Musa I ... We now have evidences
> of African contacts with America going back at least
> three thousand years; and the researches of Professor*

Leo Wiener have convinced us, beyond all doubt, that
people of the Mali Empire sent trading expeditions to
America and made cultural contributions to the New
World in pre-Columbian times. (pp. 234, 235)

According to Jackson, Mansa Musa relates this
story to the scholars of Cairo while he was enroute to
Mecca during his famous pilgrimage in 1324:

Mansa Musa's predecessor wanted to discover
the extent of the sea. He sent two hundred ships,
equipped with enough gold, water, and supplies to
last the men for years. He told the ship commanders
to "Return only when you have reached the extremity
of the ocean or when you have exhausted your food
and water." After a very long time, only one ship
returned, and the captain of the ship reported that
the other ships had disappeared in a strong current.
He did not enter the current, but instead chose to
turn and come back.

The head of the Mali empire did not believe it,
and decided to set sail to explore for himself. He
equipped two thousand vessels, a thousand for
himself the men who went with him and a thousand
for water and supplies.

"He conferred power on me and left with his
companions on the ocean. That was the last time I
saw him and the others, and I remained absolute
master of the empire," Mansa Musa said.

There is evidence that these two expeditions
brought the ruler of Mali and his men to America.
As observed by Abdullah Hakim Quick in his book,
Deeper Roots: Muslims In the Caribbean Before
Columbus To The Present:

This report reveals that the Mandinka monarch
made great preparation for the journey and had

confidence in its success. His captain, who reported the violent river in mid ocean, must have encountered a mid-ocean current. This current was either the North Equatorial or the Antilles Current, either of whose distances from the West African coast at that latitude would place the fleet at the doorstep of the Americas. (p. 14)

According to the author, the Mandinkas made contact with the closest land mass to the West African coast, Brazil, which they apparently used as a base for exploration of the Americas. Traces of Mandinka cities of stone and mortar were seen by early Spanish explorers and pirates. One of them, a native of Minas Geres, provided an example of the Mandinka script and described the Mandinka cities in a document written in 1754.

Quick continues:

In this document, written in 1754, we are told that a city in Minas Geres near a river, was well laid out and had superb buildings, obelisks and statues. On the statue of a young man, naked from the waist up without beard, underneath the shield were the following characters:

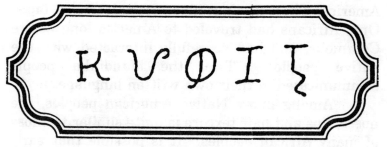

meaning, "ahn na we fe nge" ("He is of the maternal aunt, the pure side," or in other words, "He is heir to the throne.") (p. 15)

Could this have been a possible message from Mansa Musa's predecessor? Other signs indicate that Mandinka explorers, under the Mansa's instructions, explored many parts of North America. This is evident from the appearance of mounds throughout the United States, especially in the vicinity of the Mississippi River, which they used for exploring America. In Arizona, they left inscriptions which show that the Mandinka explorers also brought a number of elephants to America with them. Writings and pictographs were also found in Arizona. In a 1920s document entitled "Africa and the Discovery of America" it was proven that the Mandinka had not only spread throughout the Caribbean, Central and South America, but had reached Canada, and were trading and intermarrying with the Iroquois and Algonquin Native American nations! In Columbus' third voyage he wrote about his discovery that Africans were already trading with the native Americans.

The map on the next page was drawn by an Arabian map maker about four hundred years before the ruler of Mali sent his ships across the Atlantic ocean. The area entitled "Unknown Territory" is apparently the continents of north and south America. These findings illustrate at least two facts: One, Africans had traveled to America long before Columbus, and had peacefully interacted with the native people. Two, the Mandinka people communicated in their own written language.

Among many Native American peoples, the noses, lips and hair texture is quite similar to those of many African peoples. It is possible that early African explorers intermarried with the native people, and produced mixed race children with distinctly African features.

"Ard Majhula"
or unknown territory

4B
Arab Seaman's Map
*A map drawn by an Arabian before the tenth century shows that
sea travelers from the east were aware of the land mass known
today as America many centuries before Columbus' voyage. By
turning the map upside down, one can clearly see the outline of
the American continents.*

4C
A Sign Of African Visitation?
A Mongoyo-Camacan native of Brazil, South America has physical features which reflect a Negroid strain, possibly resulting from intermarriage between Africans and Native Americans before the coming of Columbus. (Reprinted from Sex and Race, Volume II, page 4, by J.A. Rogers, Copyright 1942 by J.A. Rogers, Photo by Koch Grunberg).

MOORS OUSTED FROM SPAIN

The landing of Columbus in America created a new market for colonial expansion. The following series of events allowed the European slave to take root and gradually destroy the continent of Africa.

The Christians of Europe, having absorbed the science and culture of the Moors, were able to bring an end to the long night of the Dark Ages. Europe formed a united front to drive the Moors back to Africa. The marriage of Queen Isabella, head of one leading family in Spain, to King Ferdinand, head of a rival family, gave Europe a strong alliance by which to drive the Moors out of Spain. The Christians, though not free from internal disputes, were finally united by the marriage of Ferdinand and Isabella, which joined in peace the formerly hostile royal houses of Aragon and Castile. The Muslims, because of religious and political differences, began to split into factions and wage war among themselves. As they fought for supremacy among themselves, the Christian forces conquered one great city after another, taking Valencia in 1238, Cordova in 1239 and Seville in 1260. By 1492, the Moors had lost all of Spain except the kingdom of Granada.

The second rise of Europe again brought the destruction of knowledge and high culture. It was said that in the land where science was once supreme, the Spanish doctors became noted for nothing but their ignorance. The Spanish Inquisition, designed to seek out and destroy all non-Christians, ushered in a brutal period, where non-Christians were tortured, jailed or exiled. After the Inquisition, a darkness fell over Spain. Libraries disappeared, the land grew impoverished and neglected, and beggars and bandits took the place of

scholars and merchants. The united Christian forces,
by 1610, through expulsion and migration, had rid
Spain of the Moors, many of whom returned to
North and West Africa, creating more dissension.
The Moors had introduced the manufacture of
gunpowder into Europe. Later, the Europeans used
it as a weapon against them.

EUROPEAN EXPLORERS RAID
AFRICAN CITIES

Then came the European explorations.   In
1498, when King Fualail reigned over Kilwa, a city
on the coast of East Africa, three ships from Portugal
arrived, under the command of Admiral Vasco Da
Gama.   The ships passed by Kilwa and docked at
Mafia, an Island city a little north of Kilwa. At first
the ruler of Mafia rejoiced, thinking that these were
honest, upright men. But soon it was confirmed that
they were corrupt and dishonest people who only
came to spy out the land in order to seize it.

When the first explorers from Portugal sailed
up the east coast of Africa, they were dazzled by a
series of seaport cities, such as Malindi, Mombasa,
Sofala, Kilwa, and Zanzibar. The greatest of these
cities seems to have been Kilwa. According to
Jackson in *Introduction To African Civilization,* in
1331, famous Moorish traveler Ibn Baluta, during his
travels, describes it this way:

*We spent a night in the Island of Mombasa and
then set sail for Kilwa, the principle town on the
coast, the greater part of whose inhabitants are Zanj,
of very black complexion ... Kilwa is one of the most
beautiful, and well constructed towns in the world.
The whole of it is elegantly built. (p. 280)*

Duarte Barbosa, a Portuguese royal commercial agent, had visited the trading cities of the Swahilis in the early sixteenth century before the later invasion and looting by the Portuguese. He described Kilwa as "A Moorish town with many fair houses of stone and mortar, with many windows after our fashion, very well arranged streets, with many flat roofs." (In the middle ages, Europeans mistakenly called all Africans Moors, just as in ancient times the Greeks had called all Africans Ethiopians).

He also noted that the town had plenty of gold. A Portuguese fleet in 1505 captured the cities of Kilwa and Mombasa and proceeded to sack them. Jackson states that as soon as the town of Kilwa had been taken without opposition, the Vicar General and some of the Franciscan fathers came ashore carrying two crosses in procession and singing a Christian hymn. They went to the palaces and there the Grand Captain prayed. Then everyone started to plunder the town of all its merchandise and provisions.

Magnificent tales of cities of gold brought more European explorers to the West coast of Africa in search of wealth. Although a few Africans were captured and enslaved in the early fifteenth century, the real African slave trade did not begin until about a century later. The real catalyst to the slave trade was Europe's desire to seize the American continents.

Spain was anxious to become a dominant power in the world. When Christopher Columbus arrived in South America, he sent word back to Queen Isabella and King Ferdinand that, by converting the native people into slaves, he could create tremendous wealth. The Native Americans were then murdered and tortured by Columbus' men in order to break them down and force them to work the land for Spain. However, they could not last under this harsh treatment. Many of them died.

When the native population of South America was either killed off, maimed, or forced to flee into the hills to escape Spanish oppression, Spain began to look elsewhere for slave labor.

INTERNAL CONFLICTS INVITE INVASION

Many historians imply that most Africans were already enslaved by another people. We are led to believe that somehow slavery and blackness were synonymous. But the fact is that African nations were engaged in a series of wars between themselves for control over territory, wealth, and political power. As was customary since ancient times, those who were defeated in war were captured as political prisoners. They were often held for ransom, or were obliged to work in servitude to the conquering nation.

In the 1500s in North Africa, the old Egyptian empire was under foreign rule. After the armies of Rome and the Vandals came, many family groups migrated farther south and created rural villages.

In Morocco, the Moors were fleeing the Spanish Inquisition, and many sought to establish dominion within the Songhay empire. The Sultan of Morocco gained control of Songhay's salt mines in Taghaza, and five years later Songhay was invaded by a Moorish army. Armed with guns, imported from England, the Moors attacked the Songhay empire. Their use of firearms overpowered the Songhay army. As noted in the last chapter, this led to chaos and decline of the empire.

In *Introduction To African Civilization*,

Jackson quotes the observations of a Sudanese
scholar of the time. The Sudanese notes that after
the Moorish invasion, "Everything changed. Danger
took the place of security, poverty of wealth, peace
gave way to distress, disaster and violence."

As Songhay fell, the base of power moved
eastward to the Central Sudan, into the hands of
Kanem Bornu and the Hausa States. The nucleus of
each of these states was a city or town, in which was
located the seat of government. The prosperity of
these cities was based on agriculture and trade. The
local farmers traded their products for goods
manufactured by the craftsmen in their shops located
in the cities.

By the beginning of the seventeenth century,
the Golden Age of West Africa was headed for a
decline. Kanem Bornu and the Hausa States merged
to form the Kanem Bornu Empire. While none of
these nations ever rose to the levels gained by
Ghana, Mali and Songhay, there was a rise of
commercial success for a time.

Gun powder, introduced to Europe by the
Moors, had been developed into a powerful weapon of
war. Just as the leaders of the falling Mali empire
had considered making deals with the Europeans to
help them conquer rival nations, other African
leaders saw possible advantages in working with the
whites as well. Europeans were often able to bargain
with African leaders and buy prisoners of war for the
price of some guns and some whiskey.

The Portuguese had already begun to scope
out the wealth of the coastal cities. The Spanish
were racing to colonize the Americas after Columbus'
voyage. England, steeped in internal conflict, was
soon to begin the colonization of North America.

The stage was set. As Jackson relates in

Introduction To African Civilization:

> *Soon after the onslaught on the trading centers of the East African coast, a systematic traffic in slaves in West Africa was inaugurated by European invaders. A few Africans were reduced to slavery and transported to Europe early in the fifteenth century; but the African slave trade did not begin in earnest until about a century later. This evil enterprise was the outcome of the Spanish conquest of Mexico and Peru. The natives of Peru and Mexico were reduced to slave status and forced to work in mines. Their death rates were so high that their European masters were impelled to look elsewhere for slave labor; but the question was where? Bartoleme de las Casas, Bishop of Ciapa, in 1517 came to their rescue by proposing that each Spanish gentleman be permitted to import twelve African slaves. This advice was adopted by the king of Spain who issued a patent to one of his friends giving him the authority to import four thousand black slaves annually to Cuba, Hispaniola, Jamaica and Puerto Rico." (p. 305)*

Now, where does one just go and get four thousand people from Africa to make them slaves?

This trade in human cargo began as a big business venture, and there were those Africans without scruples who sought to make a profit for themselves. Weaker rulers traded prisoners of war for guns in the hopes that stronger weapons would lead to greater political power for them. Some of the Moroccan rulers, in their fight for control of the Songhay empire, are recorded as having sold prisoners of war to Europeans.

Then there were those tribes whose members were willing, for a price, to help in the raiding and

kidnapping of people in the rural areas on the
outskirts of the cities. It is important to know which
groups among the Africans themselves were guilty of
selling black people into slavery. The Ashantes, the
Yorubas, and the Bambouras, family groups which
settled on fringes of the great empires, were known
to work with European enslavers.

One may observe that those groups whose
religious teachings did not forbid the use of alcohol
were most likely to cooperate with European
enslavers. Alcohol was a powerful negotiating tool in
the hands of Europeans, and those whose practices
still involved the use of intoxicating drinks were most
likely to trade human flesh for guns and whiskey.

Europeans bought prisoners of war from
conquering nations, and, with the help of paid
kidnappers, also stole quite a few people from the
rural areas surrounding the cities. At first, some
Africans made a profit from this business. Later on,
as they realized too late, they would also become
helpless victims. As Lerone Bennett points out in
Before The Mayflower:

*Slave traders testified that it was not unusual
for an African to sell an African today and to be
captured and sold himself tomorrow. The story is
told of a slave merchant who sold a parcel of slaves
and unwisely accepted a social drink to seal the
transaction. One drink led to another -- and to
America. The slave merchant woke up the next
morning with a hangover and a brand on his chest.
He was in the hold of a slave ship·with his victims
and over him stood the captain, laughing to beat the
band. (pp. 38-39)*

Battles for supremacy over the Songhay

empire grew fierce. Would-be conquerors followed the age-old war time practice: first seize all men of learning and skilled craftsmen for enslavement and service to the conquering nation. Many of Songhay's educated scholars were among those captured and traded off to the Americas.

The first African slaves were shipped from the coast of Guinea to Haiti in 1510, and by 1576 there were 40,000 black slaves in Latin America. Quite a few agricultural experts from Morocco, Songhay, and other parts of Africa proved valuable in the development of the American continent. The demand for Africans, skilled in mining and farming and strong enough to withstand harsh physical labor, became great. In a short time, all of the nations of Europe were participating in the traffic. They raced to export workers to the Americas, where fast fortunes were being made.

RELIGION AND THE SLAVE TRADE

The Christian church soothed the consciences of European enslavers by giving its endorsement to the trade. The Pope gave his blessing on it as a means of spreading Christianity. Captain Sir John Hawkins, Treasurer of the British Navy, was the first Englishman of importance to engage in this trade. With the blessings of Queen Elizabeth I, he sailed along the coast of Africa, burning and spoiling as he went. He kidnapped a number of Africans, and smuggled them overseas in his ship, named Jesus. They were sold to settlements in Latin America for a handsome price.

While Western writers have often blamed the slave trade on Islam, the fact is that no Muslim leader ever endorsed the slave trade. Quite the

contrary; participation in the slave trade was sharply
denounced by the Sheriff of Mecca in a statement
issued to Muslim nations, a few years before Sir John
Hawkins in 1562 took three cargoes of slaves to the
West Indies.

In his book, *Islam in Africa*, Mirza Mubarak
Ahmad produces documentation:

It is possible that some individual Muslims
might have engaged themselves in this business; but
in the whole of Islamic history not one single instance
of any Muslim leader can be found who gave his
blessings to this nefarious business. Old records of
the British Government itself go to prove that
Muslims held the Slave Trade to be not only contrary
to the Islamic teaching, but also played a prominent
part in checking it.   In this connection, a relevant
portion of the Report of The Commission of Inquiry,
Sierra Leone is of great interest and value:
"About six years before, the Sherief of Mecca
had sent a letter to the King of Fulas for circulation
through   all   these   'Mandingo'   tribes,   strictly
prohibiting the selling of slaves -- and which later
was also promulgated among the Yorubas, Fulanis
and other neighboring tribes.   The slave traffic was
declared   to   be   contrary   to   the   teachings   of
Muhammad (on whom be peace) which pronounce the
most fearful denunciations of Allah's wrath in the
world hereafter against those who persist in the traffic
with the European nations."
In the face of such authentic testimony of the
official government records, it is the height of
shameless audacity, on the part of any Christian
writer or missionary, to accuse Muslims of having
given support to the Slave Trade. (p. 5)

Some African-American writers look back on historic events and interpret them as a simple "black/white" conflict. But the modern day concept of a distinct black "race" and white "race" did not develop in its present form until the height of the slave trade. In the wars over territorial control, the battles were often between the Africans who were animists and polytheists (worshippers of idols, people, or many gods) and those Africans who descended from the Muslim empires of Mali, Songhay, and later the Kanem Bornu states. Some historians erroneously interpret all of these battles as "Arab invasions" rather than religious conflicts between Africans.

Quite a few Moors who were captured in battles or kidnapped from the sea coasts were also enslaved. A large portion of the first Africans taken overseas as slaves came from the Mandinkas, the Fulanis, and the Hausas, all part of those empires. The Mandinkas, of course are part of the Soninke family group which founded the great empire of Ghana. This was by no means an overnight affair. Even while villages were being raided and plundered, African kingdoms continued to flourish. At first Europeans bought prisoners of war, but as the profits got higher, everybody on the continent with a hint of color became a target.

Many historians assume that the Africans who were taken away during the slave trade came primarily from the west coast. Actually, the west coast was only the holding place for the slaves until they could be herded onto the ships, which launched from the west coast. The people were taken from all across the continent, and included a variety of shades of color, hair textures, and physical features.

COLONIES INCREASE SLAVE BUSINESS

In 1620 in the new colony of Virginia, a group of 20 slaves were imported; by the year 1760, the number of slaves had reached 200,000. In Jamaica, in 1767, there were 140,000 slaves. And by 1800 there were 776,000 slaves in Latin America.

African society was terrorized. The word was spreading that multitudes of people were being captured in village raids. Homes were burned, people kidnapped, entire communities left desolate. The people who left Africa were the learned class, scholars, artisans, builders, doctors, farmers, laborers, and soldiers.

Africans introduced many new crops to America which had previously been produced by the Moors in Spain and which thrived on the continent of Africa. Rice, sugar cane, cotton -- these were some of the crops which became the backbone of America's agricultural industry. The Africans' farming skills certainly increased the value of African laborers.

In *Introduction To African Civilization,* Jackson states that an estimated 250 million people disappeared from the African continent during a period of over three centuries. About 100 million died during the journey overseas. Working in American plantations, mines and cities, they created vast wealth and profits, but none of it for Africa. Imagine the gradual disappearance of 250 million people from the United States. At least 25 major cities would be empty of people!

What happened to all those brilliant people from Africa's Golden Age? In the next chapter we shall see what became of them and their descendants in America.

CHAPTER FIVE
Who Did They Really Sell Into Slavery?

5A

Prince Abdul Rahman
The son of a king, Prince Abdul Rahman rose to become a high ranking military officer at the age of 24. He was ambushed by his enemies during a battle at age 26. He was well educated and multilingual. But after being captured in war, Rahman, like many African free people, was sold into slavery. He was sold to a plantation owner in Natchez, Mississippi. (Photo reprinted from African Muslims in Antebellum America, by Allan D. Austin, Copyright 1984, Garland Publishing Company, Inc.)

CHAPTER FIVE
Who Did They Really Sell Into Slavery?

BRAINWASHING: The process of systematically, forcibly, and intensively indoctrinating a person to destroy or weaken his beliefs and ideas, so that he becomes willing to accept different or opposite beliefs and ideas. (Thorndike Barnhart Advanced Dictionary)

Imagine ... you are in your bedroom at night, laying out your clothes, preparing for the next day, when suddenly you hear screams outside and smell smoke.   Immediately you realize your neighbor's house is on fire. Then -- crash! A window is broken in your home, a fire breaks out, and you frantically cry out to your family, trying to save yourself and your loved ones from the flames.

Once outside, you see people running wildly through the streets, being chased by armed bandits. People are being hunted down, captured, handcuffed, and dragged away through the street, kicking and screaming.   Children are crying hysterically.   Men and women are desperately trying to fight off attackers with whatever weapons they can find. In the chaos, you feel strange hands roughly grab you from behind. In panic, you fight for your life, but are overpowered by a group of men, who beat you with clubs and rifle butts until you are nearly unconscious. Dazed, you cry out to your family. You don't know where they are -- have they been captured or killed? You are handcuffed and dragged away into the night, bruised and bleeding. Horrified, you wonder, "What is going to happen to me?"

This was a common experience for many of the ancestors of African Americans who were captured and sold into slavery.   In spite of all its horror,

European writers tried to make the slave trade appear to be a blessing in disguise. They have painted a picture of a naked, illiterate, idol-worshipping savage who was taken off to America to be clothed, taught proper speech, given a legitimate religion, and trained to live in a house with civilized people.

Were the writers successful? Look back at your answer to Psychic Trauma Test question Number 18: "I think blacks who were brought to America from Africa became more "civilized" than those who remained in Africa."

If you strongly agree, agree, or are even unsure, then you have been a victim of brainwashing.

In the last chapter, we saw the magnificence of the great empires of Africa. The people who ran thriving businesses, schools, hospitals, and farming industries -- what happened to them?

It is common knowledge that during slavery it was against the law for whites to teach blacks how to read and write. But what Eurocentric history books have carefully hidden was that a vast number of Africans who were brought to America already knew how to read and write -- often in several languages!

Many Mandinkas and other family groups who were part of the great African empires were brought to America as slaves. A number were well educated, and in addition to their own language, also were well versed in Arabic, and wrote in Arabic as well. Arabic was the language commonly used at many of the universities of the West African empires.

Through some of their own writings and from some of the hidden records of the slaveholders, we are able to trace what really happened to the scholars from the Golden Age of Africa.

PRINCE ABDUL RAHMAN

Prince Abdul Rahman, a military officer from Timbo, Futa Jallon, was made Captain of the military at age twenty one, and rose to Colonel by age twenty four. In *African Muslims In Antebellum America,* author Allan D. Austin recalls Rahman's narration of his ambush and capture during a war:

> *"At the age of twenty-six, they sent me to fight the Hebohs, because they destroyed the vessels that came to the coast, and prevented our trade. When we fought, I defeated them. But they went back one hundred miles into the country and hid themselves in the mountain. We could not see them and did not expect there was an enemy...*
>
> *"One came behind me and shot me in the shoulder. One came before and pointed his gun to shoot me, but seeing my cloths, (ornamented with gold,) he cried out, that! the King. Then everyone turned down their guns and came and took me." (p. 146)*

Thus the proud officer began his career as a slave. He was sold, along with fifty others, to an English ship bound for the Island of Dominica. After that he was taken to New Orleans, and later to Natchez, Mississippi, where he was bought by Colonel F., a plantation owner. He stayed there and labored 40 years.

As the son of a king, Prince Abdul Rahman had been well educated. He spoke and wrote Arabic fluently, and left many documents which described his life and the political events in his country which led to his capture. In Natchez, he got married and had five children and eight grandchildren, all of whom he desired to take back to Africa.   He impressed many whites who helped him raise money.

Prince Abdul Rahman finally succeeded in returning to Africa. He and his wife managed to get to Liberia, but failing health prevented him from traveling to Futa Jalon.   He died in Monrovia, Liberia, and did not get to see his American children or his African homeland of Timbo again.

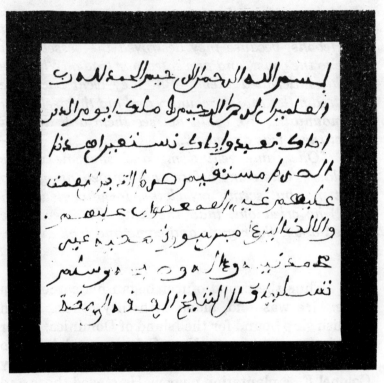

5B

Arabic Writing of Prince Abdul Rahman

Here is a sample of many of the writings of Prince Abdul Rahman. He left several autobiographical writings which gave an account of his life in Africa before his capture, his 40 years of experience as an American slave, and his eventual freedom. (Reprinted from African Muslims in Antebellum America, by Allan D. Austin, Copyright 1984, Garland Publishing Company, Inc.)

SLAVERY, INCORPORATED

South America, after the landing of Columbus, became a battle ground for European nations, who were fighting to gain control of the land and wealth. The rapid growth of sugar plantations resulted in an increasing demand for slaves. This turned what began as the purchase of a few prisoners of war into a wholesale trade in human flesh, anywhere it could be found on the continent of Africa. Slavery became big business. According to Quick's book *Deeper Roots: Muslims in the Caribbean, Columbus To The Present,* the first step was to establish an organized system for the capture, transport, and sale of human beings:

To make this possible, ships had to be built or hired, forts, warehouses and slave pens set up on the African coast and payment made to local slavers. The Dutch, English and French developed their trade in African slaves by establishing corporations with special privileges in which private persons were able to take shares. (p. 23)

The Dutch were the first to gather private investors to finance this enterprise, and in 1621 The West India Company was born. In 1660, the British government followed their example, and set up the Royal Africa Company. In 1664, the French set up its own company. Each competed for control of the slave business. The intense rivalry led to wars between the European nations. The final result was a series of treaties which divided the Caribbean region into zones of influence controlled by the Spanish, Portuguese, English, French or Dutch.

Early slave traders were well aware that many of the Africans who had been captured were highly

educated and multi-lingual. Bryan Edwards, author
of a well known work on the history of the British
West Indies, wrote about his Mandingo slave who,
although taken from Africa as a youth, still
remembered the prayers from the Quran taught to
him by his father. In Quick's *Deeper Roots*, Edwards
is quoted as saying:

> *Besides this man, I had once another
> Mandingo servant who could write, with great beauty
> and exactness, the Arabic alphabet and some passages
> from Al Koran. Whether his learning extended any
> further, I had no opportunity of being informed, as he
> died soon after he came into my possession. (p. 26)*

Robert R. Madden was a special magistrate
sent to the island of Jamaica in 1833 by the British
government. He wrote about his encounter with
three educated Africans. These Africans wrote
letters to Madden explaining their family histories.
The letters, written in Arabic, were translated into
English.

ABU BAKR SADIQ TRACES ROOTS
TO OLD KINGDOM

One letter was from Abu Bakr Sadiq, known in
Jamaica by the Christian name of Edward Doulan.
In Quick's *Deeper Roots* he writes:

> *My name is Abu Bakr Sadiq, born in
> Timbuctoo, and brought up in Jenne. I acquired the
> knowledge of the Al Koran in the country of Gounah
> in which country there are many teachers for young
> people ... My father's name is Kara Mousa Sheriff...*
> *(p. 28)*

In his book, *African Muslims In Antebellum America,* author Allan D. Austin explains that the name "Sadiq" suggests possible descent from the family of Muhammad Mustapha. Austin also points out where Abu Bakr Sadiq's narrative reveals his grandfather Omar was a magistrate in Timbuktu, and was one of the principle law officers of the state. Abu Bakr's uncle Abdur-rahman settled in the city of Kong, a place in the chain of mountains running parallel with the southern coast of Africa. (Later, Hollywood producers created fictional stories about Kong as a wild jungle, and introduced a giant gorilla called King Kong.)

In *Deeper Roots* Abu Bakr goes on to explain how a war broke out and during a battle, he was captured. He was stripped of his clothing, tied with a cord and led through various towns and cities until he was sold overseas to Jamaica. His parents, he noted, were of the Islamic faith. He continues:

They do not drink wine nor spirits, as it is held an abomination to do so. They do not associate with any that worship idols, or profane the Lords name, nor do dishonor to their parents, or commit murder, or bear false witness, or who are covetous, proud or boastful, for such faults are an abomination unto my religion. They are particularly careful in the education of their children, and in their behavior, but I am lost to all these advantages; since my bondage I am become corrupt; and I now conclude by begging the Almighty God to lead me into the path that is proper for me, for He alone knows the secrets of my heart and what I am in need of.

Abu Bakr Sadiq, Kingston, Jamaica Sept. 20, 1834 (p. 29)

"BILAL" NAME SURFACES IN AMERICA

In North America, many more educated Africans surfaced on southern plantations, but often they were forced to hide their knowledge. Some, however, managed to pass on some traditional beliefs and practices to their offspring.

One outstanding person emerged from Sapelo Island, Georgia. His name, Bilali, suggests possible family ties all the way back fourteen hundred years ago to Bilal, the renowned Ethiopian companion of Muhammad Mustapha, known as the Holy Prophet of Islam.

Bilali's own thirteen page manuscript is testimony of his knowledge and talents. From Timbo Futa Jallon in Africa, Bilali was captured and shipped to a Georgia plantation, where he rose to prominence.

According to Austin's book, *African Muslims in Antebellum America:*

Bilali was the very capable and, more often than not, the sole manager of a large sea island property and its 400 to 500 souls, whom he reportedly saved twice: In the War of 1812, and in a great hurricane in 1824. He was also prolific, producing twelve sons and seven daughters to whom he passed on African names, terms, and traditions that were clearly Muslim. He regularly wore a fez and a long coat just as he might have in Africa; he prayed the obligatory three times a day, facing East on his carefully preserved prayer rug; and he always observed Muslim fasts and feast-day celebrations. When the time came, Bilali was buried with his rug and Quran. (p. 265)

5C

A Descendant of Bilali or "Tom" From Sapelo Island
Bilali, Patriarch of Georgia, was a Muslim from Futa Jallon, who was captured and sold into Sapelo Island, Georgia, and renamed "Tom." He wrote a 13 page manuscript on his life. He has living descendants, now under the name "Bailey" who reside in what's known as a historical site in Sapelo Island called "Hog Hamhock." During slavery, the name "Bilali" often became Americanized into "Bailey." (Reprinted from African Muslims in Antebellum America, by Allan D. Austin, Copyright 1984, Garland Publishing Company, Inc.)

5D
Bilali's Manuscript
This is a copy of pages 10 and 11 of Bilali's Arabic-American manuscript script. (Photo from the Georgia State Library, Atlanta.)

Much of the information about Bilali was relayed by his friend, Salih Bilali, from the kingdom of Massinah in the Sudan.

Salih Bilali was the son of a prince of the Foulah tribe and was taken prisoner at the age of fourteen, near Timbuktu.   He ended up on a plantation in Georgia, the property of a Mr. James Hamilton Couper, and was renamed "Tom."   Salih Bilali or "Tom" often corresponded in Arabic with his friend Bilali.

Many of those who were unfortunate enough to be among the captured, whether as prisoners of war or victims of kidnapping were often quite like the many middle class professional black men and women today. Many were married and had children, comfortable   homes,   higher   education,   and professional careers.

In *African Muslims In Antebellum America*, Salih Bilali describes his homeland to J. H. Cooper of Georgia, who wrote down his narrative. The houses, Salih Bilali said, consist of two kinds, brick for the wealthier class and straw covered huts for the poorer class. The mosques are also built of dried bricks.
In the farming community of Massini, the people cultivate the soil, and keep herds of horses, cows, sheep, goats and donkeys. The great grain crop is rice.   Other crops include red maize, millet and Guinea corn, Salih Bilali noted.

As the son of a prince, Salih Bilali was undoubtedly raised to be a skilled farmer in his homeland and was probably given authority over the field workers. It is not surprising that his abilities led him to become head driver on the plantation in Georgia. It was stated that although Salih Bilali, or "Old Tom," remained a Muslim, his numerous jet-black children and grandchildren later became Christian.

5E

Salih Bilali Lookalike

The man in this drawing is an exact lookalike of Salih Bilali of Massini, also known by the American name of Tom. The son of a Foulah prince, Salih Bilali was taken prisoner and sold into slavery at age fourteen. He became close friends with Bilali of Sapelo Island, (also known as "Tom") and the two corresponded. Salih Bilali was a devout Muslim, who often read from his Arabic scriptures, which people on the plantation referred to as "Tom's Koran." (Drawing Reprinted from African Muslims in Antebellum America, by Allan D. Austin, Copyright 1984, Garland Publishing Company, Inc. From an engraving entitled "A Native Of Hausa" in James C. Prichard's Researches into the Physical History of Mankind II, p. 279. 1851)

HAFIZ JOB BEN SOLOMON

Job Ben Solomon from Bundu, (now the eastern region of present-day Senegal) was captured and sold on the Gambia and brought to Annapolis in 1731. Described as intelligent and well mannered, he escaped from American slavery and gained international fame while he was still a relatively young man.

Job, renamed "Simon" by slaveholders in Maryland, was recognized in England for being an intellectual wonder. He wrote three complete Qurans (all 6,321 verses) from memory. He was what is known as a Hafiz -- one who has memorized the entire Quran as a means of preserving it intact for future generations.

Austin notes in *African Muslims in Antebellum America* that family names reveal much about ones history. He quotes a man who recorded Job Ben Solomon's narrative:

JOB's countrymen, like the Eastern People and some others, use to design themselves by the Names of their Ancestors and in their Appellations mention their Progenitors several Degrees backward; tho' they also have Sirnames for distinguishing their particular Families, much after the same Manner as in England. JOB's Name, in his own country, is HYUBA, BOON SALUMENA, BOON HIBRAHEMA; i.e., Job, the Son of Solomon, the Son of Abraham. The Sirname of the Family is Jallo. (p. 77)

In Job's homeland, Bundu, the King was named Sambo. The name of this respected king has been given a negative connotation in America, and is now considered a racial slur against blacks.

5F
Job Ben Solomon
Born near the Senegal river in Africa, Job's family name suggests direct lineage to King Solomon. Photo from Gentlemen's Magazine (1950), p. 252. Photo from Amherst College.

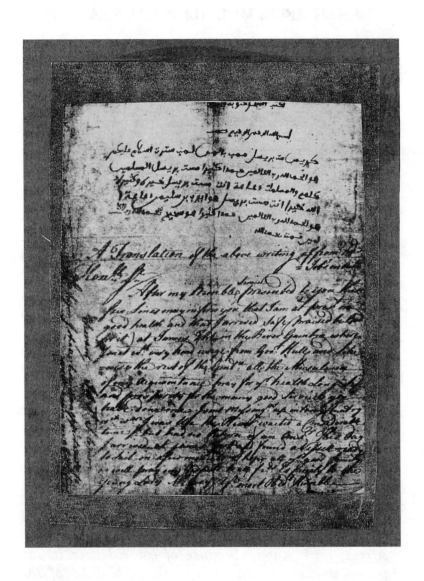

5G

Job Ben Solomon's Writings

Job's letter to Nathaniel Brassey, 1734. Photo from the British Library and Sidney Kaplan. (Reprinted from African Muslims in Antebellum America, by Allan D. Austin, Copyright 1984, Garland Publishing Company, Inc.)

LAMEN KEBE: MULTILINGUAL TEACHER

Lamen Kebe had been a promising young teacher from a very prominent clerical clan, before he was taken away from his wife and three children and sold into slavery. He spent nearly thirty years of slavery over three southern states. He was multilingual, and fluent in reading and writing Arabic. His last master, recognizing that he was a scholar and a teacher, freed him. Lamen, or "Paul" as he had been renamed in America, convinced his master that he had converted to Christianity, and claimed that he wanted to return to Africa to help Christianize his countrymen. His master tried to help him raise passage fare to Africa by arranging for him to speak before groups of philanthropists. Lamen's strategy was to convince whites that he wanted to help in the Christian missionary movement by sending Arabic Bibles to Muslim fellows in West Africa. His campaign to get back home was not successful, however.

According to Austin in *African Muslims In Antebellum America,* Lamen Kebe seems to have come from a famous clan of pragmatic, dedicated teacher-priests in Africa. Austin continues,

His name should probably be written "Lamine Kaba" -- "Lamine," because this is a standard transliteration of a common Arabic name in West Africa, and "Kaba," because of coincidences in his personal history and that of the Jakhanke of the Serahule or Soninke, his ethnic group ... Lamen said his father was a Serahule -- the founders of ancient Ghana, who were among the earliest converts to Islam south of the Sahara -- and a very black people -- and his mother a "Manenca" (Mande or Mandingo).

YARROW MAMOUT

Yarrow Mamout was known as another highly religious man, who forcefully professed his Islamic faith. He urged the slaves on the Georgetown farm where he lived not to eat hog or drink whiskey. He earned the reputation of being a hard worker and earned enough money to buy his freedom. He then worked and saved enough money to purchased $200 worth of stock in Columbia bank.

5H

Yarrow Mamout
A highly religious man, Yarrow Mamout was known for his cheerful disposition, in spite of his slave status. This is his portrait as painted by Charles Wilson Peale, 1819. (Photo from the Historical Society of Pennsylvania, from Sidney Kaplan, Northhampton, Mass.)

MOHAMMED ALI BEN SAID:
INTERNATIONAL TRAVELER, TEACHER
AND LINGUIST

Then there was Mohammed Ali Ben Said. He was a man with an unusual life story. Born around 1831, he was taken from the heart of Africa around 1850, at about 19 years of age. He went from the Mediterranean, to Mecca, and back; served three masters through Europe and part of Asia; and then, as a traveler's companion, made his way to the Caribbean and North and South America.

He had been a traveler on five continents and spoke seven languages. Part of his autobiography has been preserved, and is quoted in the book *African Muslims In Antebellum America:*

I was born in the kingdom of Bornoo, in Soodan, in the problematic central part of Africa, so imperfectly known to the civilized nations of Europe and America. Soodan has several kingdoms, the country of the Fellatahs and Bornoo, being the most powerful, -- the territorial extent of the latter being some 810,000 square miles ... Bornoo has had a romantic history for the last one hundred years. The whole of Soodan, more than two thousand miles in extent, was once under the Mai's of Bornoo; but by dissensions and civil wars nearly all the tributaries north of Lake Tchad were lost. (p. 662, 663)

Mohammed Ali Ben Said was described as "of medium height, somewhat slenderly built, complexion perfectly black, with a quiet, unassuming address." His autobiography was first published in 1867 in the *Atlantic Monthly,* where it appeared under the title "A Native of Bornoo."

51

Mohammad Ali Ben Said
Born in Bornu in the Sudan, Mohammad Ali Ben Said, renamed "Nicholas" in America, was captured at age 19 during a series of civil wars in his country. He traveled extensively and by 1863 became a teacher in Detroit, Michigan. He first published his autobiography in 1867, after the American Civil War. (Reprinted from African Muslims in Antebellum America, by Allan D. Austin, Copyright 1984, Garland Publishing Company, Inc.)

OMAR IBN SAID: AUTHOR OF
RELIGIOUS WRITINGS

Omar Ibn Said was born about 1770 on the south bank of the Senegal River in Futa Toro and was probably made a captive at Kaba to the southeast of his homeland. His portrait reflects early descriptions of his hair, color and and physical features as being "distinctly of the African character."

In his autobiography, he stressed his early African upbringing prior to being captured and sold. He said he observed the Quranic obligations on prayer, fasting, giving charity, fighting for the faith and going on pilgrimages to Mecca. He continued to fast for one month during the year as prescribed by the Islamic faith for some time even after enslavement in America. Although he never learned the English language well, he was quite prolific in Arabic. Whites recognized something distinguished in him and called him "Prince Moro." He was not a prince, but rather, a scholar educated in Africa by Africans, a teacher, a trader, and probably an aide to non-Muslim rulers. His name in his native language was Omeroh.

Omar arrived in Charleston in 1807 (the last legal year for the American foreign slave trade) and lived there about four years. He escaped and was captured and jailed, where his strange writing on the walls captured attention of the whites.

Omar was recognized as a deeply religious man. Efforts were made by whites to convert him to Christianity, and at one point it was presumed he had finally accepted the faith. However, his last known writing, passed off as "The Lord's Prayer," was, in fact, chapter 110 of the Quran which honors those remaining strong in the faith.

5J

Omar Ibn Said

Known as "Prince Moro" in America, Omar Ibn Said belonged to the Foulah tribe in Africa. The Foulahs, or Falatas, are to be found near the Senegal River, and are known as the descendants of the Arabian Muslims who migrated to Western Africa in the seventh century. They brought with them the literature of Arabia and the religion of Islam. (Photo from a dauguerrotype, from Davidson College Library, Davidson, N.C.)

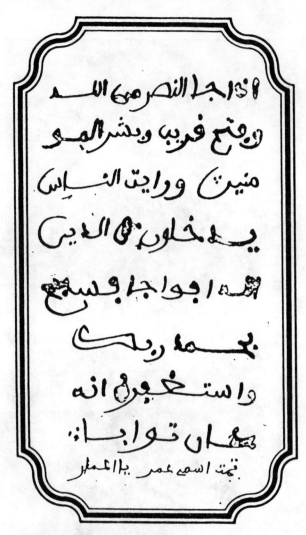

5K

Arabic Writings of Omar Ibn Said

This is a copy of a page of Omar Ibn Said's Arabic writings. He produced thirty four volumes of works in Arabic during his life in America. He died an old man in 1864 and was buried in the family graveyard on the plantation of Gen. Owen in Bladen County, North Carolina. He was said to have been a Free Mason in his native country. Several of his manuscripts and his Arabic Bible have been preserved. (Reprinted from African Muslims in Antebellum America, by Allan D. Austin, Copyright 1984, Garland Publishing Company, Inc.)

THE KINTE LEGACY

Alex Haley, author of *Roots, The Saga of an American Family,* made history as the first African American to trace his ancestry back to the first African captured and brought to America as a slave. Alex Haley's great grandfather was Kunta Kinte, a Mandinka from the Gambia. Because of Haley's work, African Americans gained a new sense of kinship with Africa. After reading *Roots,* many researchers have been inspired to seek further documentation of the genetic history, as well as the educational and religious training of Africans prior to their enslavement. Haley relates that he is told by the old Mandinka "griot" or oral historian, during his research for the book *Roots:*

> *The griot said that the Kinte clan had begun in the country called Old Mali. Then the Kinte men traditionally were blacksmiths, "who had conquered fire," and the women mostly were potters and weavers. In time, one branch of the clan moved into the country called Mauritania; and it was from Mauritania that one son of this clan. whose name was Kairaba Kunta Kinte -- a marabout, or holy man of the Moslem faith -- journeyed down into the country called The Gambia. He went first to a village called Pakali N'Ding, stayed there for a while, then went to a village called Jiffarong, and then to the village of Juffure. (p. 17)*

The book *Roots* describes the Mandinka people, and their great emphasis on higher learning.

Teachers, doctors, government officials, writers, scholars -- these are the kinds of people taken out of Africa. Some found themselves prisoners

5L
Alex Haley, Author of Roots
Thanks to Alex Haley and his indepth research of his own family's history, African Americans have gained a new understanding and appreciation of their African cultural roots. Many authors have been inspired to search further to uncover the truth about a great and ancient heritage. Those courageous men and women who survived the Middle Passage and left oral and written histories enable us to discover our true identities. (Photo copyright by Ted Gray. Reprinted by permission.)

of war after local skirmishes. Others fell victim to kidnapping. Many came from wealthy families. All trace their roots back to Africa's ancient kingdoms.

Prince Abdul Rahman was from the great Moorish empire which conquered Spain. Austin suggests that the way the name "Sadiq" was used by Abu Bakr Sadiq suggests family ties to Muhammad Mustapha of Arabia, known as the Holy Prophet of Islam. Bilali from Timbo, Futa Jallon, could be a descendant of Bilal of Ethiopia, the companion of Muhammad Mustapha. Salih Bilali, of the Foulah tribe, in the Sudan, was part of the group known to descend from the Shepherd Kings of Egypt. Job Ben Solomon traces his heritage all the way back to King Solomon and Abraham of the Bible. Lamen Kebe descends from the Sonninke people who founded the ancient empire of Ghana. Yarrow Mamout also, a Foulah, descends from the Shepherd Kings of Egypt. Mohammed Ali Ben Said was from the Sudan, the land of the old Nubian Empire. Omar Ibn Said from Senegal, descended from the Arabian Muslims who migrated to West Africa in the seventh century. And Alex Haley's ancestor Kunta Kinte traces his family to the Kante family group, the metal workers who helped launch the Golden Age of Africa in 300 C.E. (Christian Era).

Many early elected officials to the United States government were slave owners. Many wealthy and powerful American corporations which control major farming industries (the production of tobacco, rice, and sugar) gained their riches from slave labor. To this day Eurocentric history books strive to justify the barbaric behavior of those who participated in and profited from the slave trade, a bloody business of kidnapping and murder which taints some of America's greatest heroes.

CHAPTER SIX
The Making Of A Negro

Their Religious Notions, Form of Government, Laws, Appearance of the Country, Buildings, Agriculture, Manufactures, Shepherds and Herdsmen, Animals, Marriage and Funeral Ceremonies, Dress, Trade and Commerce, Warfare, Slavery, with an Account of Mahommah's Education, Capture and Slavery in Africa and Brazil, Escape, Reception by Rev. Mr. Judd, Baptist Missionary at Port au Prince, Conversion to Christianity, Baptism his Views, Objects and Aim, &c

WRITTEN AND REVISED FROM HIS OWN WORDS,

BY SAMUEL MOORE, ESQ,

late publisher of the "North of England Shipping Gazette," author of several popular works, and editor of sundry certain papers

MAHOMMAH G. BAQUAQUA,
Engraved by J. G. Darby from a Daguerreotype by Sutton.

DETROIT:
Printed for the Author, Mahommah Gardo Baquaqua,
BY GEO. E. POMEROY & CO., TRIBUNE OFFICE.

6A

Mahommah Gardo Baquaqua
This is taken from the cover of Mahommah G. Baquaqua's published biography, describing his conversion to Christianity. (Photo from the Burton Historical Collection, Detroit Public Library.)

CHAPTER SIX
The Making Of A Negro

Every immigrant who comes to America from another country brings along a language, a style of dress, family traditions, and many memories of home. An intact culture and identity gives the immigrant's family a foundation to build upon.

America's "Founding Fathers" never intended for the Africans they imported by force to develop their own stable communities based on old African cultural traditions. What America and other European colonies sought to create was a permanent labor class. Commercial investors, wealthy landowners, and colonial governments combined forces to suppress any means whereby Africans could ever become a dominant force in the land (and perhaps one day seek revenge for the brutality of slavery).

In order for the slave trade to be profitable, (remember, it's just business), all resistance to the system had to be crushed. What was needed was a non-person, a body without a mind, a basic laborer; not a Moor, or a Mandinka, or a Hausa, or a Fulani. Not a Senegalese or Sudanese or Abyssinian. Not the son of a university professor, or the daughter of a high government official. Just a slave ... a negro. Those who captured and sold Africans were calculating and methodical in their approach.

REMOVING ALL IDENTITIES

The first step was to take away all signs of personal identification. So, once captured, the African was stripped of all clothing and his head was shaved. This removed all indications of national affiliation, individual status, and personal style. In the narratives in Chapter Five, many Africans recalled the experience of having their heads shaved, clothing removed, and names changed.

Today, European history books show naked African slaves being led away to "civilization," giving the false impression that the people never had on any clothes in the first place. The stripping off of clothes was a means to totally humiliate and dehumanize the person. A glimpse of the life of Mahommah G. Baquaqua illustrates the dramatic transformation of an individual after enslavement.

In *African Muslims In Antebellum America,* Allan D. Austin states that Mahommah Baquaqua was raised in a Muslim community in the area what is now known as northern Benin. He was captured as a boy. Led by captors from the Dahomey tribe, he was forced to walk hundreds of miles to the coast. He survived the long journey in a slave ship bound for Brazil, where he was sold to a plantation. He became despondent, and, turned to drinking alcohol. He escaped from the plantation, but was recaptured. He became suicidal. He developed mental illness. He was beaten severely and sold in Rio de Janeiro. He escaped to New York, where he was imprisoned. He escaped to Boston. A confused, depressed alcoholic, he traveled to Haiti and met Rev. William L. Judd, of the Baptist Free Mission Society, who convinced him that his problems were because of his "heathen" religion. Mahommah was finally baptized as a Christian. After his baptism, however, Mahommah continued to drink heavily and experienced severe emotional problems. Just as in Mahommah's case, religious conversions rarely addressed the devastation of being taken from home, enslaved, and beaten, the root causes of a slave's psychological trauma.

6B
Procession of Slave Women
This 17th century portrait of newly arriving enslaved African women to Latin America is a demonstration of how women were demoralized by the stripping off of their clothing. They were then paraded around nude and semi-nude to the auction block to be sold. (Reprinted from Sex and Race, page 11, by J.A. Rogers, Copyright 1942.)

CREATING LANGUAGE BARRIERS

Next was to separate people who spoke the same language. This was to prevent plotting of an uprising.   The African, newly arriving to the Americas, found English (or Spanish, or French, or Dutch or Portuguese) being spoken by the other African slaves.   African languages, and in many cases, African drums which carried messages, were banned.   And writing, of course, was out of the question.

Often, the education of the African slave was superior to the European master's. But, forced to learn another language without the benefit of formal schooling in that country, often a university-educated scholar had to struggle to communicate with those on the plantation.   White enslavers pointed to the language difficulties and called the Africans "dumb."

However, the ability of the Africans to develop a common language between them, in spite of their different backgrounds, actually showed extreme intelligence. The language spoken by the slave, which forms the basis of the "black dialect" used by many African Americans today, actually has its roots in many West African languages.   In the book *Black English*, author J.L. Dillard sheds more light on this subject:

Although many of the slaves may not have had to relinquish their African languages immediately, they all found themselves in a situation in which they had to learn an auxiliary language in a hurry in order to establish communication in the heterogeneous groups into which they were thrown.   This mixing of speakers of a large number of languages, with no one language predominant is the perfect condition for the

*spread of a pidgin language, which is in a sense the
ultimate in auxiliary languages ... A pidgin language
has rules (regular principles of sentence construction)
like any other language ... It is often maintained that
a pidgin is a simple language ... It is designed to be
used by diverse linguistic groups. (p. 74, 75)*

In the colonies which became the early United
States, Pidgin English served the purpose of a
common language among the black slaves, allowing
them to communicate with each other and with
whites.   In highly segregated African-American
communities, one finds this Pigdin English still
commonly used today. J.L. Dillard gives an example
of this:

*In the United States ... such sentences as "I
been knowin' him a long time," are quite
commonplace. Detailed analysis would show that "I
been know" has the Point-of-Time Aspect. "Been"
marks an action which is quite decidedly in the past;
it can be called Perfective Aspect or even Remote
Perfective Aspect.*

*Black English resembles West African
languages grammatically in this Remote Perfective
form and in a contrasting Immediate Perfective
Aspect, for which the preverbal form is "done."
Sentences like, "I done go"; "I done gone"; "I done
went"; "I been done gone"; "I done been gone," are
frequent in Black English today ...*

*One of the more interesting facts about "done"
is its occurrence in other pidgin- and creole-related
languages (e.g., WesKos Pidgin of the Cameroons,
Fernando Poo and Nigeria). (p. 46, 47)*

Whites often mocked the language of the slave,

pointing to their speech as a sign of African ignorance. By outlawing teaching a slave to read and write, slaveholders were able to convince many American born slaves that "negroes" really were less intelligent.

INSTILLING FEAR OF WHITES

The next step was to instill such an overwhelming fear of whites that the black slave dare not rebel. This was done by the most extreme violence. Constant beatings helped to reinforce the power of the master over his slave. John W. Blassingame, in *The Slave Community*, notes:

Nowhere does the irrationality of slavery appear as clearly as in the way that slaves were punished. While generally speaking, a slaveholder had no desire to punish his slave so severely as to endanger his life, the master was only a man, subject, like most men to miscalculations, to anger, to sadism, and to drink. When angry, masters frequently kicked, slapped, cuffed, or boxed the ears of domestic servants, sometimes flogged pregnant women, and often punished slaves so cruelly that it took them weeks to recover. Many slaves reported that they were flogged severely, had iron weights with bells on them placed on their necks, or were shackled. Recalcitrant slaves received more stripes and were treated more cruelly by exasperated planters than were any other blacks. Moses Roper, an incorrigible runaway, regularly received 100 to 200 lashes from his owner. Once his master poured tar on his head and set it afire. On another occasion, after Roper had escaped from leg irons, his master had the nails on his fingers and toes beaten off." (p. 162)

6C
Back of A Beaten Slave
The criss-cross of scars on the back of this ex-slave shows the viciousness with which men and women were beaten by their masters. (Photo courtesy of DuSable Museum of African American History file, Chicago, Illinois.)

This fear of whites was deeply impressed in the minds of the black slave. Disobedience might mean torture or death. It was the duty of the parents to protect their children by instilling fear and obedience to the white man. Unknowingly, to this day some African-American parents teach their children fear of whites. How often have you heard parents or others say, "This is the white man's world -- you have to play the game by his rules"?

A white man in a position of authority has the power to destroy our lives if we displease him by showing "impudence." Or so we have been taught to believe. Has this fear been passed down to you from your foreparents? Recall question Number 5 on the Psychic Trauma Test: "When a white man wearing a business suit speaks to me in an authoritative tone, I have difficulty looking him in the eye."

If you strongly agree, agree, or are unsure, then you very likely have an unconscious fear of whites, especially those who appear to have some type of status or authority.

Many common disciplinary practices of African-American parents can be traced to the slavery time philosophy of instilling fear into the child. The child's spirit was broken early, as a means of protection against later, possibly fatal, punishment from the master.

SEPARATING FAMILY MEMBERS

Naturally, those Africans who had education and skills did not lose them just because they became enslaved. But the crushing blow to the transmission of African language and culture was the breakup of the family. Being sold away, or watching family members get sold away, was an indescribably devastating experience. Many slaves became so overcome with grief, they went insane, and in their hallucinations, talked to their absent loved ones. Others became suicidal.

Separating children from parents was perhaps the greatest factor in the loss of African culture and language. Once children were taken away, their upbringing was no longer supervised by parents who could pass down knowledge and traditions.

When the importation of Africans became outlawed in North America, this had a tremendous effect on the development of black American culture. Without a flow of new arrivals to reinforce African customs and values, American-born slaves grew more and more alienated. White masters were able to create a most repulsive image of Africa, which black slaves had no choice but to accept. The whole process of separating children from parents and teaching the children to despise their heritage is something African Americans should study closely. This technique is still being used today, within American institutions of higher learning.

SEX: A TOOL OF POWER AND CONTROL

The enslaved African always lived with the reality that marriages among slaves could never be held sacred. One could be sold away -- or, the master could take a liking to one's wife.

When slave importation from Africa was outlawed in North America in 1808, slave owners took to "breeding" slaves. Years of cotton planting had eroded the soil, and landowners needed a means to continue to generate revenue. Some states, particularly Virginia, became notorious for this. Big, strong men and women were matched up for the purpose of producing healthy offspring to bring a good price on the market. Naturally, monogamous family life would get in the way of such a system. It was merely good business sense to encourage promiscuity among the slaves. J.A. Rogers, author of the book *Sex and Race* illustrates this point:

> *Now the slaveholders, to put it crudely, but truthfully, encouraged every man they could get hold of, white and black, young and old, to get out their virile organs and fall on the Negro women. Husky bucks, black and white, were set up as "stallions for the whole neighborhood." Some white men were paid as high as $20 for each Negro woman they got with child. Robust college students were even invited to spend their vacations on the plantations and turned loose among the slave cabins at night. A. W. Calhoun rightly says, "In order to secure mulatto young, masters compelled colored women to submit to impregnation by whites and punished barbarously those that resisted. Women of color were compelled to endure every sort of insult." (p. 187)*

The powerlessness black men felt when witnessing how white men, merely by the power of their whiteness, could sexually abuse any black woman they desired, created a hostile relationship between black and white men that many say is at the root of all racial conflict today.

Historically, men have used sex as a weapon of war, a symbol of conquest and authority. Susan Brownmiller examines this in her book *Against Our Will: Men, Women and Rape:*

> *War provides men with the perfect psychologic backdrop to give vent to their contempt for women ...*

The sickness of warfare feeds on itself. A certain number of soldiers must prove their newly won superiority -- prove it to a woman, to themselves, to other men. In the name of victory and the power of the gun, war provides men with a tacit license to rape.

Among the ancient Greeks, rape was also socially acceptable behavior well within the rules of warfare, an act without stigma for warriors who viewed the women they conquered as legitimate booty, useful as wives, concubines, slave labor or battle camp trophy.

A simple rule of thumb in war is that the winning side is the side that does the raping ... Rape is considered by the people of a defeated nation to be part of the enemy's conscious effort to destroy them. In fact, by tradition, men appropriate the rape of "their women" as part of their own male anguish of defeat ... Apart from a genuine human concern for wives and daughters near and dear to them, rape by a conquerer is compelling evidence of the conquered's status of masculine impotence." (pp. 24, 25, 27)

It must be remembered that, while African men were emotionally affected by these rapes, it was the women upon whom the crime was committed; it was the women's sense of dignity and sexual integrity which had to be crushed in order for slavery to be successful.

The rape of African women served as an important means of mind control. Forced sexual relations with white masters had the effect of destroying the black woman's self esteem and feelings of personal worth -- a common response for victims of rape.

Many a slave woman had to learn to use her body as a tool for survival. Realizing they could neither protest nor prevent the advances of their masters, many women managed to use white men's physical attraction for them as a means to bargain for better treatment for themselves and their children.

After receiving better food, clothing, and living conditions as the master's concubine, some women concluded that an enslaved black man, though he may be loving and gentle and kind, could not offer the protection and material comfort that a white man could. To the black man, the sexual relationship between the white slave master and a black woman seemed to confirm his own weakness and inferior status. A vast number of African-American men still react with anger and hostility when they witness interracial relationships. In many black men's minds, a black woman intimately involved with a white man is a reminder of the black man's inability to compete with white male wealth and power.

Have you also been emotionally affected by slavery time interracial sexual behavior? If you are a male, recall your answer to Psychic Trauma Test question No. 15: "I feel resentment when I see an attractive member of the opposite sex romantically involved with a white person of my sex."

If you strongly agree, agree, or are even unsure, your own personal sense of self esteem may be so affected by those previous master/slave relationships, that you interpret every interracial couple involving a white man and a black woman as a reflection on your own manhood.

Interestingly, many women also answer "strongly agree" to question number 15, but for slightly different reasons. We will explain this further in Chapter 9, Black Beauty Standards.

Men were affected in another way by the

atmosphere of extreme promiscuity during the slave breeding era. Men who had proved their virility and ability to father children were highly prized as "studs." Sometimes they were hired out to other plantations to impregnate other female slaves. Having little else to be proud of in his state of powerlessness, sexual prowess became a means whereby a black male slave could gain status.

There were many instances when white women found black male slaves attractive. Poor white women who owned no slaves sometimes developed intimate relations with black males, (both slave and free) and in some cases tried to marry free blacks. Such an act was met with outrage by the white community. Many laws were passed forbidding such relationships; Violators were sentenced to everything from fines to public floggings. A white female who tried to marry a black male could be imprisoned. In *Sex and Race,* Rogers quotes from the Pennsylvania laws of 1725-26:

"... if a free Negro man or woman married a white person, that Negro was to be sold by the justices of the Quarter Sessions as a slave for life. For a white person offending the penalty was seven years servitude and a fine of thirty pounds, sterling. If the offense was fornication or adultery, the free Negro was to be sold a servant for seven years. The white person thus guilty was to be punished by whipping, imprisonment, or branding with the letter 'A'..."

However history records that, despite the deterrents, quite a few unions occurred between white women and black men. This issue continues to affect white and black social behavior today.

CREATING THE COLOR CAST SYSTEM

Just as rape has been a symbol of war time conquest, so has the impregnation of women of the conquered nation by those who are the victors in war. The children who are born from these pregnancies often look much different from everyone else. Their very presence is a permanent reminder of the conquest of the nation.

In America, the impregnation of black female slaves by the white master was a deliberate, calculated act, which had several benefits for the slaveholders:

One, when a slaveowner, his sons or hired white overseers got a slave pregnant, the plantation gained a new slave, at absolutely no cost to the slaveowner.

Two, it created a class of half white and half black slaves, which often became the preferred group to serve as house servants. Light skinned women who could serve as house slaves and concubines brought high prices on the market.

And three, it allowed the white masters to create a slave hierarchy as a means of preventing uprisings. Mixed race house servants and overseers, who were many times the master's own offspring, helped maintain white control over the plantation. Some of them identified so much with the master, that they reported all acts of disobedience or rebellion to the master, thereby earning themselves a greater position of trust and of authority.

It is clear that whites believed by impregnating their female slaves they were creating a better looking breed of servants. In the book, *Slavery and Jeffersonian Virginia,* author Robert McColley notes the opinions of Thomas Jefferson, third President of the United States and author of the Declaration of Independence, on this subject:

> *Jefferson ... found it a flaw in Negroes that their dark pigmentation allowed no expressive quality in their faces, asking: "Are not the fine mixtures of red and white, the expressions of every passion by greater or less suffusions of color in the [white race] preferable to that eternal monotony, which reigns in the countenances, that immoveable veil of black which covers all the emotions of the other race?"*
>
> *Pursuing his demonstation of the superior beauty of the Caucasion, Jefferson cited his "more elegant symmetry of form," and held up the advantage of "flowing" hair over the kinky, woolly kind. He capped his argument by stating that the Negro himself showed a preference for whites, which occured "as uniformly as ... the preference of the Oranootan [sic] for the black women over those of his own species." (p. 127)*

According to an article by Carlyle C. Douglas in the August 1975 edition of *Ebony* magazine, Jefferson owned more than 200 blacks, who worked his 7,500 to 10,000 acre Monticello plantation in Virginia. He fathered five children by his black concubine Sally, who was thirty years his junior. Their thirty-eight-year relationship began when Sally was just sixteen years old. Douglas reports:

> *She was known as "Dashing Sally" at Monticello and she was described in the memoirs of another Jefferson slave as being "mighty near white," "very handsome" and possessed of "long straight hair down her back." She was also the half-sister of Jefferson's late wife. (p. 62)*

The caste system measured the degrees of whiteness, upon which rested a slave's social status. First, there was the mulatto, who was half white and half black. Then there was the quadroon (one quarter black), offspring of a white and a mulatto; then there was the octoroon (one eighth black), offspring of a white and a quadroon. Of course, the highest on the social ladder was the octoroon.

Sometimes the trusted light skinned house slave, rather than serve the master, escaped to the north by "passing" for white, or acted as the plantation grapevine, sending messages to the slave quarters. Occasionally the house slaves helped other slaves escape or even helped plot insurrections.

FORCED RELIGIOUS CONVERSION

Another significant act was to force the slaves to convert to the European's version of Christianity.

In a 1988 interview, historian Muzafar Ahmad Zafar noted that a vast majority of the Africans brought to America as slaves were from the West African empires of Ghana, Mali, and Songhay. These areas were predominantly Islamic by the sixteenth and seventeenth centuries. Africans were forced to change their original names to European "Christian" names. This helped destroy cultural, economic and religious affiliations with specific nations in Africa. Zafar stated that an estimated 80 percent of those taken out of Africa were Muslims.

The need to convert "heathen" Africans to Christianity was cited as a major justification for the slave trade. Whites observed that once African slaves were converted to the European version of Christianity, they became more manageable. Religion became a political tool to control the slaves

and protect the business interests of those involved
in the slave trade. Islam, with all its guidelines for
regular prayers, fasting, prohibition of alcohol and
pork, and respect for the institution of marriage was
systematically crushed. Quick states in *Deeper Roots:*

> *Such was the case of African Muslims under*
> *the brutal system of European slavery. They were*
> *forced to forget their native languages. Arabic was,*
> *for the most part, outlawed among the slave masses.*
> *It was forbidden to openly pray, fast, or practice*
> *Islam. Pork was forced on the slaves as a main*
> *staple meat. Families were broken up and family life*
> *was not encouraged. Adulterous relationships, with*
> *all their painful and destructive consequences, became*
> *the norm. (pp. 30, 31)*

Masters were very careful in their selections of
Biblical scripture which could be read to the slaves.
Any scriptural references to Moses and Pharaoh and
escaping to freedom were strictly banned. Slave
owners would sit in on church sessions held by black
preachers, to make sure no rules were being violated.
White preachers and "Christian" masters would
expound endlessly on Bible verses which stated "Obey
your master." Slaves were told to "forebear
punishment," even if it was undeserved, and they
would be rewarded in Heaven.

THE "AFRICAN SAVAGE" MYTH

The last step in creating a successful slave
trading industry was to convince the next generation
of Africans, those born as slaves in America, that it
was better to forget a shameful past in Africa.
Forbidden to learn any other language than that

spoken by the European, the children of those first imported Africans were kept ignorant of all that their people had ever been. Sometimes sold away from their parents as young children, the only image they had of Africa was of the one created by European enslavers -- that of the "naked jungle savage."

Newly imported Africans, emerging naked from the holds of slave ships, their bruised and beaten bodies covered with open sores, were in a state of shock, rage, and despair. They were hardly in a position to give a sophisticated English discourse on the refined elegance of African civilization to their American born black brethren.

Whites painted Africa in such graphically grotesque pictures ... a place where black cannibals ate human flesh; where ape-like people put rings through their noses and swung through trees; where gorilla-faced men and women wore only tiny loincloths to cover their bodies as they scurried around in crude grass huts and spoke unintelligible gibberish. The words "African" and "savage" became intertwined. "Civilized" came to mean "white" or "European." It meant living in a house like white people, wearing clothes like white people, being able to speak like white people. To be African was to be dirty, ugly, subhuman. American born slaves turned from such an identity in disgust, and looked for something else, anything other than an African, to call themselves.

And thus we have the making of a Negro.

Suppression of knowledge has been developed into a fine art in today's educational system. How American schools are designed to produce more non-thinking, self-hating slaves will be addressed in the next chapter, "Miseducation."

CHAPTER SEVEN
Miseducation

7A
The White Man's Education
Mahommah Baquaqua, brought to America as a slave, escaped, was recaptured, jailed, resold, and severely beaten. He suffered an emotional collapse and became an alcoholic. He then converted to Christianity. This photo shows him being reeducated by William L. Judd, American Baptist Free Missionary for Haiti. (Reprinted from African Muslims In Antebellum America, by Allan D. Austin, Copyright 1984, Garland Publishing Company, Inc.)

CHAPTER SEVEN
Miseducation

In the Gambia, West Africa, a sixteen-year-old black boy is being drilled in his lessons. He is not reading from any book, and without paper or pencil, can recite centuries of history, naming details of people, places, and events in chronological order, using only the powerful tool of a well trained mind.

In the United States, on the North American continent, a sixteen-year-old black boy struggles to recall basic facts about the country he lives in. He is unable to remember the stories he read in his history book. The people, places, and events are just a blur in his mind, and he cannot pass his exam.

The boy from the Gambia is the son of a Griot, an oral historian. The boy from the United States is the son of an ex-slave.

What is happening to the minds of our children in America's school systems?

LESSONS IN INFERIORITY

Although during slavery it was against the law to teach a slave to read or write, after slavery, basic laborers were still needed to maintain the southern rural economy. Therefore some type of training was required. But even after the establishment of local schools for the freed men, education was still frowned upon by white southern landowners, as it tended to make the African American, the "negro" forget his "place" (which was, of course, the position of servant to white people).

Even though the northern industrialists welcomed cheap black labor from the south, it was still very critical for whites to maintain the social order. Blacks may learn to read and write, and may even learn a trade; but they must always recognize the inherent superiority of the white race. Education for blacks was designed to, at best, make the black student admire and seek to emulate white society. Therefore, every single subject taught in the American school system reflected the philosophy of white supremacy. Carter G. Woodson, in his book *The Miseducation of the Negro,* explains further:

> *In Geography, the races were described in conformity with the program of the usual propaganda to engender in whites a race hate of the Negro, and in the Negroes contempt for themselves. A poet of distinction was selected to illustrate the physical features of the white race, a bedecked chief of a tribe those of the red, a proud warrior the brown, a prince the yellow, and a savage with a ring in his nose the black. The Negro, of course, stood at the foot of the social ladder. (pp. 17-18)*

In history, textbooks illustrate Caucasian-looking Egyptians, said to be the creators of the first civilization. In philosophy, the Greeks Plato and Aristotle are highlighted; In art, Piccasso and Van Gogh are the creative geniuses; in science, well, of course, Thomas Edison and Ben Franklin are the heroes; and in literature, who can top William Shakespeare? Africa and Africans don't even exist -- except maybe in an anthropology class as an illustration of "primitive" people.

Education in America has historically meant indoctrination into European-American culture. An "educated" person is one who is well versed in European history, literature, and philosophy.

"PRACTICAL" VS. "CLASSICAL" EDUCATION

The public school system actually grew out of the demand for free education to be made available for newly freed slaves. After emancipation, the Freedmen's Bureau was a government agency established to supposedly provide the services to former slaves which would help them make a transition into free society. White missionary teachers were sent from the North to set up schools.

There arose a debate as to whether these schools should concentrate on a "practical" education, and equip students with agricultural and industrial skills, or "classical" education, which would focus on such subjects as literature, philosophy, and politics.

This created a heated conflict between two outstanding black spokesmen in the early 1900s, W.E.B. DuBois, noted social scientist, and Booker T. Washington, founder of Alabama's Tuskegee Institute. Their opposing viewpoints were captured in a poem by Dudley Randall. Following is an excerpt of his work, entitled, *Booker T. and W.E.B.*:

> *"It seems to me," said Booker T.,*
> *"It shows a mighty lot of cheek*
> *To study chemistry and Greek*
> *When Mister Charlie needs a hand*
> *To hoe the cotton on his land*
> *And when Miss Ann looks for a cook,*
> *Why stick your nose inside a book?"*
>
> *"I don't agree," said W.E.B.*
> *"If I should have the drive to seek*
> *Knowledge of chemistry or Greek,*
> *I'll do it. Charles and Miss can look*
> *Another place for hand or cook.*

Some men rejoice in skill of hand
And some in cultivating land,
But there are others who maintain
The right to cultivate the brain."

The sad fact is, whether the African American received a "practical" or "classical" education, the results were still the same; poverty and powerlessness. As Woodson notes that the machinery used by industrial training schools was often outmoded, and therefore, graduates from such schools were unprepared for employment. Likewise, "classical" education was equally useless. Society provided blacks little opportunities for advancementin the way of politics or literature.

The "educated negro," fully indoctrinated in the philosophy of white superiority, was equipped to do little more than inflict this attitude on the "uneducated" masses. His function, as an "intellectual" was not to develop any new ideas, but to confirm the prevailing philosophy: that in order to be acceptable to whites, "negroes" must learn to conform to European thinking and behavior. Woodson explains:

When you control a man's thinking, you do not have to control his actions. You do not have to tell him not to stand here or go yonder. He will find his "proper place" and will stay in it. You do not need to send him to the back door. He will go without being told. In fact, if there is no back door, he will cut one for his special benefit. His education makes it necessary.

The same educational process which inspires and stimulates the oppressor with the thought that he is everything and has accomplished everything

worthwhile, depresses and crushes at the same time
the spark of genius in the Negro by making him feel
that his race does not amount to much and never will
measure up to the standard of other peoples. The
Negro thus educated is a hopeless liability to the race.
(p. xiii)

Even those African Americans who had a
desire to enter the field of education in order to
change the system were at a disadvantage; educated
at white institutions or at white controlled black
institutions, all they had to rely upon was a
Eurocentric frame of reference to determine
standards of knowledge and intelligence. Black
teachers, educated in such institutions, passed on the
same attitude of African inferiority as did white
teachers. It was inherent in every subject taught.

ASHAMED OF AFRICAN AMERICAN DIALECT

Consider the study of language. An African-
American child may come to understand and
appreciate the difference in sentence structure and
phonetic pronunciation in the Spanish or German
language. English, spoken with a French accent,
might even be considered "charming" to English-
speaking Americans.

But students learn to scoff at the African-
American dialect as some peculiar defect which
should be despised. Never are African Americans
directed to study the background of this language as
a broken down African tongue, in order to
understand their own linguistic history. This would
certainly have more relevance than the study of
French Phonetics or Historical Spanish Grammar.

Have you also been taught to be ashamed of the African Dialect? Go back to question No. 1 on the Psychic Trauma Test: "While watching an African American being interviewed on a television program, when I notice that the person is using "incorrect" grammar with a very heavy "Black dialect," I get embarrassed."

If you strongly agree, agree, or are unsure, consider yourself indoctrinated in the philosophy of white supremacy.

Why does one feel personally embarrassed? Possibly because this is the unconscious thought one may have as one observes the African American's television interview:

"White people might be watching, and they'll think we're all "ignorant" like that."

Fear of white disapproval is the motivation here. Proper understanding of the history of such a dialect, along with proper self esteem (why should a white person's opinion be more important than your own?) would eliminate feelings of personal embarrassment.

Do you fear that whites will see you as "unintelligent" if you do not master the European standard of English pronunciation? Look at your answer to question No. 2: "When speaking to whites, I consciously try to alter my grammar and pronunciation so that I sound more like them, "proper."

If you strongly agree, agree, or are unsure, then you have defined "proper" speech according to European white standards. Your "education" has removed any knowledge, understanding or appreciation of African language patterns, phonetic pronunciation or sentence structure, all of which are an intricate part of the African-American dialect.

HIGH AMBITIONS DISCOURAGED

All during this last century, the professional fields of study African Americans chose depended not on their personal interests or talents, but on what white society decided to make available. Teachers discouraged their students from making any career plans which did not fit into the accepted areas for "negroes" at that time.

El Hajj Malik El Shabazz (Commonly known as Malcolm X) relates in his autobiography how his eighth grade teacher promptly squashed his ambition to be a lawyer. After being elected class president, and recognizing himself as a gifted speaker, Malcolm had expressed his career choice to his teacher, feeling that he could succeed. But his English teacher, Mr. Ostrowski, convinced him otherwise.

Mr. Ostrowski looked surprised, I remember and leaned back in his chair and clasped his hands behind his head. He kind of half smiled and said, "Malcolm, one of life's first needs is to be realistic. Don't misunderstand me, now. We all like you, you know that. But you've got to be realistic about being a nigger. A lawyer -- that's no realistic goal for a nigger. You need to think about something you can be. You're good with your hands -- making things. Everybody admires your carpentry shop work. Why don't you plan on carpentry? People like you as a person -- you'll get all kinds of work."

So, eventually Malcolm, disillusioned with school, dropped out to become a hoodlum in the streets of Detroit. His career in crime eventually landed him in jail. It was there that the genius in him, crushed by the American school system, blossomed.

African Americans often feel restricted by the bounds of racial discrimination when making career choices. Education may even be perceived as futile if the development of ones talents and interests cannot lead to employment. However, in many African societies, there is a different attitude toward education. Family groups provide specialized areas of expertise, therefore, education has a defined purpose. Children are often trained to fill specific roles in the community.

Foday Musa Suso, a Mandingo griot from Gambia, West Africa, explained this system in more detail in a 1989 interview. He said that rather than a few wealthy individuals owning the neighborhood businesses, or a few major corporations controlling all the industry, all the services needed for the community are provided by each of the family clans:

One group of families are the blacksmiths; another group of families are the traders; another group of families are the builders. My family members are historians. When one begins to tell the story of history, one begins with the family -- who was the first person in a family, how he got his name, where the family spread, what they do ...

I can look at people here and see what region in Africa their ancestors came ... The way African Americans speak, the rhythm and tone in their voices, it sounds just like the Fulani language."

In addition to family lineages and patterns of migration, an African historian also had to know the physical features, habits and customs of the people. Such knowledge involved the mastery of several disciplines -- sociology, geography, language, ethnology. All this was necessary in order for a griot to become a skilled recorder of history. Such an education is more than just abstract bits of knowledge. When students complete their course of study, they are well equipped to do whatever it is they set out to learn. Suso noted that by age eighteen he had retained some 1900 years of history. He was ready to take his place among the family of historians.

At eighteen, what do African American high school graduates know how to do? What profession have they been prepared for? What trades have they mastered? And where can they go to put their skills to use? Seeing themselves so ill prepared for survival, even after twelve years of formal schooling, African-American youth begin to ask themselves, "If education doesn't get me a decent job, what do I need to go to school for?"

The student has recognized that in order to excel in society, more is needed than basic mathematics and reading; and of what practical use is knowledge of European literature, history, and art? None of these things create a means for one to provide food, clothing and shelter for oneself or one's family. The answer, some argue, is more technical training schools. But often students in these schools are being trained to use outdated equipment and are learning systems no longer in use in today's ever-advancing business world. We have never really advanced beyond the inadequate post-slavery choices of "classical" education versus "practical" education.

African Americans are so extremely conscious of racial discrimination that they automatically

African Americans are so extremely conscious of racial discrimination that they automatically expect their progress to be blocked by whites. In school, they experience repeated discouragement from educators, who steer them away from lofty career pursuits. As adults, they experience repeated denial of promotions on jobs by employers. As a result, African Americans conclude that white approval or disapproval is the deciding factor on whether they achieve educational and career goals.

Look back at your answer to Psychic Trauma Test question Number 8: "I believe that I would be further along in my career if I were white." If you strongly agree, agree, or are even unsure, then your perception is that whites not only have the ability to control who succeeds, but that they have purposely blocked your own professional progress.

This perception, whether true or not, can have a negative effect on one's drive toward success. If one is not careful, the focus can easily become not on striving to gain knowledge, but on striving to gain white approval. In the long run, this proves to be a grave mistake; while true knowledge can never be taken away, white approval is often fickle, and can easily turn into resentment or hostility.

Awareness of obstacles such as racial discrimination is important; it helps one develop a strategy to overcome them. But the search for knowledge must be greater than a simple goal of white approval. Each person must strive to achieve the highest possible level of personal excellence, in order to make his or her own unique contribution to mankind. Those who allowed their minds to transcend the confines of white expectations discovered they possessed a special ability which, when developed, changed the course of history.

GENETIC MEMORY

Intelligence is widely regarded to be a product of heredity, environment and education. Europeans were often able to convince Africans born in America that their foreparents were dumb and therefore they, too, were dumb. Some African Americans became so convinced of this, they didn't dare approach fields of study that whites had warned them were "difficult" -- such as chemistry, biology, physics, trigonometry.

But a mere three hundred years of deprivation cannot erase eight thousand years of advanced intelligence. In spite of poor education, and sometimes no education, the hidden genius in African Americans continues to burst forth. African Americans appear to have inherited a great mental capacity that transcends formal training. It's something we call "genetic memory."

GENETIC: Pertaining to those characteristics of an organism due to inheritance or actions of the genes, the chemically complex unit which is assumed to be the carrier of specific physical characteristics from parent to offspring, being transmitted through the chromosomes.

MEMORY: The power of retaining and recording past experiences; the accumulated experiences of the mind, considered as influencing present and future behavior.

We use this expression to describe the continuous reappearance of superior talents and abilities in African Americans, in spite of being denied schooling for generations.

BANNEKER: AFRICAN AMERICAN MATHEMATICAL GENIUS

Recall the awesome structures created during ancient Egypt's dominance on the world scene. Many still stand today as a testimony to the brilliance of the African in the field of engineering. Such a mathematical mind was passed down to Benjamin Banneker, the engineer and architect who helped design the United States capital, Washington, D.C. A black man born in pre-Civil War America, Banneker's genius was not dimmed by time nor circumstances. A self taught mathematician, Banneker was born near Baltimore, Maryland, in 1731. He was the only child of a free mulatto mother and African father, who purchased his own freedom from slavery.

Banneker showed an early gift for mathematics and an interest in astronomy. His aptitude in mathematics and knowledge of astronomy enabled him to predict the solar eclipse that took place on April 14, 1789.

Banneker was appointed by President George Washington to serve on the six man team which helped design the blueprints for Washington, D.C. When the chairman of the civil engineering team, Major L'Enfant abruptly resigned and took the plans home to France with him, Banneker's photographic memory enabled him to reproduce the entire set of plans. (Although Banneker is responsible for the completion of the project, it is interesting that the plaza in D.C. is today called "L'Enfant Plaza.")

Acting as a surveyor for the engineering team, Banneker helped select the sites for the U.S. Capitol building, the U.S. Treasury building, the White House, and other Federal buildings. It is interesting to note that Banneker's designs were amazingly similar to the layout of Egyptian cities, where the major government buildings stand at the middle point of of the city and all roads lead away from the center. The Egyptians designed their cities this way as a protection from military attack.

FREDERICK DOUGLASS: GREAT ORATOR

Originally named Frederick Bailey at birth in February, 1818, Frederick Douglass rose to become one of history's most remembered orators.

Raised by his grandparents Betsy and Isaac Bailey in their cabin on a farm in Talbot County, Maryland, Frederick grew up with the knowledge that his birth was the result of a union between Betsy and Isaac's second daughter Harriet, and one of the white slave masters.

At age 20, Douglass married a dark skinned seamstress named Anna Murray, who sewed his clothes to look like a sailors outfit, and helped him escape to New York. In his early twenties, Frederick met the controversial white anti-slavery advocate William Lloyd Garrison who prompted Douglass to become a spokesperson for the abolitionist movement.

Douglass trained himself to become a master of words and developed the ability to project his powerful voice in such an eloquent fashion, that his white associates often urged him to try to get "a little of the plantation" in his voice when speaking, so that audiences would indeed believe that he had once been a slave.

Douglass rose to become an internationally known human rights advocate. He published a newspaper called The North Star, and wrote several books based upon his life experiences from slavery to freedom. He was appointed to several government posts, including ambassador to Haiti.

In the book *Frederick Douglass,* a biography written by William S. Feely, Douglass' mother Betsy is described as a "tall, strong, copper-dark woman" whose great-grandfather's name was "Baly." He, like many other Talbot County slaves, may have been imported into the British West Indies before being sold to Maryland tobacco planters. His name became the family name "Bailey" which was passed down for many generations. Feely observes:

...but "Bailey" may have had an African source. In the nineteenth century on Sapelo Island, Georgia (where Baileys still reside), there was a Fulfulde-speaking slave from Timbo, Futa Jallon, in the Guinea highlands, who could write Arabic and who was the father of twelve sons. His name was Belali Mohamet. "Belali" spelled in various ways, is a common Muslim name; indeed, Bilal was the name of a black slave who was a muezzin, a caller to prayer, much admired by the prophet Muhammad ... "Belali" easily slides into the English "Bailey," a common African American surname along the Atlantic coast. The records of Talbot county list no white Baileys from which the slave Bailey might have taken their name, and an African origin, on the order of "Belali" is conceivable.

Just as Bilal became famous for his powerful voice, so did the fiery anti-slavery spokesman, Frederick Douglass. And just as Bilal was part of a revolutionary movement for the upliftment of humanity during a time of barbaric slavery and oppression, Frederick Douglass was a fighter for the spiritual reform of pre-and post-Civil War America.

7B
Young Frederick Douglass
A fiery young Frederick Douglass began preaching against
slavery while in his twenties. This portrait was used for his
book, "My Bondage, My Freedom." (Reprinted from Frederick
Douglass, by William S. McFeely, page 146, Copyright 1991,
W.W. Norton & Company, Inc.)

CHARLES DREW: BLOOD BANK PIONEER

Dr. Charles Drew, master surgeon, medical scientist and educator, was responsible for one of modern medical science's most important inventions: the blood bank. Born in 1904 in Washington, D.C., he graduated from Chicago's Dunbar High School in 1922. After he finished medical school, he began researching a process for blood preservation. In World War II, England suffered heavy casualties and called on Dr. Drew to initiate his military blood bank program. It was then that he introduced preserved blood plasma -- there on the battlefield.

Dr. Drew's medical breakthrough would have made Imhotep, the father of medicine, proud. His skill and innovation is reminiscent of the brilliant doctors and surgeons from the University of Jenne medical school, during the glorious Songhay empire.

LEWIS LATIMER BRINGS THE LIGHT

Lewis Latimer, a pioneer in the field of electricity, was born in Massachusetts, son of an former slave. He developed a skill in mechanical drawing at an early age. After enlisting in the Navy and serving in the Civil War, he returned to Boston seeking work. His skills enabled him to secure a position with Crosby and Gould, patent solicitor. He taught himself draftsmanship skills, and later became their chief draftsman.

Latimer worked with Thomas Edison in the development of the electric light bulb, the only black member of the Edison Pioneers, a group of distinguished scientists and inventors. Latimer also drew the plans for Alexander Graham Bell's telephone patent.

7C
18th Century African Surgeon
Sake Deen Mahomed (1749-1851) served as barber-surgeon to
George IV and William IV of England. He was an expert on
cholera and muscular ailments. Even during the height of the
American slave trade, black professionals from African
universities were still performing services in various countries.
This destroyed myths that slavery introduced modern education
to Africans. (Photos courtesy of the Brighton Public Library.
Reprinted from Nature Knows No Color Line, by J.A. Rogers,
page 166. Copyright 1952 by Helga Rogers).

Just as the Moors from Africa brought the light of civilization to eighth century Spain with lighted paved streets, so did Lewis Latimer bring light to the streets of New York, Philadelphia, Canada and London, where he supervised the installation of Edison's electric light systems.

ELIJAH: THE REAL McCOY

Elijah McCoy, the Canadian-born son of escaped slaves, studied engineering in Scotland but returned to the United States only to be turned down for jobs because of his race. At the Michigan Central railroad he was given the menial task of shoveling coal into the engine and oiling all of the train's moving parts. Bored with this mundane, repetitious job, he asked himself, "Why can't these parts just lubricate themselves?" He decided to explore the idea of creating a mechanical self-lubricating device, and after some experiments, invented the first automatic lubricator, called the "lubricator cup." This invention became so important to industry that anyone who owned a self-lubricating machine bragged of having a "real McCoy." This expression is still used today to signify genuine quality.

Many other African Americans, in spite of slavery, rose to become great scientists and inventors. Norbert Rillieux, born in New Orleans, was the son of a French planter/engineer and a slave mother. He revolutionized the sugar industry by inventing a refining process that reduced the time, cost and safety risk involved in producing good sugar from can and beets. His device was patented in 1846.

Granville Woods, born in 1856 in Columbus, Ohio, was awarded more than 35 patents for electrical systems and devices. He invented a furnace and boiler to produce steam heat and invented a "third rail" system for an electric locomotive.

Garrett A. Morgan, born in 1877, just after Emancipation, invented the gas mask and saftety helmet. He also invented the electric traffic signal.

In the years following emancipation, African Americans realized the vast power of knowledge, and knew that one of the main tools for keeping them subservient was denial of education. Great pioneers in the field of education set out to develop colleges and universities of higher learning.

Booker T. Washington rose from slavery in Virginia to build Tuskegee Institute in Alabama. South Carolina-born Mary McCleod Bethune founded Bethune Cookman College in Florida in 1904.

PARENTS FIGHT BACK

Today, educators are recognizing that the African-American child's natural thirst for knowledge is being crushed within a white controlled public school system by an onslaught of negative images of African people. They have begun to fight back.

In a February 1991 interview on WVON radio station in Chicago, nationally syndicated radio commentator Bob Law reported that a group of New York parents have sued the city's public school system for damages.

The time has come, stated Law, to acknowledge that the racist doctrines passed off as education within the schools these many years have led to psychological damage to black children. The aim of this lawsuit, he said, is to change the public school curriculum for everybody.

Law, a radio commentator and activist in New York, spearheaded this movement. In an address before an audience at Chicago's Kennedy King College, he pointed out that the low self esteem, lack of motivation and drive and lack of survival skills are the results of a poor educational system, designed to make blacks feel inferior:

Centuries ago, an African named Imhotep performed open heart surgery. They'll never tell you that in the public schools. They'll look at the pyramids and say they came from outer space. They teach the "Great White Man" theory, having our children believing that only whites can do anything.

Chicago and other cities have joined New York in filing lawsuits against the public school system, bringing to the forefront the controversial and hotly debated issue of Afrocentric education.

Schools are particularly hostile toward black males, as many urban studies have shown. Black boys are most often placed into "educationally mentally handicapped" (E.M.H.) classes, when they exhibit highly spirited or aggressive behavior. Public schools, rather than creatively channeling the students' energy, tend to concentrate on discipline.

INDEPENDENT AFROCENTRIC SCHOOLS

Black educators are realizing that attitudes within the public education system will not change overnight. The logical answer to the problem, for many, has been the establishment of independent institutions, which teach from an Afrocentric perspective.

In Detroit educators have recognized the importance of reinforcing strong black manhood among young boys, who continue to be systematically

driven out of the public schools. They established
Malcolm X Academy, a school which educates from
an Afrocentric perspective and provides manhood
training for black boys. Their focus is to properly
channel, rather than crush, natural male aggression.
Although within the public school system such
programs remain controversial and are challenged by
whites as "racist," many blacks agree that
conventional education is just not working. In some
cities, private schools offer alternatives, such as the
New Concept Development Center in Chicago, where
African and African-American history and culture are
incorporated in all subjects and students learn
Swahili as a second language.

However, the private school option still has its
limitations. Many parents just cannot afford to pay
tuition costs for private institutions and must rely on
a racially biased public education system.

In spite of all the obstacles, the genetic
memory of African Americans continues to surface in
young minds today. Popular young rap artists recite
long poetic verses with the rhythm and concentration
of ancient African griots. But, although the youths
of today show talent, intelligence, and great
potential, rather than being fed the knowledge
consumed by their ancestors, they are raised on a
steady diet of television commercial jingles, profanity,
and violence. So unfortunately, much of the creative
verses they compose glorify violence, promiscuity and
degradation of women.

Perhaps the greatest battle educators must
fight is against the mass media, which has had a
devastating impact on the minds of young people and
has been used to promote racism around the world.

ACTIVITY:
Tap Your Genetic Memory

The human mind has unlimited potential if encouraged to explore its vast possibilities. African Americans, as descendants from those who created some of the world's greatest wonders, have much to draw upon in terms of inborn talents and abilities.

Consider the amazing memory capacity of the African Griot, who, by remembering facts to the tune of rhythmatic music, can recite centuries of history and family genealogies. Think of ways you might use your memory to recall important facts. Think of a tune or rhythm to help you recite educational facts, such as:

1. Multiplication tables

2. States in the U.S. and their capitol cities

3. The numbers from one to one hundred, the seven days of the week and the twelve months of the year in a foreign language you are studying.

Inventions are often created by people who are seeking to save money or make their own work easier. What inventions could help you save money?

Africans developed the first communication system, long before the telephone, with "talking drums" which imitated human vocal sounds. Think of ways you might develop a system of communicating over long distances ... to family members in the next room, to a neighbor next door, or even farther.

The pyramids made practical use of solar energy for heating and cooling. Think of ways you might design a house, using windows and mirrors, to maximize the use of natural sunlight and save on electric lighting.

Look at all of the many scientific discoveries and think of other inventions you could create!

CHAPTER EIGHT
Our Media Image: The Big Lie

8A

Man or Monkey?

The caption under this photo from the book Illustrated Africa, North, Tropical and South, (p. 472, copyright 1925 by William D. Boyce) is indicative of the media image of blacks in the early 1900s. It reads: "Here is evidence for the "evolutionists." Which is more intelligent, the African native or the chimpanzee? Those who know them best say that given equal opportunities, the chimpanzee will make faster progress than the black."

CHAPTER EIGHT
Our Media Image: The Big Lie

How did Europeans portray Africans before the slave trade? Shakespeare, who became popular in England in the 1500s, wrote his classic plays during the time when Africa was still in its Golden Age. Spain was still heavily influenced by Moorish culture. European literature did not begin to reflect disdain for Africans until the transatlantic slave trade reached its peak. In Shakespeare's play "Othello," the lead character is a Moor of royal birth in Venice who marries a European woman. In 1930 Othello was played by legendary African American actor Paul Robeson in London at the Savoy.

Robeson, a remarkably gifted scholar, athlete, orator, and linguist, was a world renowned singer. He filled the largest concert halls to overflowing in America, England Germany, Austria, France and Russia. In a review by the *London Daily Express*, critic Hannen Swaffer had this to say about Robeson's performance:

He triumphed as a Moor, black, swarthy, muscular, a real man of deep color. A wonderful audience cheered Robeson's triumph.

St. Benedict the Moor, born in Sicily, the son of African blacks, became a much admired saint of the Catholic church. In paintings on church walls, he was depicted as dark skinned with crinkly hair, with a halo of light surrounding his head. Through books and paintings, the image of the African man and woman spread across the world. Powerful king, wise scholar, majestic queen, beautiful maiden.

8B

Paul Robeson Plays The Moor

A remarkably gifted athlete, orator, and linguist, Robeson transcended the barriers of racial prejudice to become an internationally acclaimed actor and singer. His performance as the Moor in Shakespeare's "Othello" has yet to be surpassed. He took a bold stand on political issues, which caused him to come under great criticism. He left the U.S. and lived abroad. (Photo courtesy of the DuSable Museum of African American History file, Chicago, Illinois.)

8C
St. Benedict, The Moor
Born in Sicily, the son of slave parents, Benedict became one of
the most revered monks of the Catholic church. This painting
reflects the legendary Divine light he was said to reflect.
(Reprinted from World's Great Men of Color, by J.A. Rogers,
page 512. Copyright 1972, Macmillan Publishing Company.)

EUROPEAN SCHOLARS SUPPORT SLAVERY

Prior to the Transatlantic slave trade, Africans were held in high esteem internationally. Then, in answer to the critics who labeled the slave trade as barbaric, European scholars began to develop "scientific" theories of black inferiority. Books were written to support these theories, which were taught in European and American universities.

Thomas Cartwright, 18th century scholar and lecturer, presented his theories before college students across the country. Negroes, he said, were naturally sinful. In the Bible, Eve is said to have been approached in the garden of Eden by a snake. The snake, Cartwright said, was actually symbolic for a Negro. This was a warning for white women to stay away from the evil temptations of black men, he advised. *The Negro, A Beast,* written in 1900 by Charles Carroll, explained how black men and women were actually a species of animal, closer to monkey than man.

Many universities in the south were highly acclaimed institutions which attracted students from all over the country.. After the Civil War, these schools changed little of their confederate philosophies. Many students who graduated from these schools went on to become book publishers and authors of textbooks. Influenced by the South's philosophy of white racial superiority, these graduates reflected such theories in their own works. The history of African people was rewritten to remove all traces of those periods when Africans ruled Europeans, Indians, Asians, Arabs and others. Any Africans mentioned in textbooks, novels, or other literary work, were usually said to be slaves.

MODERN MULTI MEDIA IMAGES

Today, images of African Americans are created and reinforced through books, magazines, newspapers, billboards, radios, television, and motion pictures.

These forms of communication have had a definite impact on the opinions of most Americans, and indeed, of most people worldwide. Read the brief descriptions of the four people listed below and along with the common images of them which come to mind.

1. *Corporate Executive:* White male, mid thirties to mid sixties, well groomed, wearing a business suit and tie, carrying a briefcase or sitting behind a desk.

2. *Welfare Mother:* Black female, late teens to mid thirties, hair uncombed, ragged clothes, in a rundown apartment full of screaming little children.

3. *Gang Member:* Black male, mid teens to late thirties, dark skinned, menacing, with a cap on sideways or backward, and gold chains around his neck.

4. *Secretary:* White female, early twenties to mid thirties, slim, shapely figure, immaculately styled hair, manicured nails, wearing well-fitting, color coordinated fashionable dress or skirt.

These are the stereotypical images which have been very carefully planted in the minds of the American public, and have been replayed over and over again by the mass media. The negative images are often accepted without question, and could be having a global effect on the perceptions of African American people.

MOTION PICTURES CREATE VISUAL IMAGES

The novel *Uncle Tom's Cabin,* written by Harriet Beecher Stowe prior to the Civil War, introduced many of today's popular negative black stereotypes.

The rise of the motion picture industry in the early 1900s enabled white filmmakers to create visual images for all the black stereotypes concocted during slavery. They developed five basic character types to portray blacks, and these basic types are at the root of most white-controlled media images of African American people today.

Donald Bogle traces the portrayal of blacks in films in his book *Toms, Coons, Mulattoes, Mammies, and Bucks: An Interpretive History of Blacks In American films.*

The first character was the Tom, a good, submissive negro. Toms may be harassed, insulted, or flogged, but never turn against their white masters. Then there was the Coon. This was the basic negro buffoon, the harmless, childlike clown, who kept white folks laughing with outrageous "darky" antics. The Tragic Mulatto character represented the yearning of the light skinned black to be accepted as white. The mulatto character allowed filmmakers to reinforce whiteness as the standard of beauty to be admired and desired. The other black female image was the big, black, bossy Mammy. She was a non-sexual, overweight, dark skinned, loud mouthed, hands-on-hips, finger shaking, head-rag-wearing woman. And the man to be feared, hated, and ultimately destroyed was the menacing Black Brute. He plotted to kill white men, preyed upon helpless white women, and even victimized his own people.

BIRTH OF A NATION
INTRODUCES THE KLAN

D.W. Griffith's 1915 film, *The Birth of a Nation*, set the tone for American political philosophy, a philosophy which today's media continues to reinforce. In many ways *The Birth of a Nation* made history. It was a record-breaking $100,000 spectacle, more than three hours in running time, whereas up to then American movies had been no longer than 10 or 15 minutes. It was a powerful piece of propaganda, to be sure, and included all the black stereotypes.

The story, which follows the years before, during and after the Civil War, centered around a good, "decent" little family in Piedmont, South Carolina, the Camerons. Dr. Cameron, his two sons and daughter live on a southern plantation where happy, childlike slaves dance and sing as they work in the fields. Everybody is having a wonderful time, until, as Bogle quotes from a movie review, "carpetbaggers and uppity niggers from the North move into Piedmont, exploiting and corrupting the former slaves, unleashing the sadism and bestiality innate in the Negro, turning the once congenial darkies into renegades." Civil War breaks out and the victory of the North creates chaos in the South. Now blacks walk down the streets, rudely shoving whites aside. After being given the power to vote, they cheat in the election to get into office. Once in Congress, they sing and dance and eat chicken legs, and drink whiskey from the bottle while sprawling with bare feet on desks. The blacks have taken over and the country is in a mess.

The Birth of a Nation was the first to introduce the "brutal black buck" characters. Gus,

big, black and menacing, sets out to marry the young
Cameron daughter, which is portrayed as being
tantamount to rape. Rather than submit, she throws
herself off a cliff to her death. Another brutal
character is the greedy, corrupt mulatto, Silas Lynch,
who once in power decides to marry the daughter of
the white man who had been his benefactor.

The Camerons, meanwhile, are grieving that
their sweet little sister had to endure such horror.
Finally, Dr. Cameron hits upon a plan. He organizes
a heroic group of men, and just when all seems lost,
the citizens in white sheets ride in to save the day.
And thus we have The Birth of a Nation ... and the
Ku Klux Klan.

It's interesting to note that the greatest wish
of the black men and, of course their greatest sin,
was to marry the white women. The film implies that
for this abomination, the men should die. This film,
though hotly debated and bitterly cursed by black
leaders, met with widespread approval by whites.
Bogle notes that at a private White House screening,
President Woodrow Wilson exclaimed excitedly, "It's
like writing history with lightning!"

The Birth of a Nation shaped the social and
political philosophies of many people raised in the
late teens and early 1920s.

A TOOL FOR SOCIAL CONTROL

As America faced one crisis after another, from
economic depressions to world wars, it became
necessary to remind blacks of their proper place in
the social order. Mass media worked hand in hand
with educational institutions in this regard. Schools
steered black students toward menial jobs as laborers
and domestic servants. Movies portrayed blacks as

laborers and domestic servants.

In the 1930s and 1940s, many actors and actresses rose to fame as butlers and maids. Bill Robinson, an extraordinary tap dancer, was forever the faithful servant in a series of films starring Shirley Temple. Eddie Anderson, as comedian Jack Benny's chauffeur Rochester, made his character a memorable buffoon during that era. Mantan Moreland and Stepin Fetchit were two more brilliant comedians, forced to play the "coon" role in order to get paid.

Plump, dark skinned actresses found themselves in the familiar maid roles. Hattie McDaniel, Ethel Waters and Louis Beavers were women who found themselves commonly typecast in films where the maid was a mere prop, to accentuate white leading ladies.

Bogle notes that Hattie McDaniel often defended her stereotypical screen portrayals of mammies and maids with the remark, "Why should I complain about making seven thousand dollars a week playing a maid? If I didn't, I'd be making seven dollars a week actually being one!"

Attractive black women were often light skinned "bad girls," whose white half made them pretty and desirable, but whose black half made them whorish women of easy virtue. Nina Kinney in the 1929 film *Hallelujah* popularized such a character. Later, Lena Horne as the adulteress in the 1943 film *Cabin in The Sky* and Dorothy Dandridge in the film *Carmen Jones* represented more modern versions of this "Tragic Mulatto" character.

The 1950s and 1960s saw an awakening of social consciousness among African Americans. Along with it came Hollywood's attempt to placate feelings of discontent with more reinforcement of old stereotypes.

Actor Sydney Poitier emerged as the dignified, respectable, intelligent negro -- the modern, more palatable "Tom." In an era where whites struggled with the issue of integration, Poitier, in his film roles, presented the perfect model of a civilized black man. He was a negro whom whites could socially accept. In the 1967 film *Guess Who's Coming To Dinner,* Poitier and his white fiancee shock both sets of parents with a sudden wedding announcement. Who else but the proper Sidney Poitier could approach such an American taboo as black men marrying white women?

However *The Great White Hope,* (1970), starring James Earl Jones as the famous champion boxer Jack Johnson, presented a more defiant character. Johnson, with his white wife, was seen by whites as more of the "brutal black buck" who had to be crushed. At the end of the film, it was clear that Jack Johnson was a beaten man ... as was usually the fate for defiant blacks.

DESTROYING AFRICA'S IMAGE

The cinema produced on screen what American textbooks had espoused for generations; namely, that Africa was a jungle of savages, waiting to be civilized by Europeans. Motion pictures, television programs, and even cartoons reinforced this image.

Perhaps the greatest damage to the African-American psyche was done by a series of films featuring a character called "Tarzan." This film was remade several times and even became a television series. As the story goes, a young white couple are on a jungle safari with their infant. The man and woman are killed, leaving behind a helpless baby, who is found and adopted by a pack of apes. (Filmmakers did not bother to make too much distinction between apes and gorillas.) The boy, named Tarzan, is raised by these apes, and of course, takes on all the characteristics of an ape, from primal grunts and screams to swinging through trees.

Naturally, having the superior intellect of a man, Tarzan rises to a position of leadership in the ape pack. In fact, after a series of challenges from tigers, snakes, bears, lions, and hostile apes, in which he emerges slightly scarred but always victorious, Tarzan becomes king of the jungle. Animals come running when he beckons them with his peculiar call. He is a sort of Superman in the wild ... able to outwrestle crocodiles in water, and able to outrun, outjump and outclimb every species of animal on land.

So, when groups of whites on safaris through the jungle are attacked by a mob of grass skirt wearing, paint smeared, spear chucking African savages, who else but the great white Tarzan should save them? Even African-American audiences find themselves cheering with relief as Tarzan, calling in the jungle animals to aid him, uses his superior skill and strength to wipe out those black savages.

For decades, the Tarzan tales provided the only image of Africa that American children ever saw. It filled an African-American child with shame to even identify with the repulsive looking "African savages" and reinforced the European-American child's sense of innate superiority. It's no wonder that in the black community, to call a person an "African" became the highest insult. Just as *The Birth of a Nation* influenced white audiences to fear black empowerment, *Tarzan* influenced black audiences to reject the African identity.

Prominent African-American leaders, raised on a cinematic diet of *Tarzan, The Ape Man* throughout childhood, often feel extreme uneasiness at the thought of identifying with Africa. New books by African-American authors attempt to correct historical misinformation. Still, many adults, raised in the 1930s, '40s, and '50s find it nearly impossible to erase those old, repulsive images from their minds.

Have Tarzan and other such media depictions affected your perception of Africa? Look back at your answer to Psychic Trauma Test question Number 17: "When I see Africans in films expressing their own cultural rituals and activities, I see them as repulsive."

If you answered Strongly Agree, Agree, or Unsure, then you have possibly been the victim of media brainwashing.

Keeping in line with the mis-education techniques of slavery, white filmmakers today set out to depict Africa in such a way as to make black Americans feel ashamed. Producers of television documentaries seek out the most remote, rural areas of Africa to film their nature specials. White narrators use words like "primitive," "crude," and "undeveloped," to describe the homes, clothing, utensils, and general behavior of the people. Customs which may seem strange to westerners are highlighted.

Areas of Africa in which great cities are known to have existed are somehow taken out of Africa. North Africa, with its renowned heritage of great Egyptian dynasties, has mysteriously become the "Middle East" when referred to by journalists. Ethiopia, Egypt's predecessor, is never examined in relation to its historical significance as the site of great kingdoms described in the Bible. Today, documentaries on Ethiopia and other East African nations focus on the starving masses in drought-stricken lands. These films, while they may evoke intense pity, do not create a sense of pride or a desire to identify with the people of the land. (And never do these documentaries mention the real reason for Africa's drought and starvation -- depletion of mineral resources by multinational corporations of the West.) We have yet to see a film produced by a European which acknowledges that some areas of Africa had paved lighted streets, sewage systems, schools and libraries centuries before Europe.

BLACKS PRODUCE POSITIVE IMAGES

In the 1930s and '40s, black filmmaker Oscar Marchaux produced a series of motion pictures featuring all black casts. His films not only gave work to many talented actors and actresses, but also presented blacks as multi-dimensional characters with personalities, who had jobs and families and problems just like white people. Comedy, romance, murders, suspense -- Marchaux offered it all to black audiences.

Marchaux struggled to get his films distributed and met with much opposition in the white-controlled film industry. Distributors resisted the idea of presenting blacks as regular people with their own lives, and not as inferior extensions of white society.

Another weapon used to counteract white propaganda against blacks was the black-controlled press. Black-owned newspapers existed in America well before the Civil War, starting with *Freedom's Journal,* first published by free blacks John B. Russworm and Samuel Cornish on March 16, 1827.

This and publications such as Frederick Douglass' *North Star* were mostly aimed at white readers (the majority of blacks in America were still forbidden to learn to read) and advocated the end to slavery. These papers reported on the intense brutality of such a system, appealing to the conscience of white society.

After slavery, black-owned newspapers continued to champion the cause of African Americans, pushing for equality of rights and an end to lynching and violence, which escalated after Reconstruction.

The 1920s saw a sharp rise in lynching and other violence toward blacks. In answer to incidences of racial discrimination reported by black papers, white newspapers would often focus on the high levels of crime among blacks, creating images of violent, irresponsible people who should be contained in areas away from white society. Such heavy propaganda would convince whites that whatever repressive tactics law enforcement officials used to control blacks were probably necessary. The climate created by the white press made it practically impossible for whites to be convicted of brutality against blacks. Officers of the law could maim and kill blacks with absolute impunity. (Things really haven't changed much, have they?)

Black newspapers sought to present the other side of black society. Business success stories, social events, and other things generally ignored by the white press were highlighted in the black press, giving readers a more positive view of black people.

Again, whites resisted attempts to change the social order. Black-owned newspaper offices were vandalized by Ku Klux Klan members, publishers received death threats. White business owners declined to advertise in black publications, and often black-owned newspapers operated on shaky financial ground, eventually going out of business due to lack of operating capital.

A BLACK CREATIVE RENAISSANCE

After World War I, a new consciousness emerged among African Americans. The great Harlem Renaissance of the 1920s and '30s, which brought to the forefront many gifted writers and artists, greatly changed how society viewed African Americans. Through novels, poetry, songs, plays, dance, and other creative expression, blacks began to define themselves.

Philosopher W.E.B. DuBois urged blacks to use the arts as a means of education and inspiration. Dr. Alvin Poussaint, in his introduction to a recent reprint of W.E.B. DuBois' book, *The Souls Of Black Folk,* observes how DuBois' own creative works influenced the arts:

In 1913, DuBois produced a pageant, "The Star of Ethiopia," and revived it again in 1925 with a cast of 350 actors. It was a tale of the "eldest and strongest race of mankind" in which he chronicled a long list of the black man's gifts to the world: the gifts of freedom, laughter, hope, faith and humility. The black man and the Semite had made Egypt the first nation of the world, and the black man alone had spread Mohammedism over half the world.
(p. xxix)

Books and theater productions exposed the world to positive black culture. But, other than the most outstanding entertainers and athletes, black people in the white press remained, for the most part, lazy, irresponsible, filthy, ignorant criminals.

THE GREAT WHITE SOCIETY

The advent of television in the 1950s revolutionized American life. The TV set was a greater tool for teaching American social philosophy than any book, magazine, newspaper, or motion picture theater had ever been.

In this post World War II era, television producers decided to focus on programs which would reinforce feelings of American patriotism.

In the 1960s a number of TV shows featuring middle class white families served to instill in both white and black Americans the proper standard of western cultural values. Each television family came complete with a professionally employed father, an always well groomed housewife mother, and cute, mischievous, but basically good, obedient children.

Some of the popular shows of that era included *Dennis The Menace,* starring Jay North; *Dobie Gillis,* starring Dwayne Hickman; *The Patty Duke Show,* starring Patty Duke; *Father Knows Best,* starring Robert Young; *The Donna Reed Show,* starring Donna Reed; and *Leave It To Beaver,* starring Jerry Mathers.

Blacks found themselves conspicuously absent in these and many other television comedies. The unspoken message was clear. "Good" neighborhoods, where the streets were clean, school teachers visited parents' homes, and local policemen were on a first-name basis with residents, were also places where blacks didn't live.

Alvin Poussaint, in his book *Why Blacks Kill Blacks,* reflects on how these shows invoked feelings of admiration in black audiences:

> *There was something so wholesome about white culture ... that's where the beauty was, and the good things in life.*

Blacks who gained economic success often wanted to purchase homes in middle class communities, much like those portrayed on TV. They were no doubt in search of the "good life."

However, often what they found was a rude awakening. These "nice" community residents often greeted them with violence and threats, making it clear that white America had no desire to integrate. Lorraine Hansberry's play, *A Raisin In The Sun*, which became a popular film starring Sidney Poitier, Claudia McNeil, Ruby Dee and Diana Sands, addresses this issue in a powerful way.

Today African Americans still find themselves fighting white resistance as they struggle to experience the ideal middle class American family life so beautifully portrayed on the television screen.

TV'S FIRST BLACK FAMILIES

In 1968 *Julia* arose as the first black family show. Julia, played by Diahann Carroll, was a widowed nurse with a young son. She was attractive, but not another light skinned "mulatto" image. Neither was she the fat, dark skinned, head-rag wearing "mammy." She was intelligent, professionally employed, and was a good mother, who raised her son to have high moral principals.

The show was considered revolutionary in its time. But, for all its breaking away from traditional stereotypes, Julia still had a major flaw. There was

no black man, no father for her son. Why were all
the white families intact, yet the first black modern
era TV family had to be headed by a single parent?

In the 1970s, TV producers came up with a
new idea, a "realistic" portrayal of black family life, so
they thought. *Good Times,* starring John Amos and
Esther Rolle, featured a black family living in the
Chicago housing projects. Forever poor and
struggling, the parents still managed to impart
values of dignity and honesty in their children.

Although there was an intact family,
nevertheless, the black male head of the house was
emasculated again and again by chronic
unemployment and helplessness. This was quite a
contrast to the strong white male breadwinners in
TV shows a decade earlier.

Next came *The Jeffersons.* George Jefferson,
played by actor Sherman Hemsley, had risen to
become a successful business man and owned a chain
of clothes cleaning establishments.

This was certainly a new twist. A wealthy
black man, with his wife and son, living among the
rich -- with a maid, even! The actors' excellent
comedic timing often helped audiences overlook badly
written scripts steeped in unrealistic dialogue.

White producers realized they had tapped a
lucrative market, and more black situation comedies
arose in the 1970s. However, rather than being more
progressive, shows still tended to reinforce negative
images, although perhaps more subtly than before.
The women tended to be heavyset and single. Black
fathers were conspicuously absent.

Some of the comedies during this period were:
That's My Mama, starring Clifton Davis and Theresa
Merritt (a widowed mother, sometimes viewed by
critics as another matriarchal mammy figure);

What's Happening, starring Ernest Thomas, (featuring another stout, single mother); *Gimme A Break,* starring actress Nell Carter, (a stout single maid in a white home), and *Different Strokes,* starring Todd Bridges and Gary Coleman (two "ghetto" boys adopted by a white man.)

TV'S BLACK FAMILIES TURN MIDDLE CLASS

The 1980s saw a change in the television industry, as black writers, directors, and producers took more control of new programs.

Comedian Bill Cosby introduced a new TV show which completely dismantled the old stereotypes of the black family. *The Cosby Show,* met with resounding success. Although criticized by some, it ran a full eight seasons, winning Emmy awards and receiving high ratings year after year.

The show featured the Huxtable family, who lived in a house in a middle class New York neighborhood. Bill Cosby, as Heathcliff Huxtable, was a pediatrician. His wife, actress Phylicia Rashad, was a lawyer. Their five children ranged from kindergarten to college age.

The Cosby Show was a big hit with both white and black audiences. The major reason for its success, many critics observed, was Cosby's ability to deal with basic family issues affecting all races of people. Unlike *Julia,* in which almost every episode addressed some encounter with racism, *The Cosby Show* was not obsessed with blackness as the main issue of each show. At last, blacks could relax and see themselves as ordinary people. They could watch a black family deal with issues such as sibling rivalry, puberty, dating, school grades, and other everyday

problems all families faced, without the overtones of
poverty and single parenthood.

"Too unrealistic," some blacks argued. Yet,
black professional couples were buying homes and
raising children every day. Where were the TV
images of these families? Certainly not to be seen in
Good Times.

A Different World emerged as a spinoff from
The Cosby Show. Here was another new concept --
black college students on a black college campus.
The show was refreshingly youthful, addressing
serious social issues while remaining lighthearted and
funny.

Both of these shows, produced by Bill Cosby,
with psychologist and author Dr. Alvin Poussaint
acting as a consultant, represented conscious efforts
by black producers, directors, and writers to do more
than just entertain. It was time for blacks to use the
television medium as a positive weapon for instilling
cultural values.

Other positive shows have emerged since that
time, with black families which had both fathers, and
mothers. Some of these include *Family Matters*,
starring Reginald VelJohnson and Jo Marie Payton-
France, and *Roc*, starring Charles S. Dutton and Ella
Joyce.

In addition to the new programs on network
TV, cable television offers a new outlet for the
producers of black oriented programming. Although
some white film producers have developed fresh new
media images of black people, many continue to
recreate the same old Toms, Bucks, Coons, Mulattoes
and Mammies. Just as Oscar Marchaux helped
create positive black images in his early films, black
film producers today realize that it is up to them to
remove harmful stereotypes.

SEX AND VIOLENCE DESTROY
WHOLESOME VALUES

As movie special effects became more sophisticated, audiences craved more realism in order to be entertained. Films became more graphic in their depiction of beatings, burnings, stabbings, shootings, and rapes. In addition to the violence, explicit sex scenes are also a regular part of TV dramas. Scenes that would once have received an "R" rating (restricted to viewers over 18) are now shown regularly on TV. Just as earlier TV programs had a powerful effect on shaping American cultural values, so did the later sex-and-violence programs.

According to an article published in the *Chicago Sun-Times* (February 26, 1992) a task force of the American Psychological Association conducted a five-year study of television viewing. In its report, the Association examined how children are affected by violent and sexually explicit shows. The *Chicago Sun-Times* article states:

The report ... found the violence on television influences viewers, especially children and teenagers, to use violence to resolve conflicts and makes them more accepting of sexual violence and rape.

Ironically, Saturday morning cartoons designed especially for pre-school and elementary-age children have four to five times the amount of violence as programs aired after children are in bed, the report said. The violence ranged from destruction of property to physical assaults that caused injury or death.

By the time a child leaves elementary school, he or she will have watched 8,000 murders and 100,000 other acts of violence on television ...

Today's horror films depict grotesque scenes of bloody mass murder with every ghastly weapon imaginable. Many films display explicit sexual activity between unmarried couples with little commitment or emotional attachment to one another. Civic and social organizations nationwide have observed the excessive advertising of these films in African-American communities. Many studies are being done to determine the connection between the rise in violence among blacks and the viewing of violent films by blacks.

THE VIOLENT BLACK MALE IMAGE

The media has always been an effective political tool, enabling whites to justify acts of aggression against blacks and other racial groups. Repeated stories of black rapists, killers and thieves saturated white newspapers during the rise of lynching and Ku Klux Klan attacks in the 1920s. Today, amidst brutal attacks by police and neo-Nazi groups, reports of a rise in crime committed by black males have sent white society into a panic.

The Brutal Black Buck has been resurrected in the form of the infamous Willie Horton, the black man whose release from prison and subsequent acts of violence became a national issue. Vice President George Bush, in his 1988 Presidential campaign advertisements, used this image to remind Americans of the dangers of being too soft on such criminals.

Suddenly, every black man became a Willie Horton, a potential rapist and murderer who must be suppressed. The violent police attack on motorist Rodney King, videotaped by a citizen, was nevertheless justified in the minds of many who had been conditioned by the media. If a black man is chased by the police, he must be guilty of something and needs to be forcibly restrained, they reasoned.

The first jury acquittal of the officers involved in the beating of King led to the 1992 Los Angeles riots, where 53 people were killed and scores injured. Property owners suffered more than $1 million in damages. The second jury trial the following year, on Federal Civil Rights violations, resulted in the conviction of two of the four officers who were tried. Nevertheless, they received light sentences.

Some black owned publications, dependent upon advertising from major white owned companies to stay in business, may end up placating their advertisers by sticking to non-controversial issues or portraying the same old negative racial stereotypes.

When blacks in the communications industry become financially independent, they are able to reshape African American media images. Nationally syndicated television talk show hosts Arsenio Hall and Oprah Winfrey formed companies to produce their own shows. Winfrey owns her own production facilities, Harpo Studios, and has produced movies for television. Some creative efforts by independent black film producers, such as Melvin and Mario Van Peebles, Spike Lee and Robert Townsend, have opened up new avenues for blacks in the film industry. Now black film makers in American are cooperating with black film makers in England and other countries to produce films internationally.

Talented journalists, publishers, writers, producers, and directors, with adequate financial backing and support, can use the mass media to entertain as well as teach and inspire black audiences. Through cooperation, African Americans can remove the racial stereotypes in the media that perpetuate The Big Lie.

ACTIVITY:
Name That Stereotype

Viewers can learn to recognize television's reinforcement of racial images by playing this game:
Participants will watch one television program together, of at least one half hour in length. This can be a comedy, a drama, or even the news. The people who appear on screen, both in the program and in the commercials, are to be examined. When a character appears to fit one of the common stereotypes listed below, the person who recognizes it and calls it out first gets one point. One person will keep score, and at the end of the period, the person who has the most points wins. Whenever opinions differ, the decision rests with the score keeper.

Common Racial Stereotypes:

1.   *Black Male Tom - non-aggressive, subservient or apologetic attitude, promoted as acceptable.*
2.   *Black Male Coon - silly, buffoonish, non-serious, makes blackness appear amusing.*
3   *Black Male Brute - angry, menacing, a criminal*
4.   *Black Female Mulatto - light skinned, straight haired, European features, promoted as attractive*
5.   *Black Female Mammy - heavyset, loud mouthed, sassy, often dark skinned.*
6.   *Black Female Bad Girl - an attractive seductress, prostitute or street woman, often dark skinned*
7.   *White Male Role Model - Financially secure, sought after by females, promoted as respectable.*
8.   *White Female Role Model - Slim, often blond, sought after by males, promoted as beautiful.*
9.   *Ethnic Male Brute - A gangster or criminal, usually Hispanic, Asian, or other race.*
10. *Ethnic Female Bad Girl - A cunning seductress, usually Hispanic, Asian or other race*

CHAPTER NINE
Black Beauty Standards

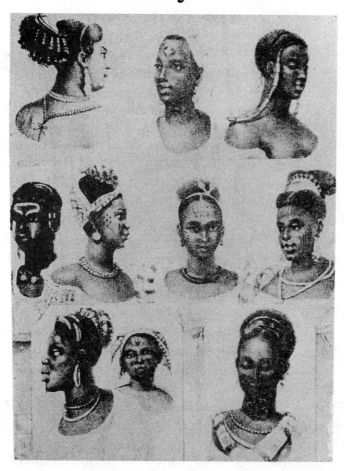

9A

African Beauties in Brazil
Slave women in Brazil, although dressed in Portuguese style, express cultural pride through traditional African markings on their faces. The markings identify the various national and ethnic groups from which these women came. (Reprinted from Sex and Race, by J.A. Rogers, page 18. Copyright 1942 by J.A. Rogers. Portraits from Debret.)

CHAPTER NINE
Black Beauty Standards

Beauty ... what is it?

Among some African people it was the smooth blackness of a woman's skin ... the fullness of her lips ... the distinguishing spread of her nostrils... the way her crinkly hair shaped her face.

The African look, with all its variations, was considered quite desirable by Europeans in times past. Ancient statues and paintings of dark skinned men and women with distinctly negroid features can be found all over the world, a testament to the international admiration of African beauty. In *Nature Knows No Color*, J.A. Rogers notes that the Greek Herodotus said, "The Ethiopians are the tallest and handsomest men in the world." Rogers continues:

Greek artists and designers of smaller objects were clearly fascinated by Negroes. Grace Beardsley in her introduction to "The Negro in Greek and Roman Civilization" says, "The popularity of this type was tremendous, and is attested by a wealth of statuettes, vases, engraved gems, coins lamps, weights, finger-rings, ear-rings, necklaces and masks from classical sites." (p. 34)

Legendary women such as Makeda, Queen of Sheba, Cleopatra, Queen of the Nile, and Nefertiti, wife of the great pharaoh Akhnaton, were praised by ancient poets for their dark beauty. Zeus, Father of the Gods in Greek mythology, was in love with Lamia, a black princess from Africa.

The African woman's style was imitated by women everywhere, even as late as the 18th century. A nude statue of a Hottentot woman of South Africa was brought to Europe. She stood erect, with large full breasts and a large, round rear end. She was known as the Hottentot Venus, and her projecting buttocks set a new fashion among European women. As J.A. Rogers states, the dresses with bustles worn by white women in the 18th century were imitations of her figure.

For thousands of years, whites and blacks intermarried, and color, or "race" was not an issue. But after the European slave trade had a firm hold on Africa, race became the determining factor as to whether one was to be treated as human or beast. Features such as hair texture, nose shape, fullness of lips, and skin complexion were carefully scrutinized. Specific categories were drawn which determined who was "white" and who was "black."

Today's society has become absolutely obsessed with racial identity. The current political and economic domination by European nations has caused African people worldwide to seek to emulate the "European look."

The slave experience has created such an inferiority complex in African Americans that the cosmetic industry reaps millions upon millions of dollars from black people determined to "fix" their hair and skin. America's first black female millionaire, Madam C.J. Walker, made her wealth from the invention of a special hair straightening comb. Skin bleachers, straight haired wigs, hair dye, and for the wealthier class, plastic surgery to thin out the nose, have been common methods used by African Americans to change themselves to appear more European.

How did this happen?

9B

Roman Ethiopian Statue
Pre-Christian Era Roman literature often reflected admiration
for African beauty.   Just as in antebellum America, many
Africans were brought to Rome as slaves and later intermarried
with the white population. This statue of an Ethiopian in Rome
reflects the woolly hair and full features characteristic of
Africans. (Statue from the Janze Collection.   Reprinted from
Nature Knows No Color Line, by J.A. Rogers, page 166.
Copyright 1952 by Helga Rogers.)

HOW PHYSICAL FEATURES ARE FORMED

What does a beautiful woman look like? How does one describe a handsome man? Opinions vary, since most races retain appreciation for their own distinct physical features. But for those who understand it, every individual is a fascinating portrait of human history, a story of migration, adaptation, and intermarriage. In each face is the tale of a nation, a clan, a family.

As noted in Chapter One, all of humanity evolved from a single black group. As the population increased, people began to travel across the earth, settling in different regions. Europe remained under a sheet of ice until only about 500 thousand years ago, and was the last continent to be settled by human beings. The "white" race did not begin to evolve until about 30 thousand years ago, while those on the continent of Africa had already passed through several major evolutionary stages. The darkest skin pigmentation takes thousands of years to develop, therefore the darkest colors are found in those hot areas of the earth where humans have inhabited the longest. As people migrated, their bodies physically adapted to the climate, producing variations in height, muscular development, skeletal structure, hair texture, nose shape, eye shape and color, lip shape, and pigmentation. According to author J. B. Birdsell's book *Human Evolution, An Introduction to the New Physical Anthropology:*

Skin color is primarily produced by two pigments, melanin, a dark brown pigment, and carotene, a yellowish one. Melanin is present in all persons, even in the albino where it only shows in traces ... In the Old World, the darkest skin colors are

*concentrated along or near the equator. Then
proceeding either north or south, skin color lightens
until one reaches northwest Europe where complexion
is so fair it represents a form of depigmentation that
amounts to partial albinism ...*

*In the case of skin color it is known that
melanin serves to protect the skin and delicate organs
beneath it from excessive exposure to ultraviolet
radiation. Heavy pigmentation in the tropics buffers
the ultraviolet rays to prevent overproduction of
Vitamin D. The moderate brown skins that
characterize so much of humankind are in proper
balance for the environments in which the populations
live. The depigmented skins found in northwest
Europeans are presumed necessary to maximize the
small amount of sunlight that falls upon the peoples'
faces and hands ... (pp. 363, 364, 366)*

Hair texture also evolved as an adaptation to
climate. Hair also contains melanin, therefore lighter
colored hair and eyes are more commonly found in
colder climates. According to Birdsell, the woolly
hair which is common among many African peoples
provided insulation for the top of the head and
protected the brain under conditions of extreme heat.
In other climates, extremes of cold made straighter
hair and faster hair growth necessary. Cold air
produced thinner noses, to prevent nostrils from
inhaling too much cold air. Wider noses allowed
hotter air to be cooled when inhaled.

Body types and sizes evolved to maintain a
correct body temperature. Long, thin bodies are
often found among tropical people living in open
country, to provide more area for the body's surface
to perspire and evaporate perspiration as a means of
cooling the body's temperature. However in colder

climates, body extremities (arms and legs) become shorter in order to reduce heat loss through radiation. In some areas, where climates fluctuate between long periods of abundant rain and food and long periods of drought, a condition known as steatopygia, which consists of massive fat deposits on the buttocks and upper thighs, develops as means to store food in the body during the dry season when food is scarce. Natural geographic boundaries (mountains, deserts, forests, large bodies of water) caused people within those boundaries to reproduce among their own group. This created dominant genetic traits among people within a geographic area. And thus, "races" were developed.

Genealogists have often tried to classify mankind into three main races, Negroid, Mongoloid, and Caucasoid, according to skin color, hair texture, eye shape, nose shape and lip shape, however these classifications are hardly adequate. Various combinations of physical traits are found on every continent. How does everyone fit in?

Migrations, from droughts, famines, explorations and wars of conquest, create new genetic combinations. Ancient paintings show that Egypt, after the first five thousand years, became a society of mixed race people, where individual status is based on something other than race. There is no "correct" skin color, hair texture, or nose shape. Beauty, as it is said, is in the eye of the beholder.

THE SKIN GAME

The gradual conquest of Africa by European nations created, over time, a change in the African self image and beauty standards.

In the sixteenth and seventeenth centuries,

some English writers introduced the philosophy that African dark skin was attributed to the supposed Biblical "curse on the children of Ham." This idea was later expressed by European Jews, and even some Muslim sects, who may have also been influenced by the Aryans of India, who introduced a caste system of light skinned superiority.

In South Africa, the Apartheid system uses this same color coded prejudice. Whites control all the land, wealth and political power; Asians are allowed certain privileges; Coloreds (mixed races) are separated from the Blacks and considered slightly better. But the Blacks are total outcasts.

After the Civil War, colleges were established for the newly freed blacks. But often these "historically black colleges" were established for the purpose of educating the white masters' mulatto children, note Nathan and Julia Hare in their book, *Black Anglo Saxons*. In terms of social acceptance on these campuses, clear lines were drawn: The darker skinned people were the lowest on the social latter. In his 1988 film "School Daze," producer/ director Spike Lee exposes this ongoing color conflict among African Americans on college campuses.

Movies, television, and magazines reinforced images of this European standard of black beauty. Light skinned women were all that were featured as models in black magazines. In *The Souls Of Black Folk,* W.E.B. DuBois recalls how he printed a dark skinned black person on the cover of one edition of his *Crises* magazine, and greatly offended some black readers, who considered the gesture a racial insult.

After World War II, jobs which had been previously closed to blacks began to open up. White bosses would often choose the lighter skinned females for office positions over the darker skinned females, again reinforcing light skinned superiority. The message blacks got was that in order to be accepted into white society and get decent employment, one had to look as "white" as possible.

So, out came the hair straighteners, the bleaching creams, the light makeup, the wigs, the hair dye ... and a cosmetic industry was born. Dark skinned women put on layer after layer of light make-up and dyed their newly pressed-and-curled hair brown, red, and even blond, looking as close as they could to white. Men found products, some which contained harmful lye, to straighten their hair and make it "look white."

People who have been affected by the color caste system have even developed their own coded language to describe the preferred European look: "Good hair" referring to hair which has a straighter texture, indicating possible European ancestry. "Pretty eyes," usually referring to lighter color eyes, also indication of possible European ancestry.

Many recall hearing the little children's rhyme which clearly outlined America's race and caste system: *"If you're white you're all right; if you're brown, hang around; but if you're black, get back."*

Has the American color caste system affected your opinions about black beauty? Consider your answer to Psychic Trauma Test question Number 13: "The people I find most attractive tend to have lighter skin and curly or straightened hair."

If you strongly agree, agree, or are unsure, then it's quite possible you have been conditioned to believe that light skin and straighter hair is better than dark skin and crinkly hair.

The issue of beauty is a political and economic one. If European physical features are considered "correct," then everything else is "incorrect." That means it must be "fixed."   This, of course, costs money. In the 1930s, '40s and '50s advertisements for skin bleaching cream could be found throughout publications which targeted black readers.   Many thought that, by some miracle, they could bleach themselves white, and all their troubles would be over. Since degrees of lightness were a measure of social status, if one could just lighten the skin a few shades, one could rise on the social latter. Whether these bleaching creams worked is another matter. The fact is, they presented a hope for the dark skinned that somehow they would turn their "ugly" blackness into "pretty" light skinned-ness.

Do you also have a desire to transform yourself into the European ideal?   Look at your answer to Psychic Trauma test question Number 12: "I think I would be more attractive if my skin were a few shades lighter."

If you answered strongly agree, agree, or unsure, then perhaps you feel a certain shame about your dark skin.   This feeling puts you at a disadvantage when interacting with whites. As long as you believe that your dark skin is unattractive, you will feel inferior to some degree to every white person, and may even feel inferior to every lighter skinned black person. In his book *Black Skin, White Masks*, Algerian psychiatrist Franz Fanon draws this conclusion about a black patient who expresses a yearning for lighter skin:

1. My patient is suffering from an inferiority complex. His psychic structure is in danger of disintegration. What has to be done is to save him from this and, little by little, to rid him of this unconscious desire. 2. If he is overwhelmed to such a degree by the wish to be white, it is because he lives in a society that makes his inferiority complex possible, in a society that derives its stability from the perpetuation of this complex, in a society that proclaims the superiority of one race; to the identical degree to which that society creates difficulties for him, he will find himself thrust into a neurotic situation.

In order to undo an often subconscious self hatred, dark skinned blacks must aggressively seek out positive images of dark skinned people.

LIGHT SKIN, BLACK RACE

The same caste system often works in favor of those on the other side of the fence. Lighter skinned children may sometimes be favored by parents over their darker skinned siblings. Lighter skinned children may be reprimanded and disciplined less than darker skinned siblings who commit the same offenses. Even in school, teachers may perceive the lighter skinned children as being "nicer" or even "smarter" than the darker skinned children. When a squabble breaks out between two children, adults may tend to perceive the lighter child as the victim and the darker child as the one likely to be at fault.

Dark skinned parents with light or white spouses sometimes send unconscious signals to their lighter skinned children that they are "better" because of their lighter skin. Such children are praised for their "good hair" and "pretty" lighter colored eyes, and sometimes so fawned over by their darker parents and relatives that they come to expect a certain deference by blacks in general.

Parents may make it clear that they want the family to maintain its higher caste position. Light skinned parents may frown upon a son or daughter who chooses a darker skinned mate. Many African-American men and women recall specific advice from their parents to "get you somebody light skinned."

Today, just as in slavery days, having a lighter skinned mate could raise a person's social status. Popular black magazines, with their light skinned, straight nosed, straight haired models, define attractiveness for African Americans. They continue to reinforce the European standard of beauty. Men and women may openly express a preference for people with lighter skin or wavy hair. Such behavior by the general society can create a sort of "superiority complex" in lighter skinned blacks, who are often raised with the belief that they are more attractive than darker skinned people, and should automatically be considered more desirable by the opposite sex.

Have you been affected in such a way by America's color caste system? Consider your answer to Psychic Trauma Test question Number 16: "I feel that I am more attractive than my darker skinned associates."

If you answered strongly agree, agree, or even unsure, you quite possibly have been taught to believe that lighter skin is a mark of superiority.

Those who are lighter skinned and unconsciously feel themselves to be "better" than darker skinned blacks face another dilemma. Since the standard of beauty is whiteness, then those who are merely light skinned will forever fall short. By declaring themselves superior to darker blacks, they are also declaring inferiority to whites.

Many light skinned blacks, particularly those from integrated marriages, remain in a perpetual state of confusion over their identities. Rejected by whites because of blackness and resented by blacks because of whiteness, they often switch from one racial identity to another, struggling to find acceptance.

In the April 1993 edition of *Ebony* magazine, actress Halle Berry, who starred as the bi-racial grandmother of *Roots* author Alex Haley in the TV miniseries *Queen,* reflects on her own experiences as the daughter of a white mother and black father:

> *Like the character she played in* Queen, *her internal turmoil started early in life, largely because of her confusion about her racial identity. "I saw a lot of the young me in* Queen," *she confesses. "The confusion, the uncertainty, not really knowing if you should be Black or White."*
>
> *That confusion created some agonizing moments. "I had a lot of problems in high school," she confides. "It was predominantly White and I wasn't really accepted there. I was in a fight practically every week. The Black kids assumed I thought I was better than they were, and the White kids didn't like me because I was Black. And I didn't know who I felt comfortable with, Black people or White people."* (p. 119)

This caste system creates bitterness between blacks particularly in the entertainment industry, where lighter skinned females often appear to be given preference over darker ones for movie roles, recording contracts, and modeling careers.

THE POLITICS OF HAIR TEXTURE

Hair texture is more than a fashion statement. It has deeply political overtones, particularly in America. In slavery times, when blacks would escape north and "pass" for white, hair texture was one of the things that could be a dead giveaway. A little too much curl to the hair could draw suspicion. A person could even escape to a Native American community and blend in, if the hair was straight enough. But that kinky hair definitely sealed one's fate. It was the mark of a slave.

After the Civil War, lighter skinned blacks found that they could sometimes pass as members of other European ethnic groups. The Spanish were often darker skinned and curly haired (no doubt due to intermarriage with Moors during their 800 years of rule in Spain). And it was always more acceptable to be a Native American, or "Indian" rather than a "Negro" in those days. But, again, that hair had to be straight enough!

With the advent of the straightening comb and chemical hair straighteners, blacks could, once and for all "fix" that "kinky" hair. Even the dark models and popular entertainers had slick, curly hair. Straighter hair, like lighter skin, elevated one on the social ladder, made one acceptable.

To be seen in public with unstraightened, "nappy" hair was shameful. One woman recalls her experience, early in the 1960s, when she became one of the first females to wear a "natural" hairstyle:

I was living in Washington, D.C. at the time. I was just tired of trying to figure out what to do with my hair everyday, so I went to the barber and had him cut it all off and shape it in a nice short style. I didn't straighten it, I just wore it natural, like a man's. You wouldn't believe the stares I got when I took the bus home that day. The women on the bus looked at me with such hostility, and rolled their eyes. They just glared at me, as if to say, "How DARE you come out in public with your hair like that!"

Many black women seemed to feel embarrassed about whites discovering their real hair texture. Then, for a brief moment during the late 1960s and early 1970s, the political significance of hair texture was recognized. African Americans wore their hair "natural" or in what became known as the "Afro" hairstyle as a symbol of cultural pride. It began as a symbol of rejection of European beauty standards, a symbol of defiance of white society, a sign of political militancy.

Then came the 1972 movie "Superfly" starring a light skinned, straight haired Ron O'Neal as a successful drug pusher. Young men admired his cool mystique, young women saw him as absolutely gorgeous. Overnight the Afro became just another faddish hairstyle, and young men raced to the hair salons for chemical treatments, so they could have "good hair" like Superfly.

Black magazines complied with the changing styles. The dark skinned, Afro-wearing women were gradually phased out and light skinned, straight haired women again dominated the pages of popular black publications. A whole new wave of hair straightening products have emerged, and black hair care companies continue to build fortunes on the desires of African Americans to "fix" their hair. New words describe the process (possibly so as not to offend anyone by saying they would be better off with straighter hair). Now hair straightening products are called "hair relaxers."

Relaxed hair. What was it before -- tense? Nervous? Uptight?

Many may say, "Oh, come on, now, it's really not that serious. It's just a style. There's nothing political about that."

Many African Americans, mostly women, find

it difficult to admit that they don't dare wear their hair in public unstraightened. Various excuses are given:

"It's just so inconvenient. I need to be able to comb my hair in a hurry."

"I don't think I look good in an Afro."

"That's out of style. Nobody is wearing naturals anymore."

"That's just not professional. Girl, you can't move up in these corporate jobs with a nappy head."

This is not to castigate people for choosing any particular hairstyle. The point is that when people feel that their natural hair texture is incorrect, then they have accepted the idea of racial inferiority.

Do you feel that your natural hair is a badge of inferiority? Look at your answer to Psychic Trauma Test question Number 11: "When a member of the opposite sex whom I want to attract sees my hair before it is pressed and permed, I feel embarrassed and unattractive."

If you strongly agree, agree, or are unsure, then you have been indoctrinated to believe that your own natural hair is somehow wrong.

LONG HAIR VS. SHORT HAIR

Hair length is also a main focus when determining who is beautiful. Most Europeans genetically grow hair at a faster rate than most Africans. Among blacks, long hair might also be a sign of "white blood" in one's family. (Even Native American ancestry could raise ones social status.)

Short haired black women often feel compelled to buy wigs and hair pieces to make themselves acceptable. Children learn early that short hair is somehow tied in with the whole undesirable African image, nappy hair, dark skin, "black and ugly."

During the period after the straightening comb and before the Afro, girls knew that if they had short hair, they must at least straighten it to make themselves acceptable. And if they were lucky, they might be able to find a hairpiece to attach to their heads. So many men have been attracted to black women with long hair, only to later turn away in disappointment when they found out the hair was not really their own. To this day, hair length is such an issue that women who wear hair pieces are often afraid to admit to the men that pursue them that the hair they wear is false, for fear of losing the man's interest.

Actress/comedienne Whoopi Goldberg, in one of her comedy routines, imitates a young black girl who hangs a shirt from her head as a way of pretending to have long blond hair. The skit, funny to some, embarrassing to others, again points to the early conditioning of young black girls: To be beautiful, you must have long hair!

This is certainly not to imply that all long haired styles are European. Many African people grow long, thick hair. When the 1979 movie "10" starring white actress Bo Derek popularized multiple braids decorated with beads (a hairstyle worn by African women for centuries), black women saw a new way to give themselves long hair. Cornrow braids (sometimes called "French braids" though it is unknown how France got the credit for this ancient African style) had become popular during the era of the Afro, but were gradually being replaced by the latest "relaxed" hair styles. For some, the braids with extensions have become a means of expressing pride in African culture.

9C

Ancient Egyptian Beauty

Ankhesenamun, the granddaughter of Queen Tiye of Egypt's Eighteenth Dynasty, shows that in the era of 1400 B.C., full noses and lips and elaborate braided hairstyles were marks of beauty for the Nubian people. Separated from African culture for generations, African Americans lost much of the knowledge of how to style their own natural hair. (Reprinted from Great Black Leaders: Ancient and Modern, by Ivan Van Sertima. Copyright 1988 by Journal of African Civilizations, Ltd., Inc.)

Dreadlocks, the long, knotted twists of hair popularized by some Jamaicans, have also become a common sight among blacks in other countries. This style, like the braids, goes back to antiquity, and creates a long haired look that is uniquely African.

BEAUTY STANDARDS AND SELF ESTEEM

Hair that is "nappy." Lips that are "too big." Noses that are "too wide." Legs that are "too skinny." Behinds that are "too big." Skin that is "too dark."

When people become convinced that their natural, God-given physical features are offensive looking, they learn to feel ashamed. The low self esteem that results from feelings of ugliness makes it difficult for them to establish healthy relationships with others. Often they spend a lifetime trying to compensate for feelings of inadequacy.

Men and women continually look to the opposite sex to confirm their desirability. In this society, for women especially, great importance is placed upon physical beauty as a necessary trait to attract a mate. If society determines that a woman, because of her natural physical features, can never be considered beautiful, then the woman may fear she will never be able to attract a suitable mate, never experience a satisfying relationship, never get married, never have children, never be fulfilled as a woman. When black women observe black men selecting white women as mates, it's as if their worst fears are being confirmed:

"Black men consider white women more beautiful and more desirable than black women. White women can take away all the available men."

Fears of loneliness, because of an inability to compete with "beautiful" white women, can cause black women to overreact at the sight of an interracial couple. A black woman may react with hostility toward a black man who becomes romantically involved with a white woman, even if the black woman is totally unacquainted with the couple, as if his personal choice for a mate represents her loss of a fulfilling relationship.

Do your fears of physical inadequacy cause you to react negatively to the sight of a black man and white woman? If you're a female, consider your answer to Psychic Trauma test question number 15: "I feel resentment when I see an attractive black member of the opposite sex romantically involved with a white person of my sex." If you strongly agree, agree, or are unsure, perhaps you fear you will not find a mate because of black men's preference for the more "beautiful" white females.

In most cultures, beauty standards reflect the physical appearance of the people in that culture. In the book *Human Evolution*, Birdsell observes:

Europeans have long referred to other populations as yellow, brown, red, or black. Embedded in the European value system is the idea that the color white stands for purity and goodness, and any deviations from white indicate the less than pure. This climaxes in the belief that black is particularly undesirable. The phrase, "as black as satan," is, of course, derived from ancient religious dogma invented by white-skinned peoples. This idea is ironic, since fossil evidence suggests, of course, that Africa was the continent of our origins, and the implication is that the skin color of all of our ancestors was very dark. (p. 363)

After so many years of indoctrination, many African Americans believe in the European standard of beauty and accept Europeans as authorities on who is beautiful. Some blacks secretly consider their own people as less attractive, while actually admiring whites' physical features. As a result, they tend to value a white person's opinion more than a black person's opinions regarding their own attractiveness.

Do you tend to accept whites as greater authorities on beauty? Look at your answer to Psychic Trauma test question Number 14: "When a white member of the opposite sex finds me attractive, I consider it a greater compliment than when a black member of the opposite sex finds me attractive."

If you strongly agree, agree, or are unsure, perhaps you value whites' opinions more because you unconsciously believe their physical features to be more attractive than your own.

Negative self images can stifle one's self confidence. Many personalities are warped by lifelong feelings of inferiority. Sometimes a person becomes abusive to others, as a means of self defense. Or a person willingly accepts abuse from others, believing himself or herself deserving of no better.

Self esteem plays an important role in mate selection. The low self esteem many African Americans experience actually affects marriage and family stability. This and other factors will be examined further in the next chapter, "Modern Marriages: Why They're Not Working."

ACTIVITY:
Discover Your Natural Beauty

African beauty is as ancient as the old kingdoms of Egypt. But centuries of European domination have caused many African Americans to consider their natural physical attributes as defects which need to be "fixed." Hair texture has become a sensitive issue, particularly with women. Try this experiment and see what happens:

1.   If you are a female and you usually straighten your hair, for thirty days, style your hair without the use of any hair straighteners, chemical relaxers, or even synthetic extensions. Try to develop styles using just your own natural hair.
> *a. Observe the reactions of those people who see your hair on a regular basis. Do they respond negatively or positively?*
> *b. Observe your own reactions. How do you feel about yourself? Do you feel more or less attractive? Are you overly self-conscious?*

2.   If you are a male or if you are a female and usually do not straighten your own hair, urge someone close to you, a wife, mother, sister, daughter, or friend to try the above experiment.
> *a. Observe their reactions. Do they adamantly refuse? Are they offended at the thought? Do they try it?*
> *b. Observe your own reactions. Do you respond negatively or positively to their new hair style? Do you consider them more or less attractive?*

CHAPTER TEN
Modern Marriages:
Why They're Not Working

10A
Sojourner Truth Fights For Moral Values
Described as an irrepressibly articulate abolitionist, Sojourner Truth left her slave master's home and traveled across the United States, speaking out against slavery. After abolition she fought for programs to rehabilitate the freedmen, predicting that the slave breeding practices on slave plantations would translate into irresponsibility in family life among blacks. (Reprinted from Frederick Douglass, by William S. McFeely, page 146, Copyright 1991, W.W. Norton & Company.)

CHAPTER TEN
Modern Marriages:
Why They're Not Working

Since the beginning of civilization, marriage has served as a means to bind individuals together for the purpose of expanding family ties, raising children, increasing wealth, and perpetuating cultural traditions.

Marriage represented the very foundation of African society. It defined social, political and economic relationships. Through marriage, individuals became a part of a family and a clan; their children were raised under the protection and jurisdiction of the clan. The economy was built upon a system of cooperation between husbands and wives. Survival depended upon a division of labor, in which each individual performed a crucial function. In some communities, the men tended the livestock and worked the land while the women sold produce at the market; or the men hunted and fished while the women did the farming. Children were greatly valued because they represented the future, and insured a perpetuation of the family and the culture. A major part of marriage preparation was the training of men and women to perform certain duties in managing property, providing food, and raising children.

The system of slavery dismantled the very cultural foundations of marriage for African Americans. On the plantation, the union between a black man and woman was more of an economic benefit for the slavemaster rather than a means of strengthening family ties. Children from such a union represented increased wealth for the master, not for the parents. A slave owned no property and all food and clothing was provided by the master. Slaves could often not even choose their own mates and had little say in the rearing of their own children. Slavery destroyed the sense of permanency of marriage, and removed the social training which prepared a young man and woman for the role of spouse.

In today's Western culture, the decision to marry is often made without consultation with parents and without consideration of how the marriage will affect the rest of the family. Couples also tend to divorce without considering the effects on other family members, particularly children. In America, where the divorce rate is 50%, marriage has become a failing institution. As a result, more and more children are being raised by only one parent. *The Negro Almanac, A Reference Work On The African American,* by Harry A. Ploski and James Williams, notes these statistics:

A February 1989 release from the Census Bureau reported that 54% of black children now lived in single-parent families, nine-tenths of which were headed by women. This growth of one-parent families has been called "one of the most startling social developments of the past quarter century." (p. 509)

Why are families collapsing? Blacks in America, cut off from cultural ties to Africa, find it difficult to create the necessary social structures to keep modern marriages together. However, today's American culture, with its 50% divorce rate, does not present a viable model for African Americans to follow. Roles and responsibilities for husbands and wives are often undefined and attitudes toward children are sometimes ambiguous and even hostile.

SOJOURNER TRUTH SPEAKS
OUT FOR MORAL VALUES

The practice of slavebreeding often prevented blacks from creating permanent relationships. Men and women were matched together for the purpose of producing offspring for the market. Once the woman became pregnant, the man would then be assigned to another female, to impregnate her also. Slavery removed the sacredness of the sex act altogether.

Sojourner Truth, legendary orator, abolitionist and women's rights advocate, often spoke of the forced sexual immorality caused by slavery. Born a slave named Isabella in Hurley New York around 1797, she was forbidden to marry the man of her choice from another plantation, but was instead "married" to an older slave for the purpose of producing children. She gave birth to thirteen children, most of whom were sold. She was also sold to a series of masters before being officially freed in 1827. She moved to New York City and in 1843 she declared that she had received a revelation from God that she was to journey across the land and proclaim the truth. She changed her name to Sojourner Truth and set out on a mission to tell the world of the moral evils of slavery. She became a powerful orator for the cause of abolition.

According to the book *Sojourner Truth, Narrative and Book of Life,* produced by Ebony Classics, after the war, Sojourner directed much of her preaching to the newly freed black masses. Seeing the almost total reliance on handouts from the Freedmen's Bureau, she warned the freedmen that they must not become dependent on government charity programs or else they would lose the will to work. She urged them to cast aside the irresponsible attitudes towards marriage and childbirth learned in slavery and warned them that the breakdown of morals between black men and women would affect future generations to come. Unfortunately, many of her predictions seem to have come true. Some black families, economically unstable since Emancipation, have now become second and third generation single parent welfare dependents. According to *The Negro Almanac:*

> *Among blacks, the major reason given for the one-parent family was that the parent had never married (54%). The same reason applied to Hispanics (33%). Among whites, however, the chief cause of single-parent families was divorce (50%). (p. 509)*

For African Americans, the rise of female-headed households is rooted in the condition of male powerlessness introduced during slavery.

EMASCULATION OF THE BLACK MAN

Slavery was an American institution, aimed at destroying African traditions and their strong family ties. Under slavery, the black man was powerless. He could not protect his family, and thereby lost his role as protector of the wife and children. As Lerone Bennett, Jr. states in his book *Before the Mayflower:*

> *Fatherhood, under this system, was a monstrous joke; fatherhood, in fact, was virtually abolished. Masters sometimes made the husband subject to the wife. The husband, for example, lived in 'Dinah's cabin' and he was often called 'Dinah's Tom.' (p. 86)*

Since a black man had no claim to his children, the father of a slave was unimportant. If his wife became pregnant, the child was master's property and could be sold away at the master's whim. Fatherhood, in effect, was outlawed. Slave women learned, after witnessing repeated beatings and lynchings of the men, that the men were powerless. Women slaves trained their sons to be submissive, to protect them from floggings. They constantly warned their husbands against making the master angry. In a sense, they became the protectors of the family, repressing the anger and aggression of the men in their lives as a means of protecting them from punishment and even death. In *The Slave Community,* author John W. Blassingame observes:

Many slaves tried to drown their anger in a whiskey bottle, and if not drowned, the anger welling up was translated into many other forms. Sometimes the slave projected his aggression onto his fellow slaves: he might beat up, stab, or kill one of his fellow sufferers. Generally, however, he expressed his resentment in rebellious language in the quarters. William Webb, for instance, frequently heard the slaves talking about wreaking vengeance on their masters, killing them, and appropriating their homes, food, clothes, and women. In addition to their empty threats of vengeance, the slaves customarily gave contemptible nicknames to their masters. (p. 209)

Whatever anger and violence the black man expressed in the privacy of his slave cabin, the fact remained that in the eyes of his woman, the institution of slavery had made him weak and powerless.

Today men (and women, too) often turn to a

whiskey bottle to drown their anger and frustration. And now, very potent drugs can also produce a temporary "high," allowing one to escape the pressures of reality for a while. Physical and psychological addiction results from alcohol and drug use, as well as some unpleasant, unpredictable personality distortions. This problem wrecks the stability of many families. The frustrations of oppression become compounded by the emotional strain of periodic violence, and the financial strain of supporting an expensive drug habit.

While black men faced psychological emasculation, black women suffered severe demoralization. The white woman was placed upon a lofty pedestal of untouchable purity, yet the black woman was treated as a mere piece of meat, to be bought, sold, borrowed, used, and cast aside. The black woman was made to feel that her body could be violated with impunity by any man. Under slave law, a black woman's body had no sacred value. In the book *Before The Mayflower,* Lerone Bennett notes that a Mississippi court ruled that there was no such legal thing as the rape of a slave woman. Even after abolition, under the protection of the law, white men raped and beat black women, and sometimes killed the black men who protested such actions.

THE CONFUSION OF THE "SEXUAL REVOLUTION"

Just as the women's suffrage movement arose during the fight for abolition of slavery, the women's protest movement of the 1960s grew out of the black liberation struggle, which began as a drive for civil rights and grew into a demand for everything from a new cultural identity to separate nationhood.

White women joined in on the attack against white male supremacy, demanding an end to their role as mere playthings to suit the male ego. White women, who had stood by for centuries and watched as men had enjoyed their illicit sexual affairs without social stigma, demanded the same rights of "sexual freedom."

In came the birth control pill. Now women could be sexually active without the fear of unwanted pregnancy. Somehow, the right to have sex outside of marriage was all tied in with the right to work for equal wages, the right to hold traditionally male jobs, and the right to choose a professional career over the traditional role of homemaker. This movement hardly addressed the real problems of black women. Most of the time black women worked outside the home anyway, out of the sheer necessity for survival. Often they were maids, washerwomen, and cooks. Sometimes they were schoolteachers, office clerks and nurses. But rarely were they bored housewives, forbidden by their husbands to hold a job.

The 1960s "sexual revolution" created a myth of "sexual freedom" for women that changed "old fashioned" values and made such beliefs as sexual abstinence before marriage a social stigma. Men and women who came of age during this era raised sons and daughters with vague, undefined beliefs about marriage and family. The results have been disastrous. Unlike in traditional African cultures, sex has been taken out of the context of marriage and family and left to be defined by the mass media. Today, the natural desires of youth are present, but gone is a community responsibility for ushering the young man and woman into a proper adulthood. Consider the differences:

Africa, 1694

A girl, 16, meets a boy, 17, from her community. They fall in love. The boy asks the girl's parents permission to marry her. Her parents discuss the matter over with his parents, asking questions about the boy's character and his preparedness to provide for a family. The boy's parents question the girl's parents regarding her personality and compatibility with their son.

The parents consent to the marriage and approach the community's Council of Elders for permission for their children to marry. Permission is given.

The children wed. The girl gets pregnant. There is a celebration of the birth of the child, who symbolizes the union of two families.

America, 1994

A girl, 16, meets a boy, 17, from her community. They fall in love. They decide to have sex. The girl becomes pregnant. She is afraid, but finally confides in her parents.

They are filled with despair. They discuss whether she should have an abortion. After discovering she is too far along in the pregnancy, she has the baby.

The boy has no job or means of support. He even denies being the father of her child. He finds another girlfriend, and does not see her anymore.

The girl's parents are angry and want to file a paternity suit. The girl is emotionally devastated.

In cultures where sex is expected to be confined within marriage, problems such as escalating teen pregnancies and irresponsible young fathers are rare. However, as *The Negro Almanac* states, in 1985, 60% of all births to black females were out of wedlock. Parents and educators today throw their hands up in despair over the loss of control of teenage sexuality, which leads to unwed motherhood, poverty, child neglect, and a host of other problems. Teaching abstention until marriage, many say, is "unrealistic," given the pervading social values. Better to educate the children on "safe sex," they insist. But pre-marital sexual activity, even when it does not result in pregnancy, is still destructive to the society. People who have sex with individuals who are not their spouses encourage within their partners attitudes of non-commitment to marriage, irresponsibility for children, and disrespect for the sex act itself. These are the same attitudes that were created during slavery.

The dating ritual, although it supposedly helps men and women select compatible mates, often leads to physical intimacy but not marriage. After a man and woman discover they are attracted to each other, next comes, according to the media, an exciting romantic interlude. Dinner, dancing, movies, then, at some point, sexual intimacy is expected in the modern day relationship. According to romance novels and soap operas, somewhere during all of this, they are supposed to fall in love and want to get married.

However, in reality, to many people's dismay, their partners don't follow the script. There is companionship, fun and sex for a while. Then, for various reasons, the relationship breaks up. People are often bitter afterward, feeling cheated somehow. Some men become angry and resolve to never form emotional attachments again. Some women conclude that all men are just "no good." Rarely do people realize that there is something wrong with their criteria for choosing a mate in a first place.

According to television and movie theaters, the desirable man is handsome and rich and the desirable woman is young and beautiful. Issues such as character, personality, values, or family upbringing are seldom considered. As a result, two people find themselves intimately involved, yet totally incompatible. In order to create lasting marital relationships, African Americans must study the positive attitudes and behavior which strengthened families before slavery destroyed African cultural values.

Sojourner Truth advocated spiritual reform as a means to combat the effects of slavery. Often the African-American church played a role in restoring constructive values to a population of ex-slaves. Preachers often exhorted their followers against the evils of "fornication" and "adultery" (sex outside of marriage). The church became the center of black social life, the place where men and women found mates, and children learned proper social behavior. It taught people the values of honesty, integrity, hard work, respect for elders, and respect for the institution of marriage. It reinforced the values of family and community.

ECONOMIC PRESSURES ON THE MARRIAGE

After emancipation, African-American men sought to regain dignity and a sense of manhood, by working hard to provide for their families. Whether this took the form of sharecropping, working on the railroad, or working in northern factories, men prided themselves on being able to take care of their wives and children.

As whites sought to relegate blacks to the lowest paid jobs and thereby maintain white dominance in society, black couples realized the necessity of working together to make ends meet. Often black women would get jobs as domestics, or in the case of the southern sharecroppers, they would work in the fields along with their husbands.

During World War II, many more women entered the job market, some taking traditionally male jobs. As black soldiers returned from overseas, greater demands were made to open up professional positions for African Americans.

Today, with American corporations relocating abroad, carrying many factory jobs with them, and jobs increasing in fields traditionally dominated by women, in many cases women are able to find work while their husbands are being laid off. This tends to cause havoc in a marriage by creating financial and emotional strain.

Conflicts over money are the most destructive to a harmonious relationship. In this society, where manhood is measured by one's income, black men often find them themselves coming up short. They may feel low self esteem because of their low wages or denial of promotions on jobs. Despite realization of deliberate racial prejudice in the work force, men still tend to subconsciously question their own adequacy when experiencing financial setbacks.

When economic hard times hit the family, couples find themselves defensively blaming each other. Black women angrily attack the men for their inadequacy, and black men lash out in rage at the women for their lack of understanding. The husband's loss of a job and subsequent total dependence on his wife has such a dramatic effect on the marriage that it can literally drive couples to the breaking point. Abdul Alim Bashir, in his book, *Passport To A Happy Marriage*, explains why:

> *The man was established as the breadwinner for the home by long held universal traditions based on physiological and psychological reasons ...*
>
> *When a man is not functioning in this capacity, he will feel that his position as the leader in the home is threatened.*
>
> *When a man is deprived of his ability to provide for his family, he is robbed to some degree of his pride in his manliness. He feels his self-esteem slipping. He feels his worth as a father is put in question ...*
>
> *It is when man is in this very vulnerable state that he is in need of his wife's understanding and compassion...*
>
> *If the wife detects during this period that the man has surrendered to adversity, it will cause her to lose faith in him as a provider. This loss of faith can also deteriorate into a loss of respect, which will spell a loss of the original state of marital happiness. (pp. 72, 73)*

Black men's reaction to economic hardship may take the form of one of two extremes:

Sometimes the man, out of extreme fear that his wife will become the dominant partner in the relationship because of her potential superior earning capacity, will constantly criticize and belittle her. This is in order to lower her self confidence and self esteem, and keep her psychologically dependent upon him, and thereby protect his sense of manhood. He may forbid her to work outside the home, or may insist upon control of her paycheck as a means of asserting his authority.

Or the man, raised in a household in which the father was either economically dependent or physically absent, may see the woman as the natural financial provider. Such a man may even purposely seek out professionally employed women who can "take care of" him. He may not feel that this arrangement is in any way an affront to his manhood; On the contrary, he may pride himself in being able to use his masculinity, charm, sex appeal, or whatever, to convince a woman to support him financially.

During economic hard times, couples often end their marriages with bitter financial disputes over control of money and property. Both sides lose in this case. The divided family must now pay two rents, (or mortgages), two electric bills, two gas bills, two telephone bills, and two heating bills. Furnishings and supplies must be purchased for two homes. One parent, usually the mother, ends up with the added burden of taking care of the children while working full time. Entire families are weakened financially when marriages fail.

In western society, couples tend to make such decisions without the input of other relatives, who are also affected by the divorce. In his book, *Facing Mount Kenya,* Jomo Kenyatta takes a look at the Gikuyu community as an example of the African attitude toward marriage and family:

In the Gikuyu community, marriage and its obligations occupy a position of great importance. One of the outstanding features in the Gikuyu system of marriage is the desire of every member of the tribe to build up his own family group, and by this means to extend and prolong his father's mbari (clan). This results in the strengthening of the tribe as a whole ...

> *On signing the matrimonial contract the marriage ceases to be merely a personal matter, for the contract binds not only the bride and bridegroom, but also their kinsfolk. (p. 163)*

Some African-American men point to the modern western practice of having multiple sex partners, and try to liken it to the system of polygamy as practiced in some African communities. However, polygamy, whether practiced as part of traditional African culture, or as part of the Islamic religion, was a legal system with specific guidelines.

Among the Gikuyu people, marriages are based on mutual love between individuals, Kenyatta notes. In polygamous marriages, the objective is the same as in monogamous marriages: to expand one's family and strengthen kinship ties through the birth of children. The system of polygamy was designed specifically for the purpose of providing financial support for women. It is often the wife who urges her husband to marry a second woman, Kenyatta explains. She considers the second wife as her companion and helper in performing household duties, and may even select the woman she prefers her husband to marry.

In the religion of Islam, a man is permitted to marry up to four wives. However, as author Mildred El-Amin points out in her book *Family Roots,* the Quran only mentions this arrangement in Chapter Four, verse four, in connection with the care of orphans. After a war, the male population has been drastically depleted. The children are left fatherless and the women husbandless. Quranic verses clearly outlaw the traditional abuse of women during wartime, such as rape or the taking of concubines. Polygamous marriages allowed a society to maintain social stability during a generation of rebuilding, and prevented the exploitation of widows by strictly forbidding sex outside of marriage. Again, the husband's economic capability is a major factor.

However, in America, men may produce a number of children, some or none of them within a binding marriage. These children, born to different mothers, are not raised as part of one family; on the contrary, the mothers may be bitter rivals, enemies, or complete strangers to each other. If a man is married, but fathers children by another woman who is not his legal wife, those children born out of wedlock may carry a certain social stigma. The father may not even openly acknowledge them as his children. They may not receive adequate financial support and may be denied the same rights of inheritance as the children born to his legal wife. In some cases, a man may father children by several women, none of them his wives. He may be financially incapable of supporting any of them.

In African societies, it was understood that out of wedlock births created major family conflicts. Disputes would arise over the father's responsibility for the child, the mother's position within the father's family in relation to other wives, and the child's legal right of inheritance. The social disorder this creates makes it clear why some societies consider adultery and unmarried sexual relationships crimes against the community.

THE BLACK FEMALE STEREOTYPE

A hostile society which disrespected black men and preyed upon black women left black women in a vulnerable position. As a result, African-American women developed an aggressive independence.

The media created and continues to promote the image of the loudmouthed, bossy, overbearing black woman and the timid, lazy, irresponsible black man. Today, men and women find themselves reacting to these deeply ingrained stereotypes. This often creates a bitter power struggle between husbands and wives.

In societies where women take a less aggressive role in the protection and provision of the family, it is because the males are able to provide a home, food, clothing, and protection from hostile outside forces. The violent slave experience and subsequent years of racial oppression have caused African American women to feel that they can expect neither protection nor provision from African-American men. They often unconsciously develop a posture of suspicion and hostility toward all men, out of fear and mistrust.

White men have often made a point of publicly humiliating black women to emphasize the point of black male powerlessness to protect the woman's dignity. In his autobiographical book *Black Boy,* Richard Wright recalls an incident which happened while he was employed as a hotel bell hop in the south in the 1920s:

One night, just as I was about to go home, I met one of the Negro maids. She lived in my direction, and we fell in to walk part of the way home together. As we passed the white night-watchman, he slapped the maid on her buttock. I turned around, amazed. The watchman looked at me with a long, hard, fixed-under stare. Suddenly he pulled his gun and asked:
"Nigger, don't yuh like it?"
I hesitated.

"I asked yuh don't yuh like it?" he asked again, stepping forward.

"Yes, sir," I mumbled.

"Talk like it, then!"

"Oh, yes sir!" I said with as much heartiness as I could muster.

Outside, I walked ahead of the girl, ashamed to face her. She caught up with me and said:

"Don't be a fool! Yuh couldn't help it!"

This watchman boasted of having killed two Negroes in self-defense.

Women frequently overlooked insults and abuse from whites and urged their men to do the same to avoid possible physical harm or death themselves. However, each time she compromised her own dignity, the woman lost a little more respect for her man because he was unable to protect her from abuse.

MUTUAL LOW SELF ESTEEM AFFECTS UPBRINGING OF CHILDREN

Fears of being disrespected, disregarded and ultimately humiliated create extreme paranoia and insecurity in both black men and women. This insecurity is at the root of the power struggle most couples find themselves embroiled in today. Most confrontations between husbands and wives are the result of each suffering from low self esteem.

People who have been taught to feel badly about themselves cannot give praise and encouragement to others, something which is essential to building a healthy relationship. One's mate should be able to act as a source of comfort and reassurance. Both men and women look to their mates to boost their self esteem by providing the amount of attention, encouragement, and respect they need. However, in many modern day marriages, neither is equipped to provide what the other desires. They have not been properly trained.

Whereas in most African societies, men and women were prepared for the role of spouse, by learning how to be pleasing to their mates, in America, such is not the case. There is no formal training program which takes a child from adolescence to adulthood. So children learn from the bad examples set by their own parents, who have learned to abuse each other verbally and physically as a means of venting frustration.

When entering a marriage, men and women bring with them all their personal insecurities about their own physical attractiveness, intelligence, cultural background, financial status, sexuality, and general competency as a human being. They expect their mates to resolve all of these insecurities and, of course, their mates cannot.

Just as the great empire of Ghana was built by stable family groups, African Americans must establish stable family groups based on principals of unity, cooperation and a strong commitment to marriage, if they are to develop a prosperous, well ordered society.

How has your upbringing prepared you for the role of spouse? One must honestly assess how their own experiences, good and bad, have influenced their current attitudes and behavior. The activity following this chapter is a questionnaire to help determine whether or not you are really ready for marriage ... or, if you are married, this may help discover the things you and your spouse need to address in order to keep your marriage together.

ACTIVITY:
Take The Marriage Test

Marriages fall apart largely due to conflicting attitudes about the essential things which can make or break a relationship. Answer these questions and discuss them at length with your spouse or your perspective spouse.

1.   What do you consider to be the responsibility of a wife? Regarding wage earning? Childrearing? Cooking? Cleaning? Household financial management?

2.   What do you consider to be the responsibility of a husband? Regarding wage earning? Childrearing? Cooking? Cleaning? Household financial management?

3.   How do you feel about housekeeping? Are you a meticulously neat person? Are you somewhat relaxed about neatness and order? How often do you clean your home?

4.   What are the five most important qualities you desire in a mate? What five traits do you consider most intolerable?

5.   Did your parents remain together throughout your childhood until your adult life? Did you grow up in a two parent home or a single parent home? Did either of your parents remarry? How did this affect you?

6.   Describe your parents' relationship: Were they friends? Did they get along? Were they affectionate toward each other? Do you expect the same kind of marriage your parents had?

7.   How did your parents resolve problems? Did they calmly discuss the differences? Did they argue? Did they stop speaking to each other? Did they become physically violent?

8.   Describe your relationship with your mother: Were you friends? Did you get along? Was she affectionate toward you? How do you feel about your relationship?

9.   Describe your relationship with your father: Were you friends? Did you get along? Was he affectionate toward you? How do you feel about your relationship?

10.   How do you express affection? Are you demonstrative? Are you reserved?

11.   How do you feel about the various expressions of sexual intimacy? What things do you prefer? What makes you uncomfortable?

12.   Do you think your mate should have sexual experiences before marriage?

13.   *Do you think you should have sexual experiences before marriage?*

14.   *If you have been sexually active in a previous relationship, what kind of expectations do you have regarding your current mate?*

15.   *If you have not been sexually active in a previous relationship, what kind of expectations do you have regarding your current mate?*

16.   *Have you had a negative sexual experience, such as a sexual assault? If so, how did it affect you?*

17.   *How do you express anger? Do you yell? Do you become silent? Do you pretend everything is okay on the outside, but harbor inner resentment which may later explode?*

18.   *What are your career goals? Do you plan to continue your education after marriage? After children are born? Do you expect your spouse's financial support while you are in school?*

19.   *How do you manage money? Do you like to spend freely? Do you maintain a tight budget? Are you generally on time paying bills? Do you tend to accumulate debts?*

20.   *How do you feel about your financial status? Would it bother you if your spouse made more money than you? Would it bother you if your spouse made less money than you?*

21.   *How do you feel about family gatherings? Do you like to be around family members? Do you avoid holidays and special occasions with family members?*

22.   *How do you feel about your mate's family? How does your mate's family feel about you?*

23.   *Do you have children from a previous relationship? Are you actively involved in rearing the child? Is the other parent actively involved in rearing the child? Have you and the other parent come to an agreement about your respective responsibilities for rearing the child?*

24.   *Does your mate have a child from a previous relationship? How do you feel about being actively involved in rearing the child? Have you and your mate come to an agreement about rearing the child?*

25.   *How do you feel about socializing? Are you a public person or a private person? How do you feel about guests in your home? How do you feel about visiting others' homes?*

26.   *How do you feel about your spouse or your potential spouse having friends of the opposite sex? Should your spouse still socialize with members of the opposite sex? If so, under what limitations, if any?*

27.   *Have you been married or engaged before? How was your previous relationship resolved? Is there still bitterness, hurt or anger between you and the previous person with whom you were involved?*

28.   *What is your concept of God? Are you actively involved in an organized religion? How important are your religious beliefs?*

29.   *How do you feel about your mate's religious beliefs? Are your mate's beliefs the same or different from your own?*

30.   *How do you feel about yourself? Do you like the way you look? Do you like your personality? Are you pleased with what you have achieved in life so far?*

Analyzing Your Answers:

Questions 1-3: If you disagree on responsibilities and roles, this will be a continuous cause of friction. For orderly household management, couples must agree on how responsibilities are to be shared.

Questions 4-9: You should be aware of how family background affects the current attitudes and behavior of you and your mate. People tend to imitate what they have experienced.

Questions 10-17: You must be able to discuss your most intimate feelings and desires with your spouse without fear of ridicule or disgust. Physical intimacy is a sensitive issue which should be addressed without hostility.

Questions 18-20: Pursuit of personal career goals, as well as changes in financial status and conflicting attitudes toward financial management can have a great impact on a marriage.

Questions 21-27: Understand how your mate expects you to interact with family members and friends. Negative feelings toward family members, ex-spouses, children, or old friends can create jealousy and hostility if not resolved.

Questions 28-29: Religious beliefs often define ethical standards and influence social behavior. Agreement on ethical standards can eliminate certain problems.

Question 25: Personal self esteem is important. You cannot love another person until you love yourself.

If you and your mate have major conflicts over more than five of these questions, and you still want to maintain the relationship, consider couples counseling before you get married. If married, consider professional counseling to help resolve conflicts before they develop into irreconcilable differences.

CHAPTER ELEVEN
African American Childrearing:
The Making Of A Slave

11A

Protect The Children
The future of the world begins with the children, as illustrated by this young Panamanian woman and her baby. What have we planted in the minds and hearts of our children to allow them to grow into emotionally healthy adults? (Photo by Ted Gray. Reprinted by permission.)

CHAPTER ELEVEN
African American Childrearing:
The Making Of A Slave

In every society, the birth of a child represents the family's future. In *Roots,* Alex Haley gives us a glimpse of West African culture, with its deep respect and regard for children, from the very moment they are born. At the birth of Kunta Kinte, in the village of Juffure in the Gambia, the entire community gathered for a special naming ceremony. During this event, the village historian recited the names of Kunta's ancestors, going back more than 200 years. Each child's birth was considered special, because of that child's connection to the ancestors. Kunta was named after his grandfather, Kairaba Kunta Kinte, who had come from his native Mauritania into the Gambia, where he had saved the people of Juffure from a famine and served as the village holy man.

In American society, young life has come to have very little value. Violent child abuse is increasing at alarming rates. According to a report published in 1990 by the National Committee for Prevention of Child Abuse (NCPCA), black children account for approximately 10 to 15 percent of America's child populace, yet in some regions represent 20 to 40 percent of all reported cases of child abuse. As a result of physical, verbal and psychological abuse, children are growing into angry, violent teenagers, who are committing crimes at younger and younger ages. Teenage suicide is shockingly high. What are we doing to our children to destroy them so?

Most African-American parents learned their childrearing skills from their own parents, who themselves were raised according to old slavery time methods. Slave masters used violent force to crush the child's spirit and produce a docile, non-threatening human being who could be trained to perform basic manual labor. Unaware of how to provide the special manhood and womanhood training their sons and daughters would have received in an African community, today's parents make harmful mistakes in the process of raising their children to adulthood.

THE EXTENDED FAMILY

What is a family? The idea of the "nuclear family" (the husband, wife, and children), is pretty much a new western industrial concept. In African society, family ties extend far beyond this, to include grandparents, aunts, uncles, cousins, in-laws, and even neighbors. As one African proverb states, "It takes a whole village to raise a child."

Contrary to what many sociologists have concluded when studying the African-American family, all African culture and tradition was not lost during slavery. In spite of the mixing up of nationalities and language groups in America, African people, under the yoke of slavery, still banded together to form close-knit families as much as possible. In *The Slave Community,* Blassingame observes that it was within the family that the slave found love, companionship, sexual intimacy, and self esteem. Children were given ethical values and instructions on how to avoid punishment.

But the institution of slavery robbed African people born in America of that all important understanding of ancestral ties. Slave owners took pains to remove any notion of family honor and tradition from those enslaved. Their offspring, as noted earlier, were taught to distance themselves from Africa as much as possible. So, two generations after the first African arrived in chains to America, the black child grows up asking the black parent, "Where did we come from?" Unlike Kunta Kinte, the child had no village historian to recite more than two hundred years of history of a great people from whom that child descended.

In America, a black child is raised with a sense of nobodyness. One of the first mistakes African American parents often make is to disconnect themselves from the extended family of relatives and neighbors who can help reinforce proper values.

Although the African family connection was disrupted by slavery, African-American children still need to be taught, as they grow up, that they are connected to an ancient past far beyond that of an American slave plantation. Parents must teach family history beyond "Grandma and Grandpa, who came from Mississippi." Even if blood lineage cannot always be traced to a specific location in Africa, black parents should still claim kinship with the people from those great African nations.

LEARNING WITHIN THE WOMB

A child's life actually begins to take shape even before its birth. The attitude of the family into which the child is being born determines whether the child will receive a happy or a hostile welcome when he or she arrives.

Today, medical doctors understand more about the stages of development of a child. The period of the most rapid brain growth is between the fourth month of pregnancy and the sixth month after birth. During this time, the baby is affected by internal and external events, which may shape its personality even before birth. A child inside the womb has ears and can already recognize the mother's voice and touch. A mother who is irritable and resentful of the child has already communicated this resentment to the child -- even before birth!

Babies who are cared for before their birth, with good prenatal care from mothers with a healthy lifestyle have a better chance of growing up feeling loved and happy. But when hostility is introduced before birth, through alcohol or drug abuse and other unhealthy lifestyles, this child has a higher chance of both physical and/or emotional problems. That hostility may continue after the child is born.

When a mother (and father) talk lovingly and soothingly to the unborn child, even read to the child and play soft, peaceful music, they are shaping within that child a calm, peaceful disposition. Doctors have observed that such children, after they are born, learn faster and are more alert than those whose mothers exposed themselves to constant noise (blaring stereos and TV sets, etc.) during pregnancy.

Diet is important during pregnancy, not only for the mother's health, but for the child's well being, also. Fortunately, many African-American slaves retained knowledge of green vegetables and herbs which promoted good health. In spite of the harsh work conditions they endured during pregnancy, many slave women gave birth to healthy babies.

A mother who will not completely eliminate alcohol and tobacco use during pregnancy is setting her child up for a life of mental or physical retardation. Those who want their offspring to grow into well-adjusted human beings must begin this process before the child's birth.

PHYSICAL AFFECTION IS HEALTHY

"Don't pick that baby up all the time, you'll spoil him!"

Many have heard such an idea, but where did this notion come from? In African societies, women carried their infants on their backs, bound up by cloth and attached to them in such a way that the child always felt the warmth of its mother's body. It has been observed that such children cry less, are calmer, healthier, and more secure. It was a common sight to see a woman working in the fields with a baby strapped to her. She may even stop periodically to breast feed the child.

However, in today's Western culture, physical contact between mother and infant may be minimal. Rather than nursing her baby, a mother might offer a bottle or pacifier to the hungry child. Some woman may choose not to breast feed, considering it an inconvenience. Small cages, called "playpens" were developed to restrict children's movement once they became toddlers. If a couple can afford it, they might even hire a nanny or someone to take care of the child daily. During slavery, black women were used as "mammies" for white children. White women, not wishing to lose the shape of their breasts, had black women to breast feed their babies.

Now psychologists understand the process of something they call "bonding" which must happen between parent and child. Children need affection for their emotional health as well as physical health, doctors have discovered. Children who are held and hugged often are found to contract fewer diseases and illnesses than those who are not.

Unfortunately, many parents never touch their children unless it is for the purpose of discipline, and then the touch is a slap or a hit, not a hug or caress. People who have not received affection as children often do not know how to give affection to their spouses or children. Psychologists have observed that sometimes men and women, seeking the physical comfort they did not receive from parents as children, become sexually promiscuous as adults. They end up using sex as a means to fulfill the desire for affection and human physical contact.

CHILD DISCIPLINE:
BREAKING THE SLAVE

What is discipline? During slavery, discipline meant punishment. It meant correcting the slave's behavior through physical force. It meant whippings and floggings. However, true discipline is not punishment, but guidance, so that a person may develop self control. *Webster's Collegiate Dictionary* defines discipline as "training to act in accordance with rules." Harsh physical punishment is often designed to instill fear, not wisdom and understanding.

During slavery, when someone was particularly unruly, he might be sent to a "slave breaker," whose profession was the breaking of a slave's will by beating the slave into submission. William S. Feely, in his biography of Frederick Douglass, recounts Douglass' experience when his master Thomas Auld sent him to the slave breaker, Edward Covey:

One cold morning, soon after his arrival, Frederick was sent by Covey into the woods with a team of oxen. The awkward, frightened boy, who had had no experience with draft animals, lost control of the difficult beasts, and there ensued a madcap dash--

described with a touch of humor--through fences and into trees. He almost had his skull crushed, but the only sympathy he received when he returned was to be told to go back to the woods. Covey "then went to a large gum-tree, and with his axe cut three large switches, and, after trimming them up neatly with his pocket-knife, he ordered me to take off my clothes. I made him no answer, but stood with my clothes on. He repeated his order. I still made him no answer, nor did I move to strip myself. Upon this he rushed at me with the fierceness of a tiger, tore off my clothes and lashed me till he had worn out his switches..." This was as close as a Victorian author could come to speaking about the sadistic abuse of males by males: Covey's savage attack strongly suggests a perversion of homosexual attraction into vicious cruelty. (p. 45)

Slave beatings often appeared to be sadistic perversions of the master. The ritual of pulling off the tree limbs to make a whip and the stripping off of clothes comes straight out of slavery. A child who is disciplined in such a manner may recover from the physical scars, but the emotional scars can be permanent. Such a beating is not only physical abuse; it can also be considered sexual abuse.

Child abuse is at the root of many of today's shocking cases of murder and suicide. In his book *Black Suicide*, psychoanalyst Herbert Hendin examines the testimony of his thirty one year old patient Ina Tracy, who had made two serious suicide attempts after violent fights with her friends:

Ina says of her childhood that there was "not a day without a beating. My mother would make me break a branch and she'd beat me with it -- hit me wherever it landed. I wanted to take her and choke

her to death. Wished that I would die or she would.
She only wanted me to go to school, work, and go to
church."...

Although Ina feared the beatings, she did what
she wanted since she was beaten anyway. (pp. 22, 23)

Some parents, claiming to follow the Biblical
philosophy of "spare the rod, spoil the child," believe
that children sometimes need a "good beating" in
order to teach them proper respect for authority.
What such beatings often produce, however, is an
angry, rebellious child. Hendin observes that rage
from abuse or abandonment by one or both parents
often causes the child to become a violent, dangerous
teenager and adult.

In addition to harsh physical punishment,
parents often verbally abuse their children,
erroneously thinking that name calling and insults
will somehow shame the child into good behavior. It
doesn't. What it does do is give the child low self
esteem and feelings of inferiority. Many adults are
still suffering emotional scars from the cruel,
insensitive remarks hurled at them by their parents
during childhood, such as "you're so stupid ... you get
on my nerves ... you're just too lazy ... you're an
ignorant little &*$#@%!!"

Rather than reprimand a child gently and
explain to them the correct behavior, parents use the
physical and verbal abuse tactics of the slave breaker.
In his book *Developing Positive Self Images and*
Discipline In Black Children, Jawanza Kunjufu
warns parents of the consequences of such practices:

When parents are strict, quick to punish (and
slow to reward), lacking in affection and physical love
expression, their children tend to lack emotional

response, appear dull and unresponsive, and perhaps, eventually to feel angry toward and resistant to any authority.

Parents affect self-esteem when they criticize the person rather than the behavior. When a parent says "YOU are a bad boy," rather than "What you DID was bad," it has the potential to be devastating to the development of self esteem. (p. 18)

The frustrated parent of an unruly two or three year old may say their child is just "bad." Accusing a child of being "bad" implies that the child has the ability to make judgments based on moral principles. A two or three year old certainly does not.

Usually, it is the parent who is bad ... bad at being patient, bad at listening, bad at understanding, bad at showing a proper example. A little child may be energetic, curious, excited, or even angry ... but very unlikely "bad."

Calling a child insulting names is the worst kind of verbal abuse and carries long range effects. People who feel badly about themselves often abuse other people. Bullies, who make a sport out of tormenting other children, sometimes are the victims of physically and verbally abusive parents.

Many harmful childrearing practices can be traced to the parent's own feelings of inferiority. People who see themselves as worthless, ugly, and stupid would more likely say such mean things to their children. Many times the harsh punishment of a child is merely the parent's excuse to vent personal anger and frustration.

Before parents can lead their children to becoming better people, they must first correct themselves.

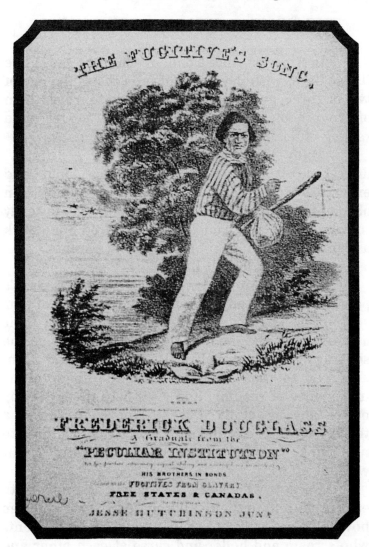

11B
Frederick Douglass Runs To Freedom
Frederick Douglass used this poster of himself escaping as an advertisement for one of his anti-slavery programs. Douglass decided to leave his master after a series of violent encounters with a slave breaker who tried to "discipline" him. (Reprinted from Frederick Douglass, by William S. McFeely, page 146, Copyright 1991, W.W. Norton & Company.)

THE HOME: A CHILD'S FIRST SCHOOL

In America, once a child reaches the age of five (these days, with daycare and pre-school, the age of two or three, even), parents are ready to whisk them off to school, considering their own job of child raising officially done.

Many times a parent sends off an unruly, disrespectful, inattentive, hyperactive child and expects the school teacher to miraculously produce an obedient, polite, mature young scholar who is ready to come home and complete all required homework assignments without prompting from parents.

This just doesn't happen.

Parents often don't realize that a child's personality is already fully formed by the age of four years old. They don't recognize the effect of their own behavior and the household environment on the shaping of that personality. Parents who read often, and read to their children teach the children the importance of reading, and even help them develop better language skills. Parents who sit in front of a television set all day and night teach their children to not think, but to expect constant entertainment without effort.

Parents who speak quietly and respectfully to each other and to their children, teach their children how to be respectful to them and to others. Parents who scream and holler and curse at each other and at the children teach their children to scream and holler and curse at everyone else ... and someday back at them as well.

A parent's most important job is to prepare the child for a responsible adulthood. This cannot be done if the parent has an "I don't want to be bothered" attitude. Children have a natural curiosity and parents have an opportunity to teach every thing from chemistry to economics by answering a child's simple question. How many times have parents heard a youngster ask curiously,"Why? Why?" and the parents impatiently tell the child, "SHUT-UP!" Black children tend to learn early that curiosity is not welcomed. They learn to keep their questions to themselves, and their later silence in the classroom prevents them from exploring the vast possibilities of the mind.

How many times do parents fuss at children for not doing chores or homework, but at the same time never sit down and actually show them how? Children are not born with knowledge of survival, and if not taught, children grow up ignorant and dependent. Where do children learn the "work ethic?" Parents who do not give their children a vision of why their labor is important, as well as why knowledge is important, will likely produce lazy, unconcerned offspring whose only philosophy is "How can I get paid for doing as little as possible?"

At two, three and four years old, a child has an open mind and wants to participate in important things. At twelve, thirteen and fourteen, after years of mindless television entertainment, the child has already become bored with life. It would be very difficult to try to arouse interest in household chores or any other kind of work at this point.

Parents have to let children participate in household management early. Let preschool children help clean the house, wash the dishes, sweep the floor, help prepare the food. Take them to the grocery store, point out the prices on the items, let them count the money and figure out the change.

Take them to the place where you work, explain what you do for a living and why it is important. Show them what you do, and explain what kind of people pay for your services. Take them to the bank, let them watch you cash your paycheck or deposit money, and explain what you are doing. Prepare them for whatever kinds of work they will later do for a living, by teaching them respect for all kinds of work. Point out what other people do -- bus drivers, plumbers, mail carriers -- and explain why they are important to the whole society. Give them an allowance for helping with chores, show them how to save and manage money. Take them with you to pay bills.

In an article in December 1989 edition of *Black Enterprise Magazine* entitled "Teaching Your Children The Financial Facts Of Life," author Pamela D. Sharif suggests that parents can open a bank account for their children, and teach them at an early age how to manage a checking account. She observes,

> *The burden of teaching children personal finance falls largely upon parents because most schools, particularly those in urban areas, do not address the importance of financial discipline ...*
>
> *By age five, most children should have learned to differentiate between coins and that money can be exchanged for goods and services. Playing "store" with your child, using a toy cash register and play money, is an effective and fun way to establish these basics ...*
>
> *By age ten, your child should understand the basics of banking and should have a savings account. Now is a good time to begin teaching solid shopping skills, such as comparison shopping, and to help your child learn the value, not just the cost, of a product. (pp. 58, 62)*

This is the way to expand children's minds, teach them to think and give them a vision and a purpose for living.

CREATING A POSITIVE CULTURAL IDENTITY

A child may be raised by loving, patient parents, yet, because of repeated psychological assaults from a racist society, may still end up an emotionally scarred adult. This is where creating a positive cultural identity is important. Parents cannot leave such things to chance. Failure to instill pride in an African heritage will result in the child first becoming confused and finally feeling inferior.

Children may be raised with the best of discipline and morals, and may exhibit exceptional intelligence, yet still end up with severe identity problems. In his book *Black Skin, White Masks,* Algerian psychiatrist Franz Fanon reviews some of his interviews with black patients who exhibit various psychological and emotional disturbances. He examines the psychological impact of slavery and colonialism on the minds of black children:

The Tarzan stories, the sagas of twelve-year-old explorers, the adventures of Mickey Mouse, and all those "comic books" serve actually as a release for collective aggression. The magazines are put together by white men for little white men. This is the heart of the problem ... In the magazines, the Wolf, the Devil, the Evil Spirit, the Bad Man, the Savage are always symbolized by Negroes or Indians; since there is always identification with the victor, the little Negro, quite as easily as the little white boy, becomes an explorer, an adventurer, a missionary "who faces the danger of being eaten by the wicked Negroes."

The black schoolboy in the Antilles, who in his lessons is forever talking about "our ancestors, the Gauls," identifies himself with the explorer, the bringer of civilization, the white man who carries truth to savages -- an all-white truth.   There is identification -- that is, the young Negro subjectively adopts a white man's attitude... (p. 146)

Children who grow up reading white comic books, playing with white dolls, and watching white television heroes, will learn to see themselves as white. In America, little black school children who learn to recite the history of "our ancestors, the pilgrims" are in for a rude awakening later on. Fanon observes:

A normal child that has grown up in a normal family will be a normal man...

But -- and this is a most important point -- we observe the opposite in the man of color. A normal Negro child, having grown up within a normal family, will become abnormal on the slightest contact with the white world...Freud wrote:

"In almost every case, we could see that the symptoms were, so to speak, like residues of emotional experiences, to which for this reason we later gave the name of psychic traumas.   Their individual characters were linked to the traumatic scenes that had provoked them...it was not always a single event that was the cause of the symptom; most often, on the contrary, it arose out of multiple traumas, frequent and repeated..."

What do we see in the case of the black man?... A drama is enacted every day in colonized countries. How is one to explain, for example, that a Negro who

has passed his baccalaureate and has gone to the
Sorbonne to study to become a teacher of philosophy
is already on guard before any conflictual elements
have coalesced around him? (pp. 142, 143, 144)

Upon contact with actual white people, the
black child realizes he or she is not white. Every
reference to color, every taunt, every insult, every
rude reply, every racial joke, is a traumatic event to
be endured. At a certain point, the child becomes
extremely self conscious of being different, of being
part of the scorned class. This self consciousness
continues on into adulthood, when by then a kind of
neurosis has developed. The black adult learns to
keep all emotional guards up when around whites,
tensed like a boxer, waiting to absorb the blow of an
offensive racial remark, ready to bounce back without
a loss of composure. After enough negative
experiences, blacks become almost paranoid about
being around whites, fearing they will be subjected to
public humiliation or embarrassment.

Have unpleasant experiences in childhood or
adulthood pushed you to the point of paranoia when
interacting with whites? Look back at your answer
to Psychic Trauma Test question Number 7: "When
I go to events where I am the only black person in
attendance, I feel self conscious."

If you strongly agree, agree, or are unsure,
then perhaps you are apprehensive that whites will
cause you some type of public embarrassment or
make you feel inferior.

A positive identity, instilled early, keeps
children from being psychologically destroyed by the
insults of others. However, the absence of
Afrocentric toys, games and literature as part of the
child's early experience makes the child feel an

emptiness, a sense of nothingness. If blackness is not defined by the parents, in terms of positive heroes in history (not just slave history!), and positive cultural activities (plays, films, music, art, etc.), white society will fill in the gaps with shameful pictures of a savage, uncivilized past, a violent, crime-ridden present, and an "endangered," non-existent future. The child will learn to reject the black identity altogether. Fanon asserts that children need early exposure to positive black literature, before they are traumatized by racism.

This is especially critical for the families who live in predominantly white communities. In some cases, because of a lack of a positive black identity, black children actually become white people, psychologically and culturally. They may actually learn to feel uncomfortable when socializing with other blacks. Parents must arm themselves with knowledge of African and African American history.

PUBERTY AND THE COMING OF ADULTHOOD

Radio stations bombard young listeners with crude, lewd, sexually explicit lyrics, while television stations flash nudity and sexual activity across the screen with every program and commercial. Sex has become the official mark of adulthood, rather than preparation for marriage and family responsibilities.

In the 1991 movie *Boyz N The Hood,* directed by John Singleton, Lawrence Fishburne plays Furious Styles, a single father who is taking care of his son, Tre (Cuba Gooding Jr.). The film shows Furious engaged in a man-to-man talk with his son, teaching him all the intricacies of sexual intercourse, ending with the warning to "use some protection."

There was no mention of marriage or being a husband and taking care of a family. Years later, when his son has become a teenager, his father (in rather crude terms) asks his son if he has had sex with a woman yet. Tre, ashamed of his virginity, lies and says yes, describing some imaginary wild encounter with an attractive young woman. Later, Tre does have sex with his teenage girlfriend, and at this point, he feels that he has finally attained manhood. This film presents a true to life condition in many families. Often parents, in their ignorance, will expect, and in the case of male offspring, even encourage their children to become sexually active upon reaching puberty. They may feel that they have done their duty by explaining the hows and whys of birth control, but as far as teaching children how to prepare for marriage and family life, most parents don't seem to have a clue as to how to do it.

In many African societies, puberty was celebrated as a significant turning point in a person's life, marked by major ceremonies. By puberty, a child will have been trained to perform as an adult. This process was effectively demolished with the European slave trade. In antebellum America, puberty for a young black girls and boys meant only one thing: it was time to start producing babies for the master. It's not surprising that today's African Americans are confused about sexual morals.

Casual attitudes toward sex and childbirth are the signs of a society which has lost its respect for women and motherhood. Such was the case in the old Roman empire, which finally collapsed due to widespread moral decay. Lewd behavior had become ingrained in Roman culture. It even pervaded Roman religious rites, traces of which can still be found in western society today.

According to *Webster's New World Collegiate Dictionary*, Easter comes from the ancient Roman celebration in honor of the dawn goddess Eastre. Young girls who had reached the age of puberty dressed in their finest clothes and marched down the street in a big parade. They carried baskets of eggs, the egg of course being symbolic of fertility. The climax of the parade was when these women publicly engaged in sexual intercourse with able bodied men.

When the leaders of Rome adopted Christianity in the 3rd century A.D., they faced the dilemma of what to do about all of the ancient customs and celebrations which the people had no intention of giving up. So, the spring festival of Eastre became the celebration of Easter and the "resurrection" of Jesus. With this new holiday, Roman leaders tried to insert the idea of a spiritual rebirth into their ancient fertility ritual. The women could continue to dress up in their finest clothes and carry their baskets of eggs, they would just have to do it with the understanding that this somehow represented Jesus and the crucifixion.

However, church leaders' attempt to "Christianize" pagan holidays did not work. The people did not, on the whole, change their overall sexually promiscuous behavior. Throughout history, whenever sex begins to be a sport rather than a respected act of creation, the society begins its final stages of decline.

Some mothers, desiring their daughters to wait until marriage before sex, may repeatedly warn them, "Now, you stay away from those boys!" Although these mothers may pound into their daughters repeatedly that sex is "wrong," they rarely create a positive anticipation of the sexual experience within a marriage. Children tend to follow the roles which they have been programmed to follow. If mothers spoke of upcoming sexual experiences with daughters in a positive context of "when you get married, you and your husband..." then girls would consider marriage the natural precedence to sex. The same must be done with boy children. Fathers must prepare their sons to be husbands; they must discuss sexual activity with their sons in the context of "when you get married, you and your wife..." and the boys will understand that manhood and marriage go hand in hand. People who desire to liberate themselves must follow higher moral standards than that of their oppressors.

BROKEN MARRIAGES, BROKEN CHILDREN

In America, children of divorced parents may find themselves suddenly cut off from relatives. Living without the protective support of a greater extended family, their upbringing is often influenced more by the society at large than by family members.

In most African cultures, when children are involved, every effort is made to reconcile a marriage. Divorce becomes a final option, only after all other avenues to keep the husband and wife together have failed. Parents on both sides strive to counsel the husband and wife, in order to keep the family together. However, in America, oftentimes it is the parents and in-laws who, rather than helping sustain the marriage, may actually instigate its break-up. Bitter court battles over alimony, custody, and child support tear families apart.

Parents whose children have lived through such emotionally distressing episodes will find it difficult to instill within their children the idea of marital bliss. Many such children tend to shy away

from marriage, not willing to risk reliving the painful
traumas of childhood. In *Black Suicide,* Hendin
notes a number of cases where adults from broken
homes develop a series of emotional problems and
often have negative attitudes toward marriage. A
child of divorced parents often grows up listening to
one or both parents spew out venomous remarks
about the ex-spouse. Children are often made to feel
that they must take sides in the dispute.

In *Black Suicide,* Hendin cited several cases in
which the men with severe emotional problems had
mothers who had vented frustration and anger
toward ex-husbands by berating their sons, with such
remarks as "You're no good, just like your no good
daddy!" Such boys often developed low self esteem,
and had difficulty achieving goals in life. Boys who
are raised by their fathers may repeatedly hear such
insulting remarks about women that they may
become angry at their mothers, and may develop
hostility toward all females. This sometimes later
translates into violence within their own
relationships with women, as Hendin noted.

Daughters of divorced parents may grow up
hearing such hostile remarks about men from their
mothers that they develop distrust for all males.
Angry at their fathers for leaving their mothers to
struggle alone, they later enter their own personal
relationships full of resentment and hostility toward
men. A number of Hendin's female patients with
suicidal tendencies were women who, in childhood,
had been abandoned by their fathers.

As marriage continues to lose its value in
American society, so does the birth and raising of
children. Crimes of child abuse and neglect,
practically unheard of in African culture, have
become quite commonplace in the west. In his

NCPCA report on child abuse, Dr. John K. Holton states that nearly 80 percent of all cases of child abuse and deaths due to neglect involve children under the age of three. More than 55 percent of the time, the child victims were black and male, and the perpetrators were disproportionately black females.

It is not African American culture which breeds such violence against children, but the conditions of poverty, stress, environmental isolation, and lack of family support services, Holton explains.

In slavery times, the birth of a black child meant increased wealth for the master. After slavery, whites made it clear, through massive lynchings, that black life was no longer profitable to them and had little value. This attitude persists today, as white sociological "experts" insinuate that perhaps low income black women should be prevented from procreating, perhaps through the use of abortions, experimental birth control methods, or sterilizations, in order to stop unwed pregnancies which drain the nation's welfare system.

However, the problem is not the natural emergence of a sex drive within young men and women. The real problem is that slavery and present day racism have created financial obstacles for African American men who strive to support their wives and children. Today, many black families recognize this fact and are now striving to combat the genocidal effect of poverty on the African American community. To discourage unwed pregnancies, parents are providing the necessary financial help to young sons and daughters who choose to get married. Despite the difficult problems they face, many young couples manage to stay together, and are therefore are able to provide a stronger foundation for their own children's futures.

ACTIVITY:
Learn From Your Child's Play

Parents can discover how their children see themselves and their society by observing them when they play. Have your children been affected by excessive violence in the home, on television, or in the surrounding community? Quietly observe your child's imaginative play in these situations:

1.   *Give your child a toy telephone to call up friends and relatives. Listen to the conversations your child creates. Are they friendly and pleasant or angry and argumentative?*

2.   *Give your child dolls which represent each member of the family. Observe the situations your child creates. Do family members participate in enjoyable activities together? Do they argue and fight a lot? Do the children get spankings? Is there extreme violence (beatings, shootings, stabbings?) Is the doll which represents your child happy or unhappy? What real life situations does your child appear to be reenacting with the dolls?*

3.   *Observe your child playing with other toys. Is there repeated pretense of killing and death? Parents may see this as harmless fun, but in today's society, violence has become very real. You should evaluate your child's toys and determine whether there is an overabundance of toy guns, knives, tanks, or other weapons which encourage violent behavior.*

CHAPTER TWELVE
Economic Genocide

12A

The Making Of A Ghetto

Rural southern black families came to the northern cities in droves seeking a better life. Because of housing discrimination, they found themselves trapped in a cycle of poverty. Restricted to certain sections of town, they crowded into old, dilapidated apartment buildings, and despite low wage jobs, were forced to pay higher rents than in the white sections of town. (Photo by Ted Gray. Reprinted by permission.)

CHAPTER TWELVE
Economic Genocide

Urban ghettos. Littered streets. Boarded-up buildings. Vacant lots overgrown with weeds. Crowded, rundown apartments. Idle, drunken black men. Young mothers on welfare. Dirty, ragged, black children.

The image of black life in America.

The nuclear family is rapidly becoming the single-parent family, with one parent (usually the mother) struggling to take care of herself and children. The result -- younger, poorer families. Government statistics show that the number of black children under 18 living in poverty reached 46.6 percent in 1987. African-American men find themselves the subject of scorn and anger from anxious women who seek protectors and providers, but instead find unemployed, unskilled men who appear to be forever locked out of the American economic mainstream. African-American women find themselves the subject of attack and resentment as they enter white America's corporate mainstream, filling professional jobs and government race and sex quotas, and being accused of "taking jobs from the men." America defines success as the acquisition of personal wealth. This philosophy teaches men and women to compete for themselves, rather than cooperate for the good of the family and community.

So, in spite of increased educational and economic opportunities, African Americans see their neighborhoods disintegrate into enterprise zones for whites, Arabs, Koreans, Jews, and every other ethnic immigrant, while they remain powerless to use their own economic power to create jobs. Black men, chronically unemployed, are reduced to street hustling, and black women, unemployed, unskilled, or unable to sustain families on a single income, are often forced to rely on government welfare.

Who is responsible for this mess?

CONTROL OF LAND: THE REAL WEALTH

In the industrialized West, making a living means having a job in an office or factory, and getting paid money, with which one can go and buy groceries. People who grow up in urban areas seldom identify land as the real source of wealth.

But contrast this experience of African farmers, before the European invasion, to that of African-American farmers, after emancipation:

Africa, 1640:
It's harvest time ... a time for celebration and thanksgiving.

This year has been a prosperous one for this group of families in a rural town in West Africa. There is an abundance of food from the crops planted and the goats are well fed, supplying healthy milk and meat for the families in the village.

When the farmers prosper, everyone in the community prospers. The women can go to the marketplace in the city and buy new goods and fabrics from the merchants who have just come from overseas. The teachers are well paid for their work in training and instructing the village children. The iron workers see an increase in their tool manufacturing business.

The families have worked together to create a self sustaining community where everybody shares in the wealth. No wonder it's a cause for celebration.

America, 1940:

It's harvest time. But a family of sharecroppers in a southern town in America finds itself in a sad dilemma.

The harvest has been plentiful. But according to the landowner's records, they are again in debt. In order to be able to plant this year's crop, they had to borrow money for seed and tools. Once this money is deducted they find themselves with little to live on through the winter.

They will either go hungry, or get into debt and try to pay off this year's bill with next year's crop.

They cannot leave without paying off this debt. The landowner would have them arrested and jailed before they could ever reach the city limits.

There is no celebration for this year's harvest ... only worry and despair over the never ending cycle of poverty.

African Americans seem to be forever on the bottom rung of the economic ladder of society. In the "land of plenty" black people never seem to control any of the money they work hard to earn. Some individuals with an aptitude for business may manage to excel in a particular enterprise. However, collective economic power is determined by a people's control of the land and wealth of their mother country. Who controls the wealth of Africa?

For more than three centuries, while tens of thousands of African farmers and craftsmen were being shipped abroad for slave labor, Europe gradually introduced its cheaply made foreign goods into the African market. Basil Davidson, in *A History of West Africa,* explains the effect of this on Africa's economy:

Cheap foreign goods, produced by Europeans or Indians forced to work for very low wages, began to ruin the market for cotton stuffs produced by self-employed and often prosperous African craftsmen. Cheap European metalware, machine-made, competed with the handiwork of African metal-smiths. Understandably, African craftsmen suffered from this rivalry ... So the slave trade removed African labor from Africa and did much to ruin the livelihood of African craftsmen. (pp. 294, 295)

There exists many examples of this kind of thing today. The increasingly popular hand woven African Kente cloth, which many African Americans wear as a symbol of pride in heritage, is being replaced by cheap imitation prints from Korea and other places. W.E.B. DuBois, in his book *The World and Africa,* describes how the destruction of African culture and industry finally led to its political and economic demise:

There came to Africa an end of industry guided by taste and art. Cheap European goods pushed in and threw the native products out of competition. Rum and gin displaced the milder native drinks. The beautiful patterned cloth, brocades and velvets disappeared before their cheap imitations in Manchester calicos. Methods of work were lost and forgotten.

With all this went the fall and disruption of the family, the deliberate attack upon the ancient African clan by missionaries. The invading investors who wanted cheap labor at the gold mines, the diamond mines, the copper and tin mines, the oil forests and cocoa fields, followed the missionaries. The authority of the family was broken up; the authority and

*tradition of the clan disappeared; the power of the
chief was transmuted into the rule of the white
district commissioner. The old religion was held up
to ridicule, the old culture and ethical standards were
degraded or disappeared, and gradually all over
Africa spread the inferiority complex, the fear of color,
the worship of white skin, the imitation of white ways
of doing and thinking, whether good, bad or
indifferent. By the end of the nineteenth century the
degradation of Africa was complete as organized
human means could make it. Chieftains, representing
a thousand years of striving human culture, were
decked out in second-hand London top hats, while
Europe snickered. (p. 78)*

Many eighteenth and nineteenth century
explorers, under the protection and encouragement
of the British government, used bribery, trickery,
deception and brutal force to divide and conquer
African nations.   One such famed explorer, Cecil
Rhodes (for whom Rhodesia and the Rhodes Scholar
award are named) was responsible for creating two
British colonies in Africa. Rhodes demonstrated the
prevailing white supremist philosophy of his day. He
stated in an 1877 publication entitled *Confession of
Faith* that the whites should form a secret society
with the sole objective being to expand the British
empire. Rhodes declared, "I contend that we are the
finest race in the world and the more we inhabit, the
better for the human race."

The governments of Europe translated this
philosophy into law.   As Jackson states in
Introduction to African Civilization, the European
powers got together and colonized Africa. At the
Berlin Conference of 1884, vast territories were
handed over to King Leopold II of Belgium. He

renamed this territory the Congo Free State, and proceeded to take control of all the land's resources. Leopold forced the native inhabitants to work the land, and in one year he reaped a profit of more than $1,500,000 from ivory, rubber and other enterprises.

With gangster-like force, the government ordered each village to collect and bring in a certain amount of rubber -- as much as they could bring in by neglecting all work for their own maintenance. In *Introduction to African Civilization,* Jackson quotes the observations of Bertrand Russell, author of *Freedom and Organization: 1814-1914,* who said that if the men failed to bring the required amount, their women were taken away and kept as hostages in compounds or in the harems of government employees. If that method didn't work, the government hired other natives to act as enforcers, according to Russell, who were:

"... sent into the village to spread terror, if necessary by killing some of the men; but in order to prevent a waste of cartridges they were ordered to bring one right hand for every cartridge used. If they missed, or used cartridges on game, they cut off the hands of living persons to make up the necessary number." (p. 311)

So Africa's resources were taken over slowly and brutally. The gold and diamond mines continue today to be controlled by British and American multinational corporations while native Africans are forced into a state of poverty.

Africa's once stable economy was shattered by the intrusion of Europeans, who slowly took over African nations by outlawing the native monetary system and introducing British and other European

1=BRITISH; 2=FRENCH; 3=BELGIAN;
4=INDEPENDENT STATES; 5=ITALIAN;
6=PORTUGUESE; 7=SPANISH

12B
**Africa Under
Colonialist Rule**
*This map, drawn by
Sultan A. Latif from
a composite of historical
sketches, illustrates that
by 1925, after slavery and
colonialism, Africa was a
jigsaw puzzle of European
controlled territories.*
*Europeans split old nations apart and grouped long time
enemies together, all under the banner of a foreign language and
culture, which laid the foundation for Africa's current political
and economic instability. The numbers on the map represent
each country's area of control.*

currency. Clearly, power is determined not by who has the most money, but by who decides what money *is*. Africans, dispossessed of the land, were then forced to work for European companies for European money. They had to pay taxes to European governments. The result was the creation of a permanent poor working class. African workers soon found themselves in a similar position to the African-American sharecropper.

THE ELUSIVE FORTY ACRES AND A MULE

The American Civil War left the South in shambles. Land was torn apart, families were devastated. Fathers, brothers and sons had been killed or maimed in the war. And the black free labor force upon which the entire economy depended was soon to be no more.

The U.S. government was faced with a dilemma: What to with the ex-slaves, many who had escaped from plantations to serve as Union soldiers, and now had no homes to which they could return? In many cases, the widows and orphans of slain confederate soldiers, bereft of slaves and crops, just packed up and left everything behind. What to do with the acres and acres of abandoned property in the south?

So, after much debate and compromise, on February 28, Congress passed a bill which became known as the act of 1865 establishing in the War Department a "Bureau of Refugees, Freedmen and Abandoned Lands."

In *The Souls Of Black Folk*, W.E.B. DuBois explains the structure of the Bureau as an arm of the government which was created to last for only one year after the Civil War. The Bureau was to

supervise and manage all abandoned lands and issue
food and clothing to the destitute war refugees. The
abandoned Southern property was to eventually be
divided up into 40 acre parcels and sold or leased to
the ex-slaves. The Bureau set up refugee and relief
stations and in fifty months, twenty-one million free
rations were distributed at a cost of more than four
million dollars, DuBois reported. The Bureau could
be said to be the government's first Welfare system.

Sojourner Truth, in a speech to freedmen
living in refugee camps in Washington, D.C., warned
them that by living perpetually on free government
rations, they were in danger of losing themselves to
another form of slavery. She campaigned heavily for
the resettlement of freedmen on the land out west,
claiming that the government should offer this land
as a way of repaying blacks for their centuries of free
labor. Some freedmen took up this challenge, and
headed west, settling in areas now known as Nevada,
Texas, Arizona, and California.

Supposedly the Freedmen's Bureau was
designed to help the freedmen make a transition
from slave labor to paid labor. But the vague,
unstructured, underfinanced Bureau failed in its aim
to bring about the long awaited economic justice.
DuBois explains:

*First, thirty thousand black men were
transported from the refuges and relief stations back
to the farms, back to the critical trial of a new way of
working. Plain instructions went out from
Washington: the laborers must be free to choose their
employers, no fixed rate of wages was prescribed, and
there was to be no forced labor ...*

*But the vision of "forty acres and a mule" -- the
righteous and reasonable ambition to become a*

landowner, which the nation had all but categorically
promised the freedmen -- was destined in most cases
to bitter disappointment. (p. 69, 70)

In most cases, the abandoned southern land,
confiscated by the government, remained in the
hands of the government. Some land was leased out
to former slaves, and the government made big
profits off of the rental fees it received from blacks.
But the promised forty acres and a mule per
freedman never did materialize.

Southern plantation owners, dependent upon
cotton, tobacco and other crops for the survival of
their farms, still needed a large labor pool to keep
their businesses going. These former slaveholders
were determined to perpetuate slavery, just under
another name. A few freedmen had tools and capital
with which to buy and work the land independently.
But most black farmers, beginning with nothing,
worked the land under the sharecropping system.
Basically, this meant that the farmer would borrow
tools and seed against the proceeds of his crop, in
exchange for a parcel of land on which to live and
work. Half of the crop went to the landowner, the
other half was kept by the farmer.

In theory, this system may have seemed
workable. But, according to the landowner's
mathematics, the sharecropper started out in debt,
and his crop never quite paid the debt he owed -- in
fact, the debt grew deeper and deeper each year,
until he was forced to stay on the land and work, if
for nothing else, just to pay his debts. Many poor
sharecroppers desired to leave in order to escape
payment of farming debts. Law enforcers (who were
sometimes also members of the Klan or other white
citizens groups) were often violent in retrieving those

who attempted to leave the south. After all, without abundant black labor to work the land, the white landowner's wealth would disappear.

The same terrorist tactics used to subdue Africans for labor in the fields, coal mines and diamond mines, were also used to frighten African Americans back into the fields (and in some states, like West Virginia, into the coal mines). Jackson stated that blacks could be jailed for "vagrancy" if they didn't have a job, or could be fined for being late to work or for quitting a job. Frequent lynchings, burnings, and beatings served to remind blacks that whites were still in control.

If caught trying to escape, a man could be thrown in jail, or even lynched. The sharecropper's condition still exists in many remote parts of the south. One Chicago resident, Mr. Karim, recalls how his family, in 1950 had to sneak away from the Mississippi farm where they were sharecroppers:

"We packed up everything we could in the car, and said we were just going to visit some relatives. We left everything in the house -- the furniture, the supplies, everything -- and drove away, in the opposite direction from the road which led out of town. This was to throw them off. We drove a long way out of the way, just so they wouldn't suspect we were leaving town and come after us."

Forced to leave valuable possessions behind in order to evade patrollers, the family arrived in the north with practically nothing, and had to start all over. Often, such a secret escape was the only way a black sharecropping family could break the never-ending cycle of debt to white landowners.

CREATION OF THE NORTHERN GHETTOS

At the turn of the century, the steady exodus of black farmers to the northern cities was usually prompted by the promise of racial equality and better jobs. But the North was not the promised land of prosperity they expected. Segregation laws and practices were designed to keep blacks out of economic competition with whites. African-American blacksmiths, bricklayers, cabinet makers, painters, and other skilled workers met with stiff opposition from white artisans wherever they sought employment. In many instances, white opposition to black skilled labor led to violence, in the North as well as in the South. Allan Spear, in his book *Black Chicago, The Making of a Negro Ghetto 1890-1920*, examines how a restricted job market created a permanent poor class of urban blacks:

Chicago Negroes in the early twentieth century were confined to the domestic and personal service trades and were unable to gain even a foothold in industry and commerce ... Over 45 per cent of the employed Negro men worked in just four occupations -- as porters, servants, waiters, and janitors -- over 63 per cent of the women were domestic servants or laundresses ... Relatively few Negroes could be found in the legal, medical, and teaching professions ... (pp. 29, 31)

Restricted to a lower income bracket, the next challenge blacks faced was to obtain decent housing. As black immigration to northern cities increased, efforts were made to contain them into the designated "black areas." Spears states that black families moving into all-white neighborhoods often

met with violence from neighbors. This forced blacks
to stay within certain neighborhood boundaries. Real
estate agents took advantage of the conditions which
limited the housing choices for blacks.   They
frequently   converted   buildings   in   marginal
neighborhoods from white to black and demanded
rents 10 to 15 percent higher than had been paid by
white tenants.   African Americans, hired in the
lowest paying jobs, and forced to pay more for
housing, were locked into another cycle of debt,
almost as bad as the sharecropping system.

THE RISE OF BLACK-OWNED BUSINESSES

There seemed to be only one other method
African Americans could achieve the "American
Dream" and break the forced cycle of poverty: Go into
business.   Tuskegee Institute, under the powerful
leadership of Booker T. Washington, provided a
means for blacks to learn trades which could give
them skills to earn an independent living. Many
followed the Washington philosophy of self help and
came North seeking their fortune.

In many cases, white discrimination was a
strong motivating factor in establishing black-owned
businesses. Segregation laws kept blacks out of
certain neighborhoods where theaters, dance halls,
and other amusements were located. Often, some
stores would not serve black customers.   This
presented a number of opportunities for the black
entrepreneur.

Jesse Binga, a successful real estate agent,
used the money he made in the real estate business
to launch the Binga Bank in 1908, the first black-
owned financial institution in Chicago. Sandy Trice
opened a small clothing store as a sideline while

working as a porter for the Illinois Central Railroad, and eventually was able to put in a complete line of men's, women's and children's clothing. Anthony Overton, a lawyer and former municipal court judge, established Overton's Hygienic Manufacturing Company in Kansas City in 1898. He manufactured baking supplies, then entered the cosmetic industry and introduced a brand of face powder for black women. Madame C.J. Walker had developed the first successful hair-straightening preparation in 1905, and by the eve of World War I, she was a millionaire with a large factory in Indianapolis. Robert Abbott founded the Chicago Defender newspaper in 1905, which soon became one of the largest black-owned businesses in the country.

But these successes were not without some severe struggle. Spears observes how a strong philosophy of racial unity helped some of the early black-owned businesses:

> *Such individual Negro business ventures as Binga's real estate and banking operations, Trice's store, Overton's factory, and Abbott's newspaper had strong ties with the Negro business philosophy. They all tried consciously to secure Negro customers by emphasizing the importance of their enterprises to the cause of race advancement. In the case of Overton and Abbott, the businesses were geared to special Negro needs. (pp. 115)*

Today, blacks watch as immigrants enter the country in droves and set up businesses, often within the heart of the African American community, and enjoy much success. However African-American neighborhood businesses struggle and fail repeatedly. Why is this happening?

When Irish, Polish, Italians, Arabs, Chinese, and Koreans immigrate to America, they come bringing a merchant tradition, and often ties to a mother country where the import and sale of goods can bring some measure of wealth. African Americans, having lost or sold most of the land previously owned in the south when the families moved north, have no direct connections with farms which could supply produce for resale in northern grocery stores. They end up having to buy produce from whites, at higher prices than their white competitors, because they cannot purchase food in the larger bulk quantities. And while white multinational corporations control the land and industry in Africa, African Americans have no direct links to African manufacturers who could ship large supplies of items to African American retail stores.

The black would-be entrepreneur must overcome many obstacles when entering the business arena. The first obstacle, and usually the main cause for business failure, is lack of financial backing. The second obstacle is lack of knowledge about business. "Business," many black professionals have been trained to think, is all of the pomp and importance of the white corporate world: clean shaven faces, three-piece suits and leather briefcases. Blacks miss many financial opportunities by not recognizing business as the simple sale of goods and services. As Carter G. Woodson states in *The Miseducation Of The Negro:*

In the schools of business administration Negroes are trained exclusively in the psychology and economics of Wall Street and are, therefore, made to despise the opportunities to run ice wagons, push banana carts, and sell peanuts among their own people. Foreigners, who have not studied economics

but have studied Negroes, take up this business and
grow rich. (p. 5)

Those who become financially secure in
corporate jobs will rarely venture out into the arena
of business, though such entrepreneurs are sorely
needed.   Going into business means organizing
financial resources, developing production systems,
managing employees -- it is all made to seem so
difficult and complicated to the black worker.

Some African Americans, not wanting the
burden of added responsibility, often refuse
opportunities to move up into management positions
in the companies where they work. They don't see
such opportunities, as a chance to observe business
management in action, and to develop the
supervisory skills needed to operate a successful
business. In some industries, the long-time practice
of racial discrimination in hiring and promotions
actually has some blacks convinced that they are not
competent enough to handle certain jobs. They may
even tend to judge all blacks in authority as less
competent than whites in authority.

Do you perhaps subconsciously believe yourself
to be automatically less competent than whites?

Consider your answer to Psychic Trauma Test
question Number 9: "I hesitate to take on certain
professional responsibilities because I don't believe I
have the ability to master them."

If you strongly agree, agree, or are unsure, you
may be responsible for a large part of your lack of
economic progress. Many blacks have been
conditioned to be dependent upon white authority.
They become content to let whites remain in
authority over them, controlling all of the decisions
regarding their livelihood. But when decisions are

made by owners and management to close plants and move abroad, or to rearrange certain departments and lay off workers, blacks realize how helpless and out of control they are regarding their own economic survival. They have allowed themselves to become totally dependent upon whites for their survival.

Many African Americans today suffer the crippling effects of psychological dependency, so much so that they don't even try to learn ways of supporting themselves. Are you also suffering from a fear of independence? Consider your answer to Psychic Trauma Test question Number 10: "If I were suddenly to lose my present means of employment, I think I would have great difficulty surviving."

If you strongly agree, agree, or are perhaps unsure, then perhaps you have placed unnecessary limitations on your own capabilities. Ask yourself why you cannot develop strategies for self employment. Stop and think of simple things many people do in order to make a living, which you could also do, should you lose your present job.

SELF HELP AND CONSUMER CONSCIOUSNESS

Blacks, once refused service at white owned department stores and restaurants, now flock to such places as an expression of triumph over racial discrimination. But the Civil Rights protesters of the 1940s, '50s, and '60s sent the wrong signals to a new generation of black consumers. Now money is spent without the slightest consciousness of its power to make others wealthy.

Money has become a means to buy status. Expensive clothing created by European designers and expensive foreign cars represent wealth and success for those who can purchase them. Such spending choices are a reflection of the philosophy that Europeans possess some type of cultural superiority. African Americans have been conditioned by the mass media to believe this philosophy as well. African Americans spend money in support of Europe in everything from clothing to automobiles to international travel.

Do your cultural values reflect a belief in European superiority? Look at your answer to Psychic Trauma Test question Number 19: "When I consider travelling abroad to become more "cultured," my first choice is a place in Europe such as Paris or London, rather than a place in Africa."

If you answered strongly agree, agree, or even unsure, you possibly tend to see Europeans as culturally superior. As a result, you may value goods and services produced by Europeans more than those produced by Africans, and may be willing to spend more money for items made or sold by Europeans.

Consider your current shopping habits. Many blacks will go out of their way to spend money at wealthy predominantly white suburban shopping malls rather than buy food and clothes from inner city black-owned stores. Do you tend to seek out African-American owned establishments, or do you tend to avoid them, believing them to be inferior? (Remember the old joke about why blacks don't support blacks in business? "The white man's ice is colder.")

How is it that African Americans spend $300 billion a year, possessing the economic power equal to that of the ninth largest nation in the world, and yet, collectively, they control so little? Blacks in America have been conditioned to use money for individual gain rather than as a tool for collective economic power.

Many immigrants who come to America seeking financial success speak little English, have no college degree, and own no property with which to secure a bank loan. Yet, they set up small grocery stores and shops within black communities and succeed. How are they financed?

They used the same system used by the Sonninkes and others who sought economic self reliance, Cooperation between families. It's an ancient custom which works, regardless of who employs it.

In the early 1990s, major U.S. cities erupted with protests aimed at Korean merchants who were accused of being "rude" to African-American customers. The stores, mostly located in predominantly black communities, were accused of not hiring enough blacks, and were threatened with boycotts by irate black consumers.

But this is not the answer, insists many economic self-help advocates. Rather than begging others for jobs, African Americans must become economically self sufficient enough to create their own businesses. As nationally syndicated columnist and television producer Tony Brown observes in a column published in the March 28, 1992 edition of *The International Sun* newspaper:

> *The popular Black misconception ... is that this economic progress is the result of a mixture of discrimination by banks against Blacks and the same banks' willingness to make loans to Koreans...*
> *Koreans don't get money from banks when they're starting out. They first work for another Korean and borrow from other Koreans when they're ready to open their own store. Their Confucian*

morality tells Koreans to refuse welfare and to consider themselves one big family.

Therefore, they depend on the group for help -- in this case, something called a "Kae" (Black West Indians call their informal bank a "Su Su"). Every month, for example, 14 Koreans put $1,000 into a pool which then goes to the member which needs it most...

It is the culture of the Koreans -- a form of social capital -- that is making them successful -- not white banks or the U.S. government (and it suggests a dependency syndrome among the blacks who believe it).

The real frustration for blacks, I believe, comes from knowing that we should be doing what the Koreans are doing, but are too psychologically damaged by racism to do it.

The solution is to compete with the Koreans and everyone else -- fruit and vegetable stand for fruit and vegetable stand. For financial capital, we can pool our black money.

The answer is clear. However, the reality is that African Americans have no real models of such cooperation to emulate. Black business owners tend to model themselves after the unscrupulous white business owner. As author George Subira points out in his book *Black Folks Guide To Business Success,* blacks will often spend a lot of money on the images of success -- the shiny new car, the extravagantly furnished office -- striving to impress others with the appearance of wealth and importance. But as for knowledge on how to manage money, train employees, produce a better product -- many entrepreneurs appear to be woefully lacking.

12C
Advertising Black Images Abroad
This picture, distributed on flyers by angry black protesters, shows the logo of a brand of toothpaste by the Colgate-Palmolive company which was marketed primarily in Asian countries. Protests by African Americans in 1990, spearheaded by Congresswoman Cardiss Collins of Illinois, caused Colgate-Palmolive company officials to promise to remove "Darkie Toothpaste" from the shelves. The only thing they did, however, was rename it "Darlie Toothpaste." Such international promotion of stereotypical images have perhaps contributed to the negative attitudes expressed by many immigrants toward African Americans. (Courtesy of the DuSable Museum of African American History file, Chicago, IL)

African Americans observe and admire the success of unethical business owners who use ruthless, cutthroat tactics. After observing this, their objective becomes not to offer the best quality product or service at the best price, but to "get over" on as many people as possible. "Get the money" seems to often be the main goal, not to make sure the customer is satisfied.

Subira also notes that many times the family is not in harmony about whether to go into business. The wife may object to the husband's ambitions out of fear that he will fail and plunge the family into financial ruin. The husband, on the other hand, may object to the wife's ambitions out of fear that she may *succeed* and outgrow him in the process. So, with this state of affairs, not only can families not cooperate with other families to build neighborhood businesses; members of one family often cannot even get together and cooperate to build one business.

Again, we come back to the core of the problem and the key to the solution: The family.

If families can work collectively to develop and support independent business enterprises, these businesses can provide a solution to the chronic joblessness in African American communities. Without such cooperation, neighborhoods will fall prey to the growing menace of drugs and crime that is sweeping the nation. Through the underground economy, where the drug traffic flourishes, many black men and women manage to survive. Unless community members create legitimate businesses, those who participate in the drug business will meet their eventual fate:

Drug addiction ... death ... or prison, which has become the new slave system.

ACTIVITY:
Create A Money Loop

African Americans can create economically strong communities by being conscious about their spending habits. A money loop is created when the dollars spent are recirculated in the form of local employment or support of neighborhood business and organizations. If you are employed outside of your community, if you are employed within your community, if you are unemployed and living on a fixed income, if you are self employed or if you own a business, try this for the next seven days:

1.   Consciously keep track of every dollar you spend.   Before you make a purchase in any establishment, answer the following questions:

   a. Is the place owned by an African American?

   b. Does the owner employ African Americans?

   c. Does the owner live in your neighborhood?

   d. Do the owner's employees live in your neighborhood?

   e. Does the owner do business with African Americans, such as advertising in black newspapers or buying supplies from black merchants?

   f. If you are self employed, or own a business, or periodically sell items to raise funds for other causes, does the owner buy your products or services?

2.   Try to only spend money at places where you can answer Yes to at least one of the questions. At the end of seven days, determine how much of your money was spent with people who help circulate the money back into your community.

CHAPTER THIRTEEN
Prison: The New Slave System

13A

Joseph Cinque

The son of an African King, Joseph Cinque led an uprising on a slave ship bound for the Americas. Upon reaching American shores, he was captured and put on trial. Cinque was so majestic and eloquent that although his captors did not understand his language, the emotion behind his words and the power of his presence convinced them that this man did not belong in slavery. (Photo courtesy of DuSable Museum of African American History file, Chicago, Illinois.)

CHAPTER THIRTEEN:
Prison: The New Slave System

While crime and punishment is as old as mankind, imprisonment is not a universally accepted means of punishing criminals.

In many African societies, one convicted of theft or destruction of a neighbor's property may be ordered to repay the neighbor, in money or goods, the amount of the property's worth. In the case of more severe crimes, the penalty might be enslavement for life or for a period of years, until the guilty party has worked enough to pay off the debt to the offended party. In some cases, if the crime was particularly heinous, such as murder, the penalty might be death. But, placing a human being in a cage would be considered cruel according to many African cultures. In the case of war where those captured in battle were sentenced to slavery, they might be in servitude to someone in the conquering nation, or they might be sold to another nation.

GUNS AND WHISKEY BUY PRISONERS

In the sixteenth century, various factions of the Moorish empire were embroiled in a bitter power struggle, and Songhay was being attacked by rival forces from inside and outside the empire. The united kingdom of west Africa gradually disintegrated. As each rival African faction fought for control of territories, the Europeans from Portugal, Spain, France and England offered the Africans new, sophisticated weapons in exchange for black slaves. Each side, hoping to outmaneuver rivals with better weapons, eagerly sold off their prisoners of war. Perhaps it seemed like a good political decision at the time. The nation received superior weapons, and got rid of its enemies all in one trade agreement.

In addition to the guns, strong alcoholic drink was sold by the barrel. Many Africans, not used to the overwhelming intoxicating effects of hard liquor, soon became addicted to alcohol and the whiskey came to have nearly as much value in slave trading negotiations as the guns.

No more prisoners of war? But the army needed more weapons. The people needed whiskey. Slaves must be found from somewhere.

And so the kidnappings began.

Often the smaller villages on the outskirts of the cities were targeted. A strong young man or woman, having the misfortune to wander away into the woods alone, might quickly be nabbed by a group of "slatees," men hired by Europeans to assist in the capture and transfer of slaves to the border. After being captured and tied up, the slaves were then chained together and marched to the shores, where the various trading companies had built holding pens, where the slaves were kept until the slave ships were ready to load up and sail away.

These pens, made of concrete with steel bars, could be considered the introduction of Africans to the European prison system.

THE SLAVE PATROLLERS: AMERICA'S FIRST POLICE

America's police patrol actually grew out of the slave patrol system of the south. Up until that time, justice was administered by local sheriffs and deputies. After the Revolutionary War, most states developed some type of militia, in case armed soldiers were needed for national defense. But the institution

of slavery required that some type of organized law
enforcement would have to be instituted on a regular
basis, to protect white slave owners against massive
uprisings or escapes. In *From Slavery To Freedom,*
Franklin describes how the slave patrols worked:

> *One of the devices set up to enforce the Slave
> Codes and thereby maintain the institution of slavery
> was the patrol, which has been aptly described as an
> adaptation of the militia.   Counties were usually
> divided into "beats" or areas of patrol, and free white
> men were called upon to serve for a stated period of
> time, one, three, or six months. These patrols were to
> apprehend slaves out of place and return them to their
> masters or commit them to jail; to visit slave quarters
> and search for various kinds of weapons that might
> be used in an uprising; and to visit assemblies of
> slaves where disorder might develop or where
> conspiracy might be planned. (p. 142)*

The patrol system literally gave every white
person authority over every black person, whether
the black person was slave or free.

JOSEPH CINQUE AND DRED SCOTT

In 1839, Joseph Cinque, an African prince, was
kidnapped and placed aboard a ship called the
Amistad, along with 52 other blacks, to be brought to
Havana, Cuba. During the journey, they organized a
revolt and, killed the captain and the entire crew,
except for two men. They seized control of the ship
and Cinque ordered the two white crew men, Ruiz
and Montez, to sail back toward Africa. However the
two men managed to secretly steer the ship toward
America. The ship was sighted off Long Island. The

mutineers, along with their leader, Cinque, were captured and taken to port in Connecticut, where the blacks were put in prison.

Although Cinque knew no English, he spoke in his own defense at his trial, in his own language, the Mendi language. He was so eloquent, the judge was moved to free him and the other blacks so that they could return to Africa.

This case raised the question: If an African was captured to be sold into slavery, but escaped to free territory, was he still legally a slave?

Soon after, the famous Dred Scott decision answered this question. Scott, a young slave from Missouri, traveled to Illinois with his master. Years later, while the two still lived in free territory, Scott's master died. He left his estate, including Scott, in the hands of his wife. Scott insisted that his residence in a free state made him a free man and he was no longer a slave.

Scott brought a lawsuit against his master's wife, and in a widely publicized case, the Supreme Court ruled that Scott was to remain in slavery, even though he had become a free man. The court ruled that "A black man has no rights a white man is bound to respect."

WRETCHED REFUGEES OF WAR

The year was 1867. The war between the North and the South was over, and now Washington D.C., the nation's capital, was overrun with homeless black refugees.

Sojourner Truth, fiery champion for the abolition of slavery, had served in the Union army as a nurse, tending to soldiers wounded in battle. Now that the war was over, and freedom had been won,

Sojourner, now in her 70s, had a new cause to champion: The rights of the freedmen. She recognized that poverty, crime and jail would become a neverending cycle for these children of slavery, unless they obtained proper homes, education, and training for some type of employment. She spoke to audiences throughout the north and south, charging that the country which gained its wealth from free slave labor now had a responsibility to train, educate and employ those left homeless and without a way to earn a living. In *Narrative of Sojourner Truth*, an article from a New Jersey paper reports on a speech she made in Orange, New Jersey in 1874:

> She spoke of the misery and degradation she had seen among the colored people in the South, of the Black Maria full of them driving up to the Washington police court, of their being thrown into jails, and of their children growing up in vice and ignorance, and said that it was a shame and an abomination ... She had heard it said that these evils would die out in time, but they would not die out, "they must be learned out." ... She lectured four years on this matter, and had got up a petition to Congress to set aside a portion of the public lands in the West, and put buildings thereon for a home for the destitute. (p. 191)

Despite sizable support for this drive, the government insisted that such a plan could not be done. Many blacks who did go west had to fight both the white vigilante groups, who were determined to force them back to the southern plantations to serve as laborers, and the big railroad companies, who sought control over major western territories.

CHAIN GANGS PROVIDE FREE LABOR

As the United States citizenry continued to move westward, more efficient transportation systems were needed. The labor force used to build roads and railroads across the country often came from within the prisons.

The American prison system actually has its roots in medieval Europe, where those convicted of crimes were locked in dungeons and subjected to public torture.

In his book, *Discipline and Punishment: The Birth of The Prisons,* author Michel Foucault describes how convicts in many European countries were subjected to public floggings, burnings, and hangings, in much the same fashion as American slaves. He notes how the "chain gang" became an extension of the practice of making a public spectacle of prisoners:

The use of prisoners in public works, cleaning city streets or repairing the highways, was practiced in Austria, Switzerland, and certain areas of the United States, such as Pennsylvania. These convicts, distinguished by their 'infamous dress' and shaven heads, 'were brought before the public. The sport of the idle and the vicious, they often became incensed, and naturally took violent revenge upon the aggressors. To prevent them from returning injuries which might be inflicted on them, they were encumbered with iron collars and chains to which bombshells were attached, to be dragged along while they performed their degrading service, under the eyes of keepers armed with swords, blunderbusses and other weapons of destruction' (Roberts Vaux, Nocies, 21, quoted in Teeters, 1937, 24). (p. 8)

In America, in the late 1800s, a black man who dared to speak out in defense of his rights or dared to fight back when physically attacked by whites was considered "dangerous" by the local white population. Many such men found themselves falsely accused and jailed on trumped up charges, then later sentenced to the prison chain gangs, where they provided free labor to railroad companies.

BLACKS UNDER MARTIAL LAW

A 1991 study of the black population in Washington D.C. revealed that every black male born in America will, at some point in life, have a confrontation with police. The study, conducted by the National Center on Institutions and Alternatives and published in the *New York Times* newspaper, concluded that almost half of all Black men between the ages of 18 and 35 in that city "were enmeshed in the criminal justice system on any given day last year." The study noted that as many as 70 percent of Black men in Washington are arrested by the time they turn 35 and about 85 percent are arrested at some point in their lives. According to the *New York Times* article:

> *The report found that on an average day 21,800 of the District's 53,377 young Black men were involved with the criminal justice system. Of those, 7,800 were in jail or in prison, 6,000 were on local probation, 3,700 were on local parole, and 1,300 were on Federal probation or parole.*
> *The report estimated that 3,000 more were awaiting trial, on bond or being pursued on felony or misdemeanor warrants.*

13B
Runaway Osman
Defiant slaves, such as this one, Osman of Virginia, managed to escape and lived as fugitives in the woods and swamps. Even after slavery, defiant black men often found themselves running from law enforcers to avoid lynching or imprisonment and forced labor on a chain gang. "Osman" was also the name of the Turkish leader and founder of the Ottoman Empire in the fourteenth century. The name Osman could possibly indicate that the slave was an ancestor of one of the many Africans who were involved in the shaping of the Ottoman Empire. (Reprinted from African Muslims in Antebellum America by Allan D. Austin. Copyright 1984 by Garland Publishing Company.)

Across the country, conditions appear to be the same for black men. Police regularly stop black motorists, particularly young male black motorists, demanding to see a "driver's license" with the same threatening air of authority as the old slave patrollers demanded to see "passes" of blacks traveling down the road. (In South Africa, under the Apartheid system, blacks still are harassed by white patrol officers who demand to see their "pass.")

History has demonstrated all too often that a white police officer can verbally abuse, physically assault, and even kill a black person with impunity. Because of upsetting personal encounters, many blacks automatically respond with fear and dread when confronted by a white law enforcement officer.

Have you also been conditioned to fear white law officers? Look at your answer to Psychic Trauma Test question Number 3: "When stopped by white police officers in traffic, I feel fearful."

If you strongly agree, agree, or are unsure, then you possibly have a subconscious belief that white police officers have the power (and the desire) to harm you. The videotaped beatings of Los Angeles motorist Rodney King in 1991 reinforced this fear for many blacks. In an article in the May 1993 issue of *Emerge* magazine entitled, "Have Police Declared War On Blacks?" author Joe Davidson writes:

> *Police brutality is a national problem that seldom gets the attention of the Rodney King incident in Los Angeles ... A nationwide study by Gannett News Service last year showed that cops accused of brutality get promoted more often than punished. (pp. 27, 28)*

Hiring more black police officers sometimes

eliminates racial confrontations, but does not always solve the problem of police corruption. Violent confrontations with police are not always racially motivated, since many black officers have been accused of using the same kinds of abusive tactics as their white counterparts.

To avoid police abuse while driving on the road, if signalled by a police officer to pull over, always drive to a well-lit area where there are people around who can act as witnesses. Ask to see the officer's I.D. This is your right as a citizen, and lets the officer know you intend to hold him or her accountable for any improper actions. Always have a paper and pen handy and clearly write down the officer's license number, name, and badge number. Be polite and cooperative. If verbally or physically abused, file a complaint with all disciplinary agencies and any citizens' rights organizations. This action not only ensures that the officer's behavior is on file and can be used as evidence in any future lawsuits; it also protects your self esteem and removes feelings of fear and helplessness. If law enforcement agencies are ever to gain the public's trust, corrupt officers must be identified and removed.

THE DRUG TRAP: PASSPORT TO PRISON

The Washington D.C. study was alarming enough, and only included men. There is also a vast number of women entangled in the justice system, arrested for everything from violent crime to prostitution. Those convicted and sentenced to prison are getting younger and younger, notes Bertina Lampkin, trial judge in Chicago's Night Narcotics Court. In a March 1992 interview, she pointed out that the problem stems from the family.

*I've worked in over 15 different courtrooms.
I've resolved over 3,000 felony cases in the last two
and a half years. I saw that in a lot of cases, the
parents simply were not there. The children were
raising themselves. When you see your seventeen year
old son park a new car in front of your house and you
know he doesn't have a job, you don't think anything
about it? These parents know what's going on. They
just don't care.*

Parents who stay high on drugs or alcohol
themselves, or are perpetually absent, lay the
foundation for delinquent children. And when a
young drug trafficker is making enough money to pay
the household bills, it becomes a difficult situation to
fight. Judge Lampkin said she often handles up to
500 cases a night. It's the same scenario, over and
over again -- a youth arrested for sale or possession
of illegal drugs.

How does one get into the drug trap in the
first place? A 1989 interview with one former drug
dealer, referred to as "Lady M," gives an inside look
on how drug sellers and users become entangled in a
neverending cycle. "Lady M" recalls how, as a young
woman in her late teens, she migrated from the
south with her family in the 1950s. In the northern
city, she got involved with a fast crowd. Soon she
met what seemed to be a sophisticated older woman,
who offered her a job of "running errands":

*The system that they use to get a young woman
involved in dealing drugs would be to have an older
woman spoil you with money. Then she would bring
you into what the dealers and the players called, "The
Stable." Usually a man was head of the stable and
women worked as recruiters.*

A year later, I was so good at my job, the head of the stable, I'll call him "Mr. Big," called me in and gave me my own dope business. I didn't know what to do with the dope because all I had done was drop packages off and collect money.

So, I contacted my brother, who had been using drugs. He showed me how to bag it, cut it up, and distribute it. The money was fantastic.

In 1954 I got busted, and slick lawyers and bondsmen took all my money to get me out of jail. By this time, I must have been doing about a half million dollars in business a year. This was a lot of money for a woman at that time. But after I paid them to get me out of jail, I was broke again.

Out of money and having no other job prospects, "Lady M" got out of jail and went back to her old employer. Soon she was back in business, traveling across the country and earning even more money than before. However, one year later, she was arrested again, on federal drug trafficking charges, and sentenced to ten years in prison.

Four years later, with a federal prison record and no marketable skills, she was released from jail. Having no luck in the job market, she turned back to the only sure way she knew to earn a living: selling drugs. From 1959 to 1968 she handled millions of dollars as a cocaine dealer, selling mostly to doctors, lawyers, big businessowners, entertainers, politicians and policemen. Eventually she became addicted herself, was arrested again and sentenced to fifteen years in federal prison. After seven years, she was released, only to wind up again in the drug business. She stated that the drug trafficking business had escalated during the period she was in jail. She noted that it had become an open market, where anybody could get into the business. Once she resumed her career as a dealer, the cycle of police arrests and paying lawyers to get her out of jail began again. Over a twelve year period, she had lost all the money and property she once owned.

"Lady M" checked into a drug abuse treatment center and managed to dry herself out. She later opened a legitimate business and began the slow process of self reformation. Her bitter thirty five year experience serves as an example of how, for those on the bottom, the drug business eventually leads to prison, and a cycle of rags to riches to rags again.

Although officials lament the spread of drugs, it is now an integral part of the American economy. Consider who gets paid:

The farmer, the drug processor, the packager, the distributor and the dealer, all who make money from the sale of the product. Then there are the gun dealers, car dealers, pager companies, clothing store owners, jewelry store owners, and property owners, who benefit from the ready cash that the drug dealers have to spend for all the high status items that have become the symbols of their trade.

And then the government law enforcement officials, such as the police, undercover detectives, and jail prison guards, plus the lawyers and judges make money from the ongoing arrests, prosecution and imprisonment of all those involved in the drug business. Pawn shops provide a means for the desperate drug addict to get quick money from stolen goods. And last but not least, the banks can certainly appreciate the cash flow from this underground economy. Those at the top of the business, the people who control the land, the shipping companies, and the chemical processing plants, are rarely snatched from their cars, handcuffed, and dragged off to jail by police. This seems to only happen to the small dealer, who is publicly arrested, jailed, and sentenced, in order to give the appearance of a "war on drugs."

HOUSING PROJECTS: PREPARATION FOR JAIL

Although many institutions profit from the menace of drugs and crime, in order to keep it from destroying white America, it must be contained within the black community ... which itself must be contained, in order to be controlled.

In 1945, the 79th Congress' Subcommittee on Urban Affairs of the Joint Committee issued a report which helped resolve such a problem. The Joint Committee studied ways that black people could be contained in crowded living conditions and not spread out into the surrounding white community. Their conclusion, published in a pamphlet entitled, "Urban America Goals and Problems" states:

The main problem for us with the "enclaves" as it is now placed in the "Sinks" is that its size is limited. When the Negro population increases at a rate the enclaves is unable to convert them -- only two choices remain:
1) Territorial Growth (more land) or
2) Overcrowding
Apart from letting "sinks" run its course "more land" and destroy the city, there is an alternative solution:
Prepack or introduce design features that will counteract out undesired effects of the sink. But most important not destroy the enclave in the process.

A study by pathologist Charles Southwick discovered that peromyscus mice could tolerate high cage densities.

To increase density in a rat population and maintain healthy specimen:
(a) Put them in boxes so they can't see each
(b) Clean their cages
(c) and give them enough to eat.

Then you can pile them in boxes up as many stories as you wish.

And thus, the housing projects were born, and spread throughout the country. The report continues:

The creation of such ideas; principles will require the combined efforts of many diverse specialists all working secretly, closely together on a massive scale. "Coterie of Experts: City Planners, Architects, Engineers of all types, Economists, Law Enforcement Specialists, Traffic, Transportation Experts, Educators, Lawyers, Social Workers, Political Scientists, Psychologists, Anthropologists, Ethologists, and Preachers. As we know, "some of the most capable help is Negro enclave specialists, hire as many as you can and keep contact. In their presence don't talk, listen and let them talk. Remember it is important to learn about them in order to forward the desired effects. It is absolutely essential to us that we learn more about how to compute the maximum, the minimum and the density of the Negro enclaves that make up our cities. Through the process of taming, most higher organisms, including Negro men can be squeezed into a given area, provided that they constantly have a minimum amount of food provided for them, that they are made to feel safe, and their aggressions are under control.

This committee report exposes an obvious truth: the overcrowded, violent, drug-infested black community is the consequence of a carefully laid-out plan to contain and control black people.

Committee members listed on this published report are: *Joint Economic Committee:* Wright Patman, Texas, Vice Chairman; William Proxmire, Wisconsin, Chairman. *House of Representatives:* W.E. Brock, Tenn.; Donald Rumsfeld, Ill.; William B. Widnall, New Jersey; Thomas B. Curtis, Mo.; Martha W. Griffiths, Mich.; William S. Moorhead, Penn.; Henry S. Reuss, Wis.; Hale Boggs, La.; Richard Bolling, Mo. *Senate:* John Sparkman, Ala.; Charles H. Percy, Ill.; Jacob K. Javits, N.Y.; Len B. Jordan, Idaho; Jack Miller, Ia.; Abraham Ribicoff, Conn.; Stuart Symington, Mo.; Herman E. Talmadge, Ga.; J.W. Fulbright, Ark. James W. Knowles, Director of Research; John R. Stark, Executive Director. Economists: Donald A. Webster (Minority); George R. Iden; John B. Henderson; William H. Moore.

Carelessly designed high-rise buildings threaten the safety of small children. Many have fallen to their deaths from windows without screens or window guards, yet the serious problem is never addressed by housing authorities.

The rats in the experiment, when kept clean and well fed, remained relatively peaceful. But when deprived of food and clean conditions, they became violent. Housing project residents, financially deprived and hungry, and forced to live in filth because of poorly administered city clean-up services, not only become violent. With the aid of an abundance of sophisticated weapons of war, which somehow find their way into the housing projects, the residents even become deadly.

GUNS AND DRUGS BUILD PRISONS

The widescale availability of drugs has made it necessary for groups to fight for control of territories where drugs may be sold. And thus we have the present day urban Drug Wars. Just as Europeans sold guns and whiskey to rival African nations in return for their prisoners of war, much of the violence conducted on America's urban streets today are instigated by the sale of guns and drugs to rival street gang factions.

In an article in the May 16, 1992 edition of the *International Sun Newspaper* entitled "Society Creates And Maintains The Climate For Crime and Imprisonment," Stateville Prison inmate David Walker makes this observation:

In a society which deliberately manufactures people to be prison bound, illiterate, unemployable, destitute, and drug/alcohol induced, we can never afford the luxury of not taking the initiative in the welfare and safety of our communities. Prisons are a multi-million dollar industry in this state. They are springing up everywhere, and they employ mostly Caucasians. Again, our welfare is taken out of our hands. Prisons are strategically placed in regions predominantly Caucasian, that way no one having an interest in the people inside will be anywhere around should they decide to exterminate us.

Prison has become the new slave market, where those captured are chained by the wrists and locked behind walls of concrete and steel, to be given a new identity (a prison number), and forced to labor and languish in helpless hopelessness.

Just as African leaders of yesterday were

willing to sell their neighbors for promises of wealth and power, so are African-American leaders of today's street organizations, who strive to create a large drug addicted clientele, selling the lives of their neighbors for promises of wealth and power. And those who buy and sell drugs, creating criminals who must support expensive habits, eventually find themselves behind bars, locked up alongside those who were previously victims ... just like those who sold slaves often found themselves chained on the bottom of a slave ship.

Civic leaders speak out against crime, begging for more job programs for youth to keep them out of gangs, pleading for more police patrol of neighborhoods to cut down on violence. But seldom is the question asked, or answered: Where are these young people getting the guns and the drugs?

Certainly major shipments of processed drugs and sophisticated weaponry could not enter the country and circulate throughout major urban centers without the knowledge of top government officials. The drug problem is by no means confined to any one race. But despite all the signs that this is an industry controlled by big business, the mass media continues to place bulk of the blame on the shoulders of poor urban blacks.

WORDS FROM BEHIND THE WALL

Prisons were made to punish, not rehabilitate. However, in spite of this major flaw, prison provides something that many an inmate needs for self reformation, but can never find in the fast-paced day-to-day struggle for survival.

In prison, one has time to think.

Some great leaders have emerged from behind

walls of concrete and steel, after years of study, reflection, and soul searching. The light of political consciousness is often turned on inside a dark jail cell. Many a spiritual rebirth has taken place after years of enduring the hell of incarceration.

El Hajj Malik El Shabazz (Malcolm X), in his autobiography, recalls how he became transformed in prison, simply by reading books. After reading and copying the dictionary all the way through, word for word, his vocabulary improved, and from then on, it was as if he was in a whole new world. Through books, Malcolm learned about history, politics, geography, religion, philosophy and law. His mind was sharpened by mastery of the English language, and he became a formidable debater, matching wits with America's best scholars. While reading about the Opium Wars between China and England, Malcolm discovered how governments use drug addiction as a political tool for control of the people. In his Autobiography, he reflects on the politics behind the Chinese drug problem, which led China to close its doors to the world after World War II:

When the white man professes ignorance about why the Chinese hate him so, my mind can't help flashing back to what I read, there in prison, about how the blood forebears of this same white man raped China at a time when China was trusting and helpless. Those original white "Christian traders" sent into China millions of pounds of opium. By 1839, so many of the Chinese were addicts that China's desperate government destroyed twenty thousand chests of opium. The first Opium War was promptly declared by the white man. Imagine! Declaring war upon someone who objects to being narcotized! The Chinese were severely beaten, with

Chinese invented gunpowder.

The Treaty of Nanking made China pay the British white man for the destroyed opium; forced open China's major ports to British trade; forced China to abandon Hong Kong; fixed China's import tariffs so low that cheap British articles soon flooded in, maiming China's industrial development.

After a second Opium War, the Tientsin Treaties legalized the ravaging opium trade, legalized a British-French-American control of China's customs. China tried delaying that Treaty's ratification; Peking was looted and burned.

"Kill the foreign white devils!" was the 1901 Chinese war cry in the Boxer Rebellion ...

Red China after World War II closed its doors to the Western white world. Massive Chinese agricultural, scientific, and industrial efforts are described in a book that Life magazine recently published.

Inspiration and knowledge can transform the life of any individual, either before, during, or after prison. However, the conditions which lead one to end up in prison will still exist once that person returns to the outside world. Perhaps African Americans should follow the example set by China, and somehow block the flow of drugs into their communities while taking steps to rebuild, morally, spiritually, and economically.

To really create positive change on a massive scale, leaders must be willing to expose the root of these problems and dismantle forever the system of violent exploitation which maintains a permanent underclass in America.

CHAPTER FOURTEEN
Political Leadership:
Power Strategists or
Plantation Overseers?

14A

Marcus Garvey
The father of the Black Nationalist philosophy, Jamaican born
Garvey's visionary leadership inspired many movements for
black economic independence which grew and flourished long
after his death. (Reprinted from World's Great Men of Color,
Volume II, by J.A. Rogers. Copyright 1972.)

CHAPTER FOURTEEN
Political Leadership:
Power Strategists or
Plantation Overseers?

Names like Nat Turner, Denmark Vesey, and Harriet Tubman are commonly recognized as leaders in the resistance of slavery in America by those who study black history. In Virginia in 1831, a religious mystic known as The Black Prophet, whose name was Nat, and who was owned by a Mr. Turner, organized a massive slave revolt. Nat, who had taught himself how to read, studied the Bible, fasted, and prayed, and one day declared that he was told in a vision to organize a revolt and kill all the white slavemasters. He and his followers went from plantation to plantation, killing every slaveholding family they found, and recruiting blacks at every plantation. The countryside was paralyzed with terror for thirty-six hours as the organized army of blacks stalked through the countryside, wreaking vengeance on their former masters. Finally the slave patrols got organized, and caught up with the freedom fighters. The armed slave patrol officers forced Nat and his army to scatter and hide. There was a nationwide panic during the six weeks Nat and his men were still at large. When Nat was finally captured he was given a swift trial and executed.

The rise of Nat Turner represented every slaveholder's worst nightmare. As a result, repressive laws were passed to ensure that such a widescale resistance movement could never rise again. Nat Turner's rise led to the passage of laws prohibiting teaching blacks to read and write and forbidding blacks to preach from the Bible.

Nat Turner was not the only revolutionary

who was inspired by the Bible. Ten year earlier, in 1821, a free black man living in Charleston, South Carolina, Denmark Vesey, had developed an impressively intricate strategy for a widescale revolution against slavery. Vesey read about "the oppressors" in the Old Testament and compared them to plantation slavemasters. His revolt was well planned. Unfortunately, their plans were betrayed. The leaders of the revolt were all arrested, and twenty-two of the 130 leaders were hanged. Afterward, laws against assembly of blacks were passed.

Harriet Tubman from Maryland is described in the book *Flight to Freedom* by Henrietta Buckmaster as "one of the greatest freedom fighters of them all." She smuggled some 300 men and women out of the south and into northern free states without ever being captured. The reward for her capture mounted to forty thousand dollars (a lot of money in the 1850s), but Harriet insisted she was led by God, and would never get caught. She was so adept at slipping along the woods at night unseen that during the Civil War, the Union Army employed her as a spy.

These and other rebels used the Bible and strong faith in God as inspiration to fight against oppression. Slaveowners realized that the Bible, if not carefully interpreted, could become a dangerous weapon in the hands of an educated, rebellious slave. Black leaders who worked for the liberation of slaves were always branded as criminals by slaveholders. "Good negroes" were the ones who looked out for the master's interests and reported any news about possible uprisings. They were rewarded by their masters with extra privileges and titles of authority on the plantation. If they were especially loyal, they could possibly rise to the position of Overseer.

POLITICS OR EDUCATION?

At the turn of the century, Tuskegee Institute founder Booker T. Washington rose to prominence as the premier black leader in America. His famous speech at the 1895 Atlanta Exposition indicated that blacks should be willing to concentrate on agricultural and industrial training which would prepare them to be better workers rather than to seek out political power and social equality through voting rights. Southern whites, interpreting his position as an endorsement of permanent black servitude, rallied to his support.

But a young Massachusetts-born scholar from Fisk, Harvard and Berlin universities arose to challenge the Washington philosophy. W.E.B. DuBois, who received his Doctor of Philosophy degree from Harvard, wrote numerous books and essays criticizing Washington's views.

The white journalists and writers of the time analyzed the conflict between these two men, often casting DuBois in the role of an agitator, a militant advocate for integration of the races. Washington was often portrayed as the most practical, level-headed spokesman of the two.

Many African Americans who were inspired by the words of Washington, received degrees from Tuskegee Institute and went on to buy property, build homes, and even develop successful businesses. There were also many success stories of people whose academic, professional, and artistic achievements were inspired by DuBois. Both men articulated effective strategies for African American achievement during the critical post Reconstruction period. How much more effective both men could have been if they had merely cooperated!

14B
The African Cavalry
These royal horseman, serving as a sultan's bodyguard in the Cameroons, West Africa in the early 1900s are reminiscent of the excellent Senegalese horsemen who rode in perfect unison into Cordoba, Spain for the Moorish conquest. (Reprinted from Illustrated Africa, North, Tropical, and South, by William D. Boyce, page 291, copyright 1925, Rand McNally & Company.)

MARCUS GARVEY AND BLACK NATIONALISM

Perhaps one of the most dangerous threats to white supremacy was the rise of Marcus Garvey. His vision was both local and global, and he identified the root of the problem of black powerlessness: Loss of identity and loss of economic control of Africa.

His organization, the United Negro Improvement Association (UNIA), has been described by many African American historians as the most successful Pan Africanist movement of all time. He believed that the answer to the race problem for blacks was the establishment of an independent nation in Africa, where blacks could establish political and economic control.

Garvey achieved an unprecedented measure of success. He founded a newspaper, The Negro World, to further promote his ideals. Armed with his Negro World newspaper, Garvey traveled across the country, making speeches and recruiting members into the UNIA.

By 1919, Garvey had about 30 branches in various cities, and boasted a membership of more than two million people. He then launched The Black Star Line shipping company, a major victory for the UNIA. The UNIA sold several hundred thousand shares of stock worldwide to raise money for the purchase of steamships. More than 25,000 people packed Madison Square Garden on August 1, 1920, to hear Marcus Garvey address the first International Convention of Negroes.

Garvey's fame had surpassed any black man of his time, and jealousy and envy was aroused in those who believed they had a greater right to the title of "Negro Leader." Enemies of Garvey began to sabotage his efforts.

INTEGRATION VS. SEPARATION

W.E.B. DuBois, a vocal critic of Booker T. Washington, ridiculed Marcus Garvey's "Back To Africa" plan as "bombastic and impractical."

A rash of mob violence against blacks at the turn of the century had moved DuBois to organize a group of black leaders for a strategy meeting in 1905. This group met in Niagara Falls, Canada, in June 1905 and drew up a platform for aggressive action. In *From Slavery To Freedom,* Franklin states that the group demanded freedom of speech, manhood suffrage, and the abolition of all distinctions based on race. The group, attacked by some as "radical" became known as the "Niagara Movement."

In 1909, a national conference was called by Oswald Garrison Villard, the grandson of white abolitionist William Lloyd Garrison, and in addition to a body of white citizens, outraged at the atrocities of mob violence and lynchings, members of the Niagara Movement were also invited to the conference. According to Franklin, the conference was made up of "a distinguished gathering of educators, professors, publicists, bishops, judges, and social workers." Plans were made to establish a permanent organization, and thus in 1909 the National Association for the Advancement of Colored People (NAACP), was born. It absorbed the old Niagara Movement, pledging to work for the abolition of all forced segregation, equal education for black and white children, enfranchisement of blacks, and enforcement of the fourteenth and fifteenth amendments. The following year, in May, 1910, officers were elected to the NAACP. Moorefield Storey of Boston was president and William E. Walling was chairman of the executive committee.

W.E.B. DuBois was elected director of publicity and
research. He was the only black officer.

Branded as a radical organization by many
white philanthropists, the NAACP used its
publication, the *Crisis* magazine, to speak out against
lynching and lawlessness. It filed suit in court, and
in many instances won, overturning unjust laws.
Soon the NAACP had organized branches across the
United States.

Whereas the NAACP sought full integration
and acceptance into the white mainstream, the UNIA
sought the establishment of a separate power base
for African people in America and abroad. According
to Franklin, Garvey went into action, organizing the
Universal African Legion as a military wing to drive
white settlers out of Africa. He also organized the
Black Cross Nurses, the Universal African Motor
Corps, and the Black Eagle Flying Corps.

But Marcus Garvey's global plan for economic
empowerment based on a universal concept of black
nationalism was ridiculed by many black leaders of
the time. Black newspaper publishers accused
Garvey of being an insincere, selfish imposter.
Followers of Garvey's movement were said to be of
"the most primitive and ignorant element of West
Indian and American Negroes,".whereas supporters
of the NAACP were hailed as "intelligent and
respectable."

Name calling of the most juvenile kind erupted
between DuBois and Garvey. In an article in the
February 1923 edition of *Century Magazine,* DuBois
derisively called Garvey a "little, fat, black man; ugly,
but with intelligent eyes and a big head." Garvey
tauntingly referred to DuBois as "the Mulatto." In
Philosophy and Opinions of Marcus Garvey, Garvey
is quoted as saying:

Some of us in America, the West Indies and Africa believe that the nearer we approach the white man in color the greater our social standing and privilege and that we should build up an "aristocracy" based upon caste of color and not achievement in race. It is well known, although no one is honest enough to admit it, that we have been, for the past thirty years at least, but more so now than ever, grading ourselves for social honor and distinction on the basis of color. That the average success in the race has been regulated by color and not by ability and merit; that we have been trying to get away from the pride of race into the atmosphere of color worship, to the damaging extent that the whole world has made us its laughing stock. (p. 56)

Deeper reflection by both men may have resulted in the discovery that without the removal of certain discriminatory laws, a goal which the NAACP was working on, Garvey's followers would not gain access to the training and experience in the areas needed to implement the UNIA's plans. And without an economic and political alliance with the nations of Africa, such as Garvey envisioned, in spite of higher education, African Americans would remain an isolated racial "minority," at the mercy of a dominant European American society.

RELIGION AND THE GARVEY MOVEMENT

According to Tony Martin, author of the book *Race First, The Ideological and Organizational Struggles of Marcus Garvey and The Universal Negro Improvement Association,* Garvey wrote poetry, plays and even religious hymns to reflect the black struggle for independence. At a Christmas pageant Garvey

held at Liberty Hall in Harlem, Christ was depicted
as a black child. The essence of religion for Garvey,
Martin states, was the imparting of race pride, Black
Nationalism, and self reliance. By taking this stand,
Garvey managed to eliminate religious conflicts in
the UNIA. Christians and Muslims alike joined the
UNIA, and at the 1922 UNIA convention, some
delegates suggested that the Association should adopt
Islam as its official religion, since three fourths of
blacks worldwide were Muslims.

Islam appeared to be a natural transition for
African Americans, who were seeking a religious
expression which freed them from mental and
physical bondage. Garvey seemed to understand the
necessity of a spiritual component in creating a
successful mass movement.

Garvey's position that religion must also be a
tool for liberation was a philosophy which influenced
leaders for generations to come. Even though Garvey
declined to adopt Islam as the official UNIA religion,
its publication, the *Negro World* published many
articles in favor of Islam, which influenced many
UNIA members. Even the organization's Universal
Ethiopian Hymnal, compiled by Rabbi Arnold J. Ford
(who was known as a leader of Harlem's so-called
Black Jews), contained a hymn *Allah-Hu-Ak Bar*
(Arabic for God is Great) based on African lyrics.
Martin also observes:

*Among the Muslims who established
apparently close contact with the UNIA during
Garvey's American period were adherents of the
Ahmadiyya Movement, a Muslim denomination
founded in northern India a decade or so before the
end of the nineteenth century. In 1920 Dr. Mufti
Muhammad Sadiq, a missionary from this group,*

arrived in the United States. He purchased a property at 4448 South Wabash Avenue in Chicago, part of which was converted into a mosque, and began proselytizing. By 1923 we find Sadiq among the guests on the rostrum during a Liberty Hall meeting. He had recently converted forty Garveyites in Detroit, an area of intense Ahmadiyya effort ...

The Ahmadiyya Muslims apparently did not succeed in building up a mass movement, but those Muslims who did were also associated in some respects with the UNIA. It has been suggested that Elijah Muhammad, leader of the most successful of these Muslim organizations, the Nation of Islam, was a corporal in the uniformed ranks of the Chicago UNIA division. Others remember him as an active member of the Detroit UNIA. Muhammad did some of his early proselytizing in Chicago in 1933 in a UNIA Liberty Hall. He also apparently encouraged, or at least did not object, to having his movement cast in the role of successor to the Garvey movement. (pp. 75, 76)

In the book *The Judas Factor, The Plot To Kill Malcolm X*, author Karl Evanzz states that Elijah Muhammad moved his family to Detroit in 1923, the same year as Sadiq's UNIA address, and lived and worked there until 1926. Evanzz notes:

At the end of 1926, Elijah was laid off for reasons which were never made clear. It is possible, however, that he was terminated because of his political activities. Elijah had discovered Garvey's Universal Negro Improvement Association, and is believed to have joined the Detroit branch. (p. 134)

In a 1989 cable television documentary entitled

The Real Revolution: Islam, The Liberating Force In Africa and America, historian and scholar Muzafar Ahmad Zafar noted that the Ahmadiyya Movement, founded by Hazrat Mirza Ghulam Ahmad of Qadian, India, was global in scope and had missions throughout Africa. During the 1920s, Sadiq distributed Qurans, Islamic prayer books and other literature to African Americans, reacquainting them with the knowledge possessed by their ancestors. He provided positive information about the empires of Africa during a time when literature on Africa and Islam was scarce in America. The Ahmadiyya Muslims had a significant impact on the Garvey Movement and on the various Islamic sects which later sprang up in America.

Garvey's philosophy is also said to have had a heavy influence on the movement led by Timothy Drew, who was to become known as Noble Drew Ali, founder of the Moorish American Science Temples in 1913. Martin states that Drew's movements had for its major theological document a Holy Koran compounded of the teachings of the Bible, Marcus Garvey and the Quran.

Garvey recognized that the use of propaganda plays heavily in the control of the masses. In *Race First*, Martin quotes Garvey as saying:

> *The great white man has succeeded in subduing the world by forcing everybody to think his way ... He has given to the world, from the Bible to his yellow newspaper sheet, a literature that established his right and sovereignty to the disadvantage of the rest of the human race.*
> *The white man's propaganda has made him master of the world and all those who have come in contact with it and accepted it have become his slaves.*

*The Universal Negro Improvement Association
is now calling upon the 400,000,000 members of our
race to discard the psychology and propaganda of all
other peoples and to advance our own. (p. 89)*

Garvey, who had been an apprentice to a
printer in Jamaica, was trained in the art of
publishing. He became a master at propaganda, and
through newspapers, pamphlets, and magazines,
influenced the actions of black people internationally.
Martin notes that Garvey's papers were said to be a
factor in the uprisings in places such as Dahomey,
British Honduras, Kenya, Trinidad and Cuba.

The Federal Government then came down
hard on Marcus Garvey, charging him with fraud.
His old enemies, members of the NAACP as well as
several black publishers whom he had offended with
his attacks, aided in his demise. They published
stories about the financial problems surrounding the
Black Star Line, and claimed Garvey had taken
money under false pretenses. In 1925, he was
sentenced to five years prison for mail fraud. Two
years later in 1927 President Calvin Coolidge
pardoned him, and deported him back to Jamaica.

When Garvey died in 1940, his movement had
disintegrated. American history books all but erased
his memory, reducing his life to a few derisive words
about what they considered a doomed-to-failure "Back
To Africa Movement."

THE POLITICS OF RACE

In the post war period of the 1920s, many
immigrants were arriving to America from the east,
and those from North Africa, Arabia, and India were
often dark skinned and could have been counted

among the "Negro" population. If these immigrants had united with African Americans, the politics of America may have undergone a radical change. But, just as Garvey's movement was attaining worldwide credibility, the U.S. created a census classification which effectively caused many dark skinned immigrants to stop identifying themselves as part of the black community. In 1923 the U.S. Census Bureau declared that all Egyptians immigrating to America must classify themselves on U.S. census forms as "white."

In a 1990 interview, Egyptian immigrant Mostafa Hefny said that upon moving to America, he found himself in a dilemma. A dark complexioned man with negroid features, he discovered that because of his Egyptian birth, the U.S. demands that he be legally classified as white. He is part of a national drive to correct the U.S. racial classification of North African blacks in the U.S.

The Federal government's Office of Management and Budget determines racial classifications for the purpose of maintaining census records. "Directive No. 15" is the code which designates racial identity, and individuals are placed in one of the following groups:

* American Indian or Alaskan Native - A person having origins in any of the original peoples of North America or who maintains a cultural identification through tribal affiliation or community recognition.

* White, Not of Hispanic Origin - A person having origins in any of the original peoples of Europe, North Africa, or the Middle East.

* Black, not of Hispanic Origin - A person having origins in any of the black racial groups of Africa.

14C
Mostafa Hefny
Egyptian born Hefny immigrated to Detroit Michigan to teach school and discovered that according to American law, on U.S. census forms he must classify himself as "White." His physical features, like a great many native Egyptians, are obviously that of a black person.

* Asian or Pacific Islander - A person having origins in any of the original peoples of the far East, Southeast Asia, the Indian subcontinent, or the Pacific Islands. This area includes for example China, Japan, Korea, the Philippine Islands and Samoa.

* Hispanic - A person of Mexican, Puerto Rican, Cuban, Central or South America or other Spanish Culture or origin, regardless of race.

As is characteristic of other people of African descent, many North Africans and Middle Easterners have dark skin. So why are they classified as white?

After Garvey's deportation, many of his followers and supporters felt a great void. Some joined various Islamic oriented groups as a means to express black nationalism through religion. But others, however, used religious conversion as a means to hide an undesired black identity. In the television documentary *The Real Revolution*, historian Muzafar Ahmad Zafar stated:

> *The lighter skinned blacks saw this as a way to be accepted into the white mainstream. Some of them would learn a few Arabic phrases, slick their hair back, and no longer were they African American. They would pass for Arab, Indian, anything but an African American.*

Hopes of being able to "pass" for something near white, in order to be rid of the stigma of "negroness" were still held by many light skinned blacks. In addition, many dark skinned immigrants, arriving in America during a time when lynching was at a peak, were fearful of being treated with the same cruelty as the black citizens of the country. Many gladly accepted their "honorary white" status and, steered clear of radical movements. Many of the Arab Muslims who arrived in America immediately set up shops in poor neighborhoods and exploited black consumers as shamelessly as did other ethnic immigrants. They were hardly representatives of a philosophy of international brotherhood.

In *The Judas Factor,* Evanzz states that Elijah Muhammad, then Elijah Poole, met Wallace D. Fard in 1930. Fard had opened a mosque in Detroit, named The Allah Temple of Islam which Elijah Poole joined and, according to Evanzz, assumed leadership in 1931 while Fard traveled around the country opening new chapters. Evanzz notes that Elijah first changed his surname to Elijah Karriem, then late in 1931, adopted a new name, Ghulam Ali. Fard is presumed to have left the country in 1933 and the Allah Temple of Islam disbanded. Elijah changed his name to Elijah Muhammad and became the head of the Nation of Islam.

In the 1930s Elijah Muhammad presented a teaching which exhorted followers to be morally clean, industrious workers, and financially self sufficient. His motto, "Do for self" reflected Garvey's emphasis on economic independence of the black race. One of the demands of Muhammad's group, which became known as "The Black Muslims," was for the control of some territory within the United States for the black population, to govern as an independent nation. This was certainly in the spirit of Garvey's idea of establishing a nation for America's blacks on the continent of Africa.

The soldier-like uniforms of Muhammad's male members, called the Fruit of Islam, had the striking flair of those worn by the UNIA's Universal African Legion. The Islamic long white dresses and head coverings worn by the female members were

14D

Elder Frederick Douglass

Frederick Douglass is recognized by many historians as one of the greatest African American leaders. He rose from slavery to become a world renowned orator, and an Ambassador to Haiti. He traveled to Africa. In later life, he became an avid campaigner for the Republican party. (Reprinted from Frederick Douglass, by William S. McFeely, page 146, Copyright 1991, W.W. Norton & Company.)

reminiscent of the UNIA's modest white Black Cross Nurses uniforms.

Muhammad, like Garvey, aimed his message not at the black elite, but at the urban poor, the victim of economic and political exploitation, the alcohol and drug abuser, the criminal, the ex-convict. One convict, Malcolm Little, who became known as Malcolm X, joined the Nation of Islam in the early 1950s. Malcolm's father was also a Garveyite, and is believed to have been lynched in Michigan by white vigilantes who feared Garvey's teachings.

A dynamic orator, Malcolm soon became the organization's National spokesman. He organized the Muhammad Speaks newspaper and persuaded other black newspapers to run Elijah Muhammad's column. His leadership skills and organizing abilities helped the Nation of Islam grow, in just a few years, from a little over 400 followers to thousands of members across the country. During the 1950s and early 1960s, the Nation of Islam experienced phenomenal success.

GOVERNMENT CONTROL OF BLACK LEADERSHIP

Recent public scrutiny of the U.S. Federal Bureau of Investigation (FBI) under the leadership of J. Edgar Hoover, revealed that from the time of the rise of Marcus Garvey in the 1920s to Hoover's death in the late 1970s, the FBI used everything from telephone wiretaps to paid government informants to disrupt black organizations.

Differences in philosophies and leadership styles were exacerbated into bitter rivalries, such as the Booker T. Washington-W.E.B. DuBois conflict, the W.E.B. Du Bois-Marcus Garvey conflict, and later, the Martin Luther King-Malcolm X conflict. In each case, the media paints one spokesman as "acceptable" and the other as too "militant."

In America, any black leader who may have the capacity to mobilize great numbers of people and initiate an effective program is immediately vilified, slandered, and when possible, jailed ... and when necessary, killed.

In 1965 Malcolm was assassinated. Three years later, Martin was also gunned down. While political analysts continue to debate the merits of each man's philosophy, many tend to miss this glaring fact: just as each man's career reached a point where his efforts had begun to take on international dimensions (King, with his protest against the Viet Nam war, Malcolm with his plans to take the case of black Americans before the United Nations world court), the government stepped up its propaganda program, creating a climate where the leader would be ostracized by other leaders and opposed by his own people.

During the 1984 U.S. Presidential elections, Operation PUSH Founder Rev. Jesse Jackson's campaign for President had risen to unprecedented levels of success. In the introduction to Jackson's book: *Reverend Jesse Jackson, Straight From The Heart,* editors Roger D. Hatch and Frank E. Watkins observe:

After conducting a Southern crusade for voting-rights enforcement focused in Mississippi with an assistant attorney general from the U.S. Justice Department and expanding his voter registration drive to G.I.s on U.S. bases in Europe, Jackson launched his campaign for the Democratic nomination for the presidency of the United States on

November 3, 1983. His candidacy marked the first full-scale effort by an African American to capture the nation's highest office. His campaign was given a significant boost in January 1984 when he successfully negotiated with Syrian President Assad for the release of downed air force pilot Lt. Robert Goodman. This feat was expanded and duplicated in the summer when Jackson's discussion with Cuban President Fidel Castro led to the release of forty-eight American and Cuban prisoners.

The keystone of the Jackson presidential campaign was the Rainbow Coalition. Through the Rainbow Coalition, Jackson intends to give a united voice to those blacks, browns, Native Americans, Asian Americans, Arab Americans, Jewish Americans, and Caribbean Americans, and the poor who lack power. (p. xiii)

During the year 1984, as his campaign progressed, he won congressional district after district, even in areas where the black population was very small. He confounded the political analysts, and made the idea of becoming America's first black president a real possibility.

So, the U.S. propaganda machine went to work, first attacking Jackson's organization, Operation PUSH, and its educational arm, PUSH/EXCEL. Next, his international activities were called into question. The issue was raised -- had Jackson's negotiations with Syrian President Assad violated U.S. State Department regulations?

The next step was to create a division within the Jackson campaign ranks. Minister Louis Farrakhan, leader of the Nation of Islam, had pledged his support to the Jackson campaign. Farrakhan's uniting with Jackson set a historical

14E
Joseph and Pharaoh

*In his autobiography, Frederick Douglass stated that the faces
on the statues of Egyptian Pharaohs looked just like the face of
his mother, Betsy Bailey. This convinced him that the ancient
Egyptians were African, not European. This carving of Joseph
and the Pharaoh from approximately 2500 B.C. illustrates his
rise to a position of high authority under Pharaoh, as explained
in the Bible, Genesis 42:6. The story of Joseph is an example of
how a former slave, using intelligence, talent, and integrity can
rise to a position of power and control in the land. (From the
library collection of Ms. D. B. Luckey, Special Education
Consultant.)*

precedent, in that two decades earlier, Jackson's mentor, Martin Luther King, and Farrakhan's mentor, Malcolm X, had been pitted against each other as adversaries.

The mass media went to work in creating a major controversy surrounding Farrakhan. His speeches were scrutinized, analyzed, and criticized, and he was portrayed as a "militant," a "racist," and a hater of whites and Jews. The attacks on the Jackson campaign became harsh. Financial supporters threatened to withdraw support. Top leaders withheld key endorsements. National Democratic Convention officials threatened to remove Jackson from the program as a keynote speaker if he refused to "denounce" Farrakhan. In the end, in a press conference held upon Jackson's return from Cuba, Jackson stated his disagreement with some remarks allegedly made by Farrakhan, and the next day newspaper headlines screamed that Farrakhan and Jackson had split.

In the years following the 1984 campaign, both men have since warned followers to beware of how the media manipulates conflict between black leaders and organizations. In a 1988 speech at the Operation PUSH headquarters in Chicago before rival black political candidates, Jackson advised:

We should never again fight each other through the media. We may agree to agree or we may agree to disagree. But we should settle our differences behind closed doors and come out in public with a united front.

In 1990 Farrakhan addressed an audience during the 25 year commemoration of the assassination of Malcolm X, held at Malcolm X

College in Chicago. In that speech, he declared:

> *Let us unite. We've got to put a healing balm in the wounds of yesterday ... Even though we have differences, don't let your enemy exploit your differences ... Because we're always going to have some differences.*

Some blacks still believe they must seek white approval for black leadership. Have you also been conditioned to disapprove of any black leader who may offend whites? Look back at your answer to Psychic Trauma Test question Number 4: "When I hear an African American leader speak out forcefully and aggressively, I feel uncomfortable."

If you answered strongly agree, agree, or unsure, you should think about why you feel uncomfortable. Do you believe that black aggression is wrong? Do you fear that a strong black leader will inevitably be assassinated? These are some of the fears created by the violent slave experience and the subsequent murders, lynchings and assassinations.

Since the days of Nat Turner and Denmark Vesey to the present, strong African American leaders have been attacked and betrayed by blacks who fear the disapproval of whites. The media's instigation of bitter rivalries between black leaders is designed to prevent blacks from developing a unified movement and achieving collective power.

In America, with the right strategy, a growing black population has the opportunity to acquire local, national, and ultimately international political power. In order to achieve this, perhaps the greatest lesson to be learned, as Garvey stated, is "to discard the psychology and propaganda of all other peoples and to advance our own."

ACTIVITY:
Evaluate Your Leaders

Use this list of questions to help you evaluate those who seek positions of leadership. When selecting an organization or civic leader, observe how many of these questions to which you can answer Yes. Does the leader or potential leader:

1. Follow an unwavering code of honesty and ethical conduct and speak out against unfairness, injustice and corruption, regardless of who may be guilty of it?
2. Have the ability to bring together previously conflicting factions to create a stronger, unified body?
3. Appeal to the masses of people and not just those of the elite class or leadership hierarchy?
4. Propose specific solutions to problems as opposed to vague philosophical concepts?
5. Consistently represent the desires and concerns of the people, and speak or negotiate in their behalf?
6. Seek opinions and advice from followers before making important decisions?
7. Have an independent means of survival which does not depend upon financial contributions from government controlled agencies?
8. Support positive programs even when there is no public recognition or personal financial gain?
9. Demonstrate humility and understanding that leadership is a responsibility given by the people and not an opportunity for self-aggrandizement?
10. Delegate responsibility to competent people, train them to assume leadership, and prepare for an orderly transition of authority upon the end of the leader's term of service?

CONCLUSION:
How To Get Rid Of Your Psychic Trauma

15A.
The Metamorphosis of Malcolm X

The transformation of Malcolm Little, Detroit Red, street hustler and prison convict, to El Hajj Malik El Shabazz, international leader and human rights advocate, represents the potential of all African Americans to reach heights of greatness regardless of their present circumstances. Despite the lynching of his father, the break up of his family, and the discouragement of his ambitions in school, once Malcolm discovered his true heritage, he was able to develop the natural brilliance within himself. His outstanding organizing and speaking abilities are an example of the genetically inherited potential of African American people which can overcome the damaging effects of slavery. (Malcom X, "A Part of the Solution." Accra, Ghana, May 1964. Photo by Alice Windom. Courtesy of the DuSable Museum of African American History file, Chicago, Illinois.)

CONCLUSION:
How To Get Rid Of Your Psychic Trauma

Many psychological studies have been done by black psychologists who point out the social pathology which results from racism. Our purpose, however, was to correct historical misinformation by producing a well documented, scholarly work which verifies the level of social, economic, political, and educational development of Africans prior to being brought to America as slaves. We set out to investigate all photographic, written, and statistical material which seems to have not been available to the general public, in order to determine how the institution of slavery transformed African people. Our final objective was to discover how the slave experience still influences the thinking and behavior of present day African Americans, and to develop a method to reverse the emotional and psychological damage from slavery.

THE FAILURE OF WHITE PSYCHOLOGY

The fields of psychology and psychiatry have often been used by whites against black people to support slavery and racial discrimination. In *Why Blacks Kill Blacks*, Dr. Alvin Poussaint observes:

American psychiatry, like other institutions in this country, has been guilty of racism. Most practitioners and patients have been white and well-to-do ...
During slavery, white mental health workers pointed to the high incidence of mental illness among blacks in the North -- there was ten times more

mental illness in the North than in the South -- and concluded that slavery was a benign institution which protected inferior blacks from the stresses of a competitive society. Traditionally, any black who asserted himself was labelled a "crazy" or "uppity nigger" who ought to be incarcerated in a mental hospital or prison. At the peak of the Civil Rights movement in the South, both whites and blacks who protested racial oppression were committed to mental institutions as "insane." (p. 50)

Clinical psychologist Dr. Bobby E. Wright, in his book *The Psychopathic Racial Personality*, asserts:

History is replete with examples of White scientists justifying the "inferiority" of the Black race. There was the eminent Dr. Samuel Cartwright of Louisiana who diagnosed Blacks who ran away from slave owners as having a disease of the mind. Dr. Robert Bean of Johns Hopkins University in 1906 proposed that Blacks had smaller brains than Whites and since "brain efficiency" depended on the number and position of nerve cells and fibers in the brain, Blacks had less capacity for development than Whites. Dr. Carl Jung, one of the White giants of psychology stated that White Americans' sexual inadequacy was due to their having to live together with a barbaric race (Blacks). (pp. 10, 11)

Today, some white psychologists use so-called scientific studies to try to prove that blacks are naturally prone to violence. According to the November 22, 1992 edition of *All Chicago City News*, a study published by the National Institute for Mental Health claims that there are "genetic factors" which influence criminal behavior. The article states:

>   *That study was put together by Dr. Fred Goodwin, a federal psychiatrist who now heads the powerful federal National Institute for Mental Health (NIMH). In his work, Goodwin compares the inner-city to a jungle and says that the people who live there "have regressed to an earlier stage of evolution." Goodwin specifically compares young men in the inner cities to "Rhesus monkeys who only want to kill each other, have sex and reproduce."*
>
>   *Goodwin then recommends using "genetic and biochemical markers" to identify "potentially violent black children as young as the age of five for biological and behavior intervention." Apparently the "intervention" could include the use of powerful drugs and/or some forms of surgery.*

Negative theories such as these can hardly be the basis of any credible study of African American behavior.

PSYCHIC TRAUMA TEST RESULTS

The Psychic Trauma Test at the beginning of this book highlights some of the major stumbling blocks to individual and collective African American progress. Many people recognize that there is something inappropriate about the way they view themselves and about their reactions to white people. However, they may seek to justify those feelings in order to avoid admitting they have been so deeply affected by society's racism.

Look back at your answer to Psychic Trauma Test question Number 20: "I found myself defensively making excuses for my answers as I filled out this questionnaire." If you answered strongly agree, agree, or unsure, you possibly realize that some of your answers on the test reflect a negative self image, low self esteem, or fear of whites.

The Psychic Trauma Test was developed with the assistance of Dr. Florestee Vance, who received her Doctorate in Education from Illinois State University, and studied at the University of Chicago, where she specialized in statistics.

The test was designed to measure the degree to which an African American's behavior and attitudes have been affected by the social conditions in a Eurocentric society. It was first administered to several test groups which, all totaled, consisted of 500 males and females from diverse educational backgrounds and age groups, with varying economic status and religious ideologies. The results were quite revealing.

After each administration of the test, a discussion of the questions was held with members of the test group. In addition to age and sex, educational level and income level also appeared to affect the participants' answers to questions. Another strong factor which appeared to influence answers was the participant's own physical features, (skin color, hair texture, etc.) However, the greatest influence was apparently one's personal experiences with family, peers, and the society in general.

There were noticeable patterns in answers among the various age groups and among males and females. Among the 16-19 year olds, females averaged a score of 22 and males averaged a score of 19. For females in this age bracket, question number one (embarrassed when watching a black person interviewed on TV using incorrect grammar and "black dialect) and question number fifteen (feel resentment at the sight of an attractive member of the opposite sex with a white person of your sex), received high scores. For males in this age bracket, question number three (feel fearful when stopped by white police) and question 18 (think blacks brought to America became more civilized than those in Africa) received high scores.

Among 20-29 year olds, females averaged a score of 21 and males averaged a score of 20.

In this group, for females, questions one and fifteen again received high scores. In addition, question seven (feel self conscious at being the only black person at an event) and question fourteen (consider it a greater compliment when a white member of the opposite sex considers me attractive than a black member) also received high scores. Males scored high on questions one, three, seven, fourteen and fifteen.

In the 30-39 age group, females averaged a score of 18 and males averaged a score of 16. Females scored high on questions one and fifteen, and also on question eight, (believe I would be further along in my career if I were white). Males scored high on questions one, three, eight, and eighteen.

In the 40-49 age group, females averaged a score of 18 and males averaged a score of 21. Females scored high on questions one, three, eight, and fifteen and males scored high on questions one, three, seven, eight and fifteen.

The 50-59 age group had the highest overall average scores. Females averaged a score of 23 and males averaged a score of 24. Among females, questions three and fifteen received high scores and among males, questions one, three, and eight received high scores. In addition, males from this age bracket also scored high on question two (when speaking to whites, I consciously try to alter my grammar), and question four (I feel uncomfortable when I hear an African American leader speaking forcefully).

This is the generation who was often on the front line during the intense Civil Rights struggle of the 1950s and 1960s, and was perhaps deeply emotionally affected by the violently hostile reactions of whites who resisted integration and the quest for black power. They were also possibly quite traumatized to witness the beatings, jailings and assassinations of comrades involved in the struggle.

In the 60+ age group, among males and females the average score was 20 and the questions which received high scores were one, three, and fifteen.

It is interesting that males and females across the board scored high on question one. The frequency of high scores increased with age and educational level, indicating that perhaps the educational system itself reinforces a belief that intelligence is measured by ones ability to use "standard" English.

Colloquial language can sometimes be colorful and expressive and many times retains much of the rhythm and speech patterns of African languages. There is often great wisdom in the words of elders whose speech may still reflect a black southern dialect. African Americans must be careful not to let education create an arrogance within them, which can cause them to dismiss the opinions of those who may not have had access to formal speech training or exposure to European American society.

Males from all age groups scored high on

question three, indicating that there is a great concern about police brutality. Most males are painfully aware that confrontations with police may result in verbal and physical abuse, which often goes unpunished because of the media's repeated reinforcement of the "dangerous black man" image. This realization creates a constant state of anxiety for black males.

The best way to combat this situation is to first keep control of oneself. By remaining calm and dignified, men (and women) can avoid being provoked into an argument by police officers who are seeking an excuse to abuse them. Individuals who are presently employed as law enforcement officers or are seeking to become law enforcement officers should realize that these are very high stress jobs. They must constantly strive to prevent themselves from developing an abusive personality.

Question seven was an item of concern for females and males in the 20-29 age group, as well as some males in the 40-49 age group. Further conversations revealed why many said that they felt uncomfortable at events in which they were the only black person. After experiencing a segregated upbringing, many of those in the 20-29 age group felt uncomfortable upon enrolling in predominantly white colleges or entering a predominantly white professional job market. In such situations, discomfort tends to decrease as a person develops self confidence, and breaks through artificial racial barriers to make friends.

Men and women in the 30-39 and the 40-49 age groups scored high on question eight, belief that they would be further along in their careers if they were white. They perceive that they have personally experienced racial discrimination and have been prevented from reaching their full potentials.

When blacks focus on white discrimination in the form of denial of access to higher education or refusal of loans from white banks, they may develop a certain feeling of helplessness. But many now recognize the power of collective action. By developing independent educational facilities or creating the kind of financial support system to launch their own businesses, as mentioned in Chapter Twelve, they can empower themselves to reach their goals.

Men and women in the 20-29 age group scored high on question fourteen, indicating that they placed higher value on compliments from whites than those from blacks. An interesting seeming contradiction is that they also scored high on question fifteen, resentment of interracial couples. In fact, males and females of every group scored high on this question, which exposes a widely held resentment of blacks who date and marry whites.

In conversations following the test, a number of black women stated that it appeared that the "successful" black men -- the entertainers, athletes, and top executives -- seemed to prefer white women. Many black men said that professional black women with higher incomes tended to date white men because of the low economic status of black men. Both groups believed that blacks often choose white mates as a kind of status symbol of their success.

The attitude that a white man or woman represents the ultimate dream mate is something that is actually created during childhood. Stories of Cinderella, Sleeping Beauty, Snow White, Beauty and the Beast and other fairy tales, show white women as the epitome of beauty and a white Prince Charming who sweeps her off her feet and takes her to his

368   *Slavery: The African American Psychic Trauma*

castle. When black parents present such stories to their children, they are unknowingly programming their sons and daughters to desire white mates like the princes and princesses in the fairy tales.

Interracial relationships are as old as the human race. This is why there are so many physical variations of human beings. No individual should take offense at someone else's preference for a mate. The healthy attitude toward forming any personal relationship is to appreciate what you are yourself and to seek people who also appreciate who or what you are. The qualities which are necessary for building a good relationship, such as honesty and respect, transcend race and nationality.

Scores on the overall test varied, ranging from nearly the lowest possible score to nearly the highest possible score. Many who had received degrees in higher education and held impressive job titles scored just as high on the test as those who had not completed high school and were unemployed. People who professed certain religious beliefs scored just as high as those who professed no religion at all. Every African American has been affected to some degree by living in a racially biased society which reinforces the notion of black inferiority. A proper understanding of history can perhaps help undo the psychological damage.

You have read much about history, and have had a chance to analyze the whys and hows of the African American condition. Perhaps some of the things in this book have given you a new perspective. We recommend that you review the Bibliography as a suggested reading list at the end of this book. After reading some of these enlightening works, wait one month and take the Psychic Trauma Test again. See how your attitudes may have changed.

WORKING TOWARD THE COLLECTIVE GOAL

In order to develop lasting solutions, African Americans must look beyond the present racial conflict and recognize their problems as part of a human condition. Regardless of their political ideology or religion, before any people can rise to positions of leadership, they must first correct those human failings which led to their downfall ... such as greed, selfishness, envy, immorality, cruelty, and ignorance. These vices cause infighting and weaken a nation, making it vulnerable to internal revolution or foreign conquest. Regardless of one's personal beliefs, the universal laws of cause and effect always determine the fate of any individual, group, or nation.

The United States, steeped in crime and suffering an unending economic recession, finds itself slipping as an economic world power. The United Soviet Socialist Republic has disintegrated into fragmented warring factions. The empire of Great Britain, after slowly losing its colonies through wars of independence, is now a fading memory. Clearly today's world is undergoing a major transformation.

Throughout history, whenever a revolutionary change in society is about to occur, the violent upheavals and catastrophic events which precede such a change are like the labor pains which herald the birth of a new baby. As violence and corruption increases, consuming every facet of American life, one should not panic; this is only a sign that a new beginning is near. Such a transformation does not occur over night, however, but over a period of generations. This is why family and community stability is such an important first step for change.

African people are slowly reaching a level of

collective consciousness. The problems of crime and poverty, whether in Soweto, South Africa or Kingston, Jamaica, or Brooklyn, New York, are understood to be rooted in European economic exploitation, and tend to be the same world wide. As African Americans make social, political and economic gains, their next step is to reach out to the continent of Africa, to the Caribbean Islands and to black citizens of other European nations. The same psychic trauma, in various degrees, is suffered by blacks across the globe.

As African Americans seek to reestablish ties with native born Africans, they must be cautious, however. Some people seek to exploit others in the name of "African brotherhood." Some rich and influential African families today are wealthy because their ancestors made fortunes selling slaves. Some Africans today are still willing to sell out their own people and destroy their nation's economy, by participating in the international drug smuggling business. And there are those Africans who exploit the trust of African American women, marrying them only to receive a "green card" (American citizenship) and/or getting them pregnant, then abandoning the women and children.

African ancestry alone is not enough to build a unified movement. People must unite around moral principals, and judge each other according to actions.

Many leaders, activists and educators have presented various strategies to rehabilitate, reform, and redirect the multitudes of lost black youth and adults. Some have developed immensely successful programs. Every individual should be involved in some way in supporting a program, organization or institution which is working for the progress of black people.

"If you're not part of the solution, you're part of the problem."

Malcolm X

In developing successful programs and strategies, use of the mass media is important. Just as Marcus Garvey's publications helped inspire international revolt against colonialism, blacks today must communicate across the continents, and develop local and international strategies for achieving self determination. Most problems occur on a global scale, yet blacks often react with ineffective little local protests. In a recent speech at a mental health symposium in Chicago, University of Illinois political science professor and civic activist Professor Robert Starks observed:

"Blacks tend to think locally and act globally. It should be the other way around. We need to think globally and act locally."

Local strategies, such as the establishment of an Afrocentric curriculum in schools, can work in harmony with global strategies such as economic boycotts of products sold by multinational corporations who do business with oppressive governments. While boycotting products produced by such companies, blacks must consciously do business with black owned companies and when necessary, create new products to compete with those produced by the companies they are boycotting. These kinds of tactics are valuable in achieving the collective goal of ending the unjust European domination of African peoples. Once this is achieved, then nations can be built upon sound economic principals which promote the welfare of all people.

THE NEW WORLD ORDER

The future is bright for those with clear vision. In the midst of modern debates over what constitutes right and wrong moral and ethical behavior, those with understanding will continue to follow the right path, the path of those whose descendants replaced yesterday's declining civilizations.

The power of a collective consciousness is evident in the release of South African leader Nelson Mandela. In an article in the May 1990 edition of *Ebony Magazine,* writer D. Michael Cheers observes:

In 1984, when TransAfrica's Randall Robinson, U.S. Civil Rights Commissioner Dr. Mary Frances Berry and D. C. Delegate Walter Fauntroy decided to pressure the Pretoria government into making reforms by staging what was the beginning of daily demonstrations at the South African Embassy in Washington D.C., word of this act of civil disobedience soon reached Polls-moor Prison in Cape Town, South Africa, where African National Congress leader Nelson Mandela was in the 20th year of a life sentence. He says he was moved by the commitment of thousands of African-Americans and others who chose arrest to further the cause of Black South Africans.

When the fervor from the Free South Africa Movement shifted from the streets to the United States Congress where Rep. Ronald Dellums led the successful fight for comprehensive economic sanctions against the terrorist and racist regime, again, Mandela says his "spirits were lifted." The civil disobedience in the U.S. and other countries, stiff economic sanctions and growing world-wide outrage over South Africa's apartheid system finally prompted

*President F. W. de Klerk's decision to release
Mandela.*

Because of the collective action of African
people worldwide, Nelson Mandela is now free.
South Africa is at the dawn of a new age and African
Americans can be very proud that they played a part.

Today, many African Americans who have
acquired knowledge and skills are now organizing
and building independent institutions. Some of them
have been mentioned in this book. These people and
many others are raising a new breed of children who
will be prepared to usher in the new era.

While TV reports show dysfunctional black
families, escalating teen pregnancies, absent fathers
and welfare mothers, little attention is paid to the
stable black families who quietly go about the
business of producing well behaved children with
high moral principles and sound values. These are
the people who send their children to school, help
their children with homework and provide wholesome
family recreation without drugs, alcohol, or illicit sex.
They are enthusiastic about life and have an exciting
vision for the future, because they are experiencing
positive results from the choices they made. While
other families fall victim to domestic violence,
juvenile delinquency, alcoholism, and drug addiction,
these families, by their own example, provide a
strong foundation for children to grow up, get
married, and create families of their own.

The news media focuses on talented young
black athletes setting new records for speed and
endurance, and acknowledges the outstanding
physical ability of black people. But few notice the
brilliant young black scientists developing new
inventions, excelling in school, winning scholastic

awards, and completing a college education, which demonstrates outstanding intellectual abilities as well. In spite of 300 years of slavery, the genetic memory emerges within each new generation.

Chicago journalist Vernon Jarrett worked with the NAACP to create the Afro-Academic Cultural, Technological and Scientific Olympics (ACTSO) Awards, which gives recognition and encouragement to outstanding black youth across the country. Students are rewarded for their intellectual achievements with gold, silver and bronze medals, just like in the athletic Olympic competitions. Their works in the fields of chemistry, physics, biology, and other sciences are awesome and offer a glimpse into the future. They and others are tomorrow's scientists, mathematicians, writers, artists, musicians, and orators. These articulate young people, with sharp and sober minds, will be prepared to contribute to the rebirth of America as well as the redevelopment of Africa, thereby benefitting the entire world in the 21st century and beyond.

Those who have a vision for the future can plan for twenty, fifty, even one hundred years from today. Through their works, they will leave a great legacy for future generations to build upon.

What legacy will you leave behind for the future? Every individual has the power to choose. Will you strive to gain knowledge and wisdom? Will your behavior serve as a positive example for the youth? Will you teach them sound moral principles? Will you provide them with a spiritual foundation, wholesome education, valuable skills, and constructive values? Will your children, and your children's children be among those who establish the new world order?

It all begins with you.

Lesson Plan

How To Use This Book For Classroom Studies

This lesson plan outline, developed with the assistance of Betty D. Luckey, Special Education Consultant and Principal at Private Therapeutic Day School, can help teachers use this book as a supplement in the study of subjects such as history, sociology, geography, political science, language arts, economics, and science.

Introduction: What Is Psychic Trauma?
Objective: Examine social behavior between blacks and whites.
Activity: Take the Psychic Trauma Test

Chapter One: The Stolen African Past
Objective: Study the various national boundaries in Africa during the time of ancient Egypt and compare with those of today.
Activity: Discuss the ever changing political climate as illustrated by the chart

Chapter Two: Europe's First Rise To Power
Objective: Examine the role of religion in history
Activity: Compare Ancient Egyptian and Roman philosophy and culture

Chapter Three: A Hidden Spiritual Heritage
Objective: Observe how Africa influenced the European Renaissance.
Activity: Discuss the historic role of religion in the shaping of political policies.

Chapter Four: The Columbus Conspiracy
Objective: Discuss the historical significance of the celebration of "Columbus Day."

Activity: Compare European and African approaches to international trade

Chapter Five: Who Did They Really Sell Into Slavery?

Objective: Study the geographical areas identified as the homelands of the captured Africans profiled in the chapter.

Activity: Discuss methods in which displaced citizens can try to preserve old family traditions in a completely new cultural environment.

Chapter Six: The Making Of A Negro

Objective: Examine laws passed in pre-Civil War America and their effects on race relations.

Activity: Discuss the effects of present day Civil Rights legislation.

Chapter Seven: Miseducation

Objective: Explore the pros and cons of practical verses classical education.

Activity: Discuss the concept of a "genetic memory." Discuss your ideas for a scientific invention.

Chapter Eight: Our Media Image: The Big Lie

Objective: Examine the influence of the communications industry on today's society

Activity: Critique some popular films, noting any racial stereotypes

Chapter Nine: Black Beauty Standards

Objective: Locate publications (such as National Geographic) which feature people from different nationalities and cultures. Discuss the various concepts of beauty.

Activity: Critique the models of popular current magazines and compare with the models in magazines of twenty years ago.

Chapter Ten: Modern Marriages: Why They're Not Working

Objective: Examine the function of the family.

Activity: Discuss the issues raised on the Marriage Test

Chapter Eleven: Childrearing: The Making Of A Slave

Objective: Discuss the pros and cons of corporal punishment in the home and school.

Activity: Evaluate current toys for children, and discuss their possible impact on children's social behavior.

Chapter Twelve: Economic Genocide

Objective: Observe how rural farming affects the urban economy.

Activity: Compare prices in several stores of basic food items and discuss price differences.

Chapter Thirteen: Prison: The New Slave System

Objective: Examine the social and economic impact of drug use on today's society.

Activity: Discuss social and educational programs which could rehabilitate prison inmates.

Chapter Fourteen: Political Leadership: Power Strategists or Plantation Overseers?

Objective: Discuss the philosophies of African American leaders past and present.

Activity: Evaluate the performance of your local elected official.

Conclusion: How To Get Rid Of Your Psychic Trauma

Objective: Examine past experiences which may have influenced your answers on the Psychic Trauma Test

Activity: Discuss your vision of American society fifty years from today.

Bibliography

We are grateful to all the authors listed in the following Bibliography whose excellent works provided information for this book. Their books are highly recommended for further research and study.

Books and Pamphlets

Ahmad, Hazrat Mirza Bashir-ud-Din Mahmud, *The Life Of Muhammad,* The Ahmadiyya Muslim Foreign Missions, Rabwah Pakistan

Ahmad, Hazrat Mirza Bashir-ud-Din Mahmud, *The New World Order Of Islam,* Oriental Publishing Corporation, Ltd., Rabwah, Pakistan, 1946

Ahmed, Mirza Mubarak, *Islam In Africa,* Ahmadiyya Muslim Foreign Missions, Rabwah, Pakistan, 1962

Ammi, Ben, *God, The Black Man And Truth,* Communicators Press, Chicago, IL, 1982

Angelou, Maya, *All God's Children Need Traveling Shoes,* Random House, Inc. New York, NY, 1986

Austin, Allan D., *African Muslim In Antebellum America,* Garland Publishing Company, Inc., New York & London, 1984

Balwin, John D., *Prehistoric Nations,* Harper & Bros., New York, NY, 1869

Bashir, Abdul Alim, *Passport To A Happy Marriage,* New Mind Productions, Inc., Jersey City, NJ, 1992

Bennett, Lerone, *Before The Mayflower,* Johnson Publishing, Inc., Jersey City, NJ, 1961

Blassingame, John W., *The Slave Community,* Oxford University Press, Inc., New York, 1972

Bogle, Donald, *Toms, Coons, Mulattos, Mammies & Bucks, An Interpretive History of Blacks In American Films*

Boyce, William D., *Illustrated Africa, North, Tropical and South,* Rand McNally & Company, 1925

Brownmiller, Susan, *Against Our Will, Men Women and Rape,* Bantam Books, Inc., New York, NY, 1975

Buckmaster, Henrietta, *Flight To Freedom,* Vail Ballon Press, Inc., Binghamtown, NY, 1958

Chapman, Abraham, *Black Voices, An Anthology of Afro American Literature,* New American Library, New York, NY, 1968

Cleaver, Eldridge, *Soul On Ice,* Dell Publishing Co., New York, NY, 1968

Davidson, Basil, *The Lost Cities Of Africa,* Little, Brown and Company, Boston, Mass., 1959

Davidson, Basil, *Africa In History,* The Macmillan Company, New York, NY, 1968

Dillard, J.L., *Black English,* Random House, Inc., New York, NY, 1972

Diop, Cheikh Anta, *The African Origin Of Civilization, Myth Or Reality,* Lawrence Hill & Co., Chicago, IL, 1974

Du Bois, William Edward Burghardt, *The Souls Of Black Folk,* (1903), The New American Library, Inc., New York, NY, 1969

El-Amin, Mildred, *Family Roots,* International Ummah Foundation, Chicago, IL, 1991

Emanuel, James A. and Theodore, L., *Dark Symphony, Negro Literature In America,* The Free Press, New York, NY, 1968

Evanzz, Karl, *The Judas Factor, The Plot To Kill Malcolm X,* Thunder's Mouth Press, New York, NY, 1992

Fann, K. T. and Hodges, Donald C., *Readings in U.S. Imperialism,* Porter Sargent, Boston, Mass., 1971

Fanon, Franz, *Black Skin, White Masks,* Grove Press, Inc. New York, NY, 1967

Fanon, Franz, *The Wretched Of The Earth,* Grove Press, Inc., New York, NY, 1963

Foucault, Michel, *Discipline & Punishment, The Birth Of The Prisons,* Pantheon Books, New York, 1977

Franklin, John Hope, *From Slavery To Freedom, A History Of Negro Americans,* Fourth Edition, Alfred A. Kropf, Inc, Random House, Inc., New York, 1947

Garvey, Amy Jacques, *The Philosophy and Opinions of Marcus Garvey, Or Africa For The Africans,* (1923) The Majority Press, Dover, Mass., 1986

Gibson, Richard, *African Liberation Movements, Contemporary Struggles Against White Minority Rule,* Oxford University Press, New York, NY, 1972

Hale, Thomas A., *Scribe, Griot and Novelist: Narrative Interpreters of the Songhay Empire,* University of Florida Press, Center For African Studies, Gainsville, Florida, 1990

Haley, Alex, *Autobiography of Malcolm X,* Ballantine Books, New York, NY, 1973

Haley, Alex, *Roots: The Saga Of An American Family,* Dell Publishing, New York, NY, 1976

Hare, Dr. Nathan and Dr. Julia, *Black Anglo Saxons,* Third World Press, Chicago, IL, 1991

Hayden, Robert C., *A Salute To Black Scientists and Inventors,* Empak Publishing Company, Chicago, IL, 1985

Hayden, Robert C., *A Salute To Historic African Kings and Queens,* Empak Publishing Company, Chicago, IL, 1988

Hendin, Herbert, *Black Suicide,* Harper and Row Publishers, New York, NY, 1969

Hoch, Erasmus, *Clinical Psychology: An Empirical Approach*, Brooks/Cole Publishing Company, Belmont, LA, 1971

Jackson, Jesse L., *Straight From The Heart*, Fortress Press, Philadelphia, 1982

Jackson, John G., *Introduction To African Civilizations*, Citadel Press, Secaucus, NJ, 1970

King, Martin Luther, *Where Do We Go From Here: Chaos Or Community?* Beacon Press, Boston, Mass, 1967

Koestler, Arthur, The Thirteenth Tribe, Random House, Inc., New York, 1976

Kunjufu, Jawanza, *Countering The Conspiracy To Destroy Black Boys*, African American Images, Chicago, IL, 1985

Kunjufu, Jawanza, *Developing Positive Self Images And Discipline In Black Children*, African American Images, Chicago, IL, 1984

Madhubuti, Haki, *Black Men, Obsolete, Single, Dangerous? The African Family In Transition, Essays in Discovery, Solution, and Hope*, Third World Press, Chicago, 1990

Martin, Toni, *Race First, The Ideological and Organizational Struggles of Marcus Garvey and The Universal Negro Improvement Association*, Greenwood Press, A Division of Williamhouse-Regency, Inc., Westport, Connecticut, 1976

McCabe, Joseph, *Life Among The Many Peoples Of The Earth*, E. Haldeman-Julius Co., Gerard, Kansas, 1943

McCray, Walter Arthur, *The Black Presence In The Bible*, Black Light Fellowship, Chicago, IL, 1990

McColley, Robert, *Slavery and Jeffersonian Virginia, Second Edition*, University of Illinois Press, Urbana, Illinois, 1973

McFeely, William S., *Frederick Douglass*, W.W. Norton & Company, New York, NY, 1991

Mitchell, Henry, *Black Belief*, Harper & Row Publishers, Inc., New York, NY, 1975

Nasir, Dr. Khalil Ahmed, *Muhammad In The Bible*, The Ahmadiyya Movement In Islam, Inc.

Nkrumah, Kwame, *Africa Must Unite*, International Publishers, New York, NY, 1963

Pettigrew, Thomas F., *The Sociology Of Race Relations, Reflection and Reform*, The Free Press, New York, NY, 1980

Poussaint, Dr. Alvin, *Why Blacks Kill Blacks*, Emerson Hall Publishers, New York, NY, 1972

Quick, Abdullah Hakim, *Deeper Roots, Muslims In The Caribbean, Before Columbus To The Present*, The Association of Islamic Communities in the Caribbean and Latin America, Toronto, Ontario

Quresh, Sultan Ahmed, *Letters Of The Holy Prophet*, Noor Publishing House, Farashkhana, Delhi, 1986

Rogers, J.A., *Nature Knows No Color-Line*, Helga M. Rogers, New York, NY, 1952

Rogers, J.A., *Sex and Race, Volume II*, J.A. Rogers, New York, NY, 1942

Rogers, J.A., *World's Great Men Of Color, Volume II*, The Millan Publishing Company, NY, 1972

Shams, J.D., *Where Did Jesus Die?* Islam International Publications Limited, Islamabad, United Kingdom, 1989

Skinner, Elliott P., *Peoples And Cultures Of Africa*, Natural History Press, an affiliate of Doubleday and Company, Inc., New York, NY, 1973

Spear, Allan H., *Black Chicago, The Making Of A Negro Ghetto*, University Of Chicago Press, Chicago, IL, 1967

Subira, George, *Black Folks Guide To Business Success*, Very Serious Business Enterprises, Newark, NJ

Van Sertima, Ivan, *They Came Before Columbus*, Random House, Inc., New York, NY, 1976

Van Sertima, Ivan, *World's Great Black Leaders*, Journal Of African Civilizations, Inc., New Brunswick, NJ, 1988

Williams, Chancellor, *The Destruction of Black Civilization*, Third World Press, Chicago, IL, 1987

Wolseley, Roland E., *The Black Press, USA*, Iowa State University Press, Ames, Iowa, 1971

Woodson, Carter G., *The Miseducation Of The Negro* (1933), AMS Press, Inc., New York, NY, 1977

Wright, Dr. Bobby E., *The Psychopathic Racial Personality*, Third World Press, Chicago, IL, 1984

Wright, Richard, Black Boy, World Publishing, 1945

Newspapers and Magazines

Black Enterprise Magazine, December 1989, Earl G. Graves Publishing Co., Inc., New York, NY, 1989

Chicago All City News, November 22, 1992, Justice Graphics, Chicago, IL, 1992

Chicago Sun Times, February 26, 1992, Chicago Sun-Times, Inc., Chicago, IL, 1992

Ebony Magazine, August 1975, Special Issue, Johnson Publishing Company, Chicago IL, 1975

Ebony Magazine, August 1976, Special Issue, Johnson Publishing Company, Chicago, IL 1976

Ebony Magazine, April, 1993, Johnson Publishing Company, Chicago, IL, 1993

Emerge Magazine, May 1993, Emerge Communications, Inc., New York, NY, 1993

International Sun Newspaper, August 1989, Latif Publishing Company, Chicago, IL, 1989

International Sun Newspaper, December 1990, Latif Publishing

Company, Chicago, IL, 1990

International Sun Newspaper, March 1992, Latif Publishing Company, Chicago, IL, 1992

Newsweek Magazine, January 1988, Newsweek, Inc., New York, NY, 1988

New York Times Newspaper, New York Times Company, New York, NY, 1992

Religious Scriptures and Reference Books

Holy Bible, New International Version, New York International Bible Society, Zondervan Bible Publishers, Grand Rapids Michigan, 1978

Holy Quran, Arabic Text and English Translation With Commentary, Ahmadiyya Movement In Islam, London Mosque, London, England, 1981

Metaphysical Bible Dictionary, Unity School of Christianity, Unity Village, MO, 1931

Thorndike Barnhart Advanced Dictionary, by E. L. Thorndike and Clarence L. Barnhart, Scott Foresman and Company, Glenview, IL, 1974

Webster's New World Dictionary of the American Language, Second College Edition, William Collins Publishers, Inc., Printed in the U.S.A., 1980